TOWARDS AN AMERICAN ARMY

Military Thought from

Washington to Marshall

TOWARDS AN
AMERICAN ARMY

Military Thought from
Washington to Marshall

RUSSELL F. WEIGLEY

 NEW YORK AND LONDON 1962

Columbia University Press

To FRANCIS WEIGLEY

7th Pennsylvania Cavalry, Minty's Brigade,

Army of the Cumberland

A CITIZEN SOLDIER

Preface

THIS book is a history of controversies that have surrounded the growth of the United States Army, controversies that have flared over the inextricably related questions of how to attain maximum military security for the United States and how to form an army that will be appropriate to and not subversive of American democratic society.

These questions obviously have never been more relevant than they are now, and an examination of past efforts to solve them, even though in eras much simpler than ours, may aid us in approaching them today. The past perhaps never offers sure answers to questions of present policy, and the past never answered the above questions satisfactorily, even for itself. But the experience of the century and three-quarters of American history reviewed here in exploring the dimensions of the questions and the limits of possible solutions should nevertheless offer valuable guide markers to the present.

There are further suggestions for today that a study of the search for an effective American army may offer. This book examines the ideas of men in various positions who considered the problems of American military policy during the period 1776–1951. Since most of that period constituted the long epoch when civilian Americans considered military issues remote, perforce most of the men whose ideas are discussed herein were military men. A study of American ideas of military policy cannot help but be a study mainly of the ideas on military policy expressed by professional soldiers.

Therefore the book offers some measure of information on the attitudes and thought processes that have been traditional and habitual among American professional soldiers. Especially, it reveals something of their customary approach to issues of military policy where such issues merge with those of national policy in general. And to know something about the customary approach of military men to the broadest issues of military and national policy is also of manifest value to the present.

The United States has closed the most recent of its experimental inquiries into the presidential qualifications of the professional military man. But the new intimacy between military issues and every other area of national life suggests that similar experiments in the professional soldier's exercise of nonmilitary responsibilities are not ending, but are merely beginning. With professional soldiers offering leadership beyond the traditional limits of their calling, and with their calling itself now closely bound up in the most important national activities, it behooves the American citizen to study every possible indication of the sort of leadership he can expect from the professional soldier, within and beyond that soldier's professional sphere. Since the professional soldier, like the initiate of any profession, is in part the product of the history and traditions of his profession, a historical approach to our questions may again reveal their general dimensions.

How competent have the judgments of professional soldiers been in the past when issues of military and national policy have merged? What traditional attitudes of their profession have shaped their judgments on such issues? What effect may such attitudes, if they have persisted, exert upon the judgments of military men today? This book also seeks to offer the reader suggestions towards answering such questions.

During most of their history the American people faced no serious external military threat. Most Americans and even their government could afford to devote to the pursuits of peace most of the thought and energies that other nations gave over to wars and preparation for wars. But the United States won its independence in the course of a global war, found its security threatened for several decades thereafter by other global wars, and then, following the long interval of safety, discovered itself caught up in the global wars of the twentieth century. Even during the long nineteenth-century era of safety, many thoughtful Americans were sure that a country so rich and potentially powerful as theirs could not remain forever aloof from international politics and thus be forever secure, especially in a world where technology was rapidly narrowing distances. There has been no period when Americans gave no thought whatever to their military security. There has always been some concern, if not for the present, then for the future.

In a country of ocean frontiers concern for military security implied an interest in naval power, and such an interest appeared early and persisted. But the United States is a continental as well as an oceanic state, and American concern for defense has turned also on the building of an American army.

From the beginning of the national history, there was controversy as to the sort of force that would constitute an appropriate American army. Europe in that day was a continent of professional standing armies, but the English legacy and the United States colonial as well as revolutionary experience had created in America a tradition of the nonprofessional soldier, of the armed citizenry. Since the United States was embarking on an experiment in popular government, a popular army raised from the armed citizenry seemed to many Americans appropriate to their country's condition. But to seek national defense through a nonprofessional, citizen army was to run the risk that such a force might not be able to cope with the professional armies of Europe, one or more of which it presumably would have to face in any major war in the future, and the British example of which it faced at the outset. An army of armed citizens offered the advantage of vast numbers, but its numbers might be offset by the superior skill of professional adversaries.

From the beginning of American history, therefore, part of the concern for national security took the form of this controversy: should the American army be a professional force modeled on the armies of Europe or a nonprofessional force reflecting the ability of a popular government to entrust arms to its citizens. This controversy persisted unresolved when in the World Wars the United States did at last have to pit its army on a large scale against European armies, when arguments were put to the test of performance. Indeed in new forms controversy over the proper roles of professional and nonprofessional soldiers still exists. The controversy of amateur versus professional soldiers has endured as a major theme of all except exclusively naval thought about American defense. The history of American ideas on naval defense and sea power has largely been told elsewhere. This book will review the debates of those who sought to create an American army effective as a military force and appropriate to American life.

The book is not, however, a history of the official military policy of the United States. That history also has been written by others. The focus here is on the reasoning and conclusions of certain men who gave sustained thought to the issues connected with creating an American army. They were mainly, because of the nature of the period, military men. Sometimes the book will touch on general topics of American military thought, such as the nature of war or the merits of offensive or defensive warfare. Such discussion is necessary because the type of war that a writer envisions the United States as fighting obviously must influence his conception of the appropriate form of the American army. There will be a discussion of the American contribution, through William T. Sherman and his contemporaries and followers, to the appearance of total war, since a totalization of war often came to imply not only total destruction and ruthlessness but also warfare waged by mass citizen armies. But the main theme of the book is the effort of American students of war and military affairs to weigh the requirements of national security and of the American order of society so as to move toward the shaping of an American army.

Among the many persons and institutions to whom I owe a debt of gratitude for their assistance in my preparation of this work, I must mention especially the American Philosophical Society, whose Penrose Fund grant made possible the completion of the research; Dean Roy F. Nichols of the University of Pennsylvania, who graciously read and criticized the entire manuscript; and Professor Robert W. Rhoads, chairman of the department of social science of the Drexel Institute of Technology, who has always sought to be helpful in keeping time and opportunities open for research. Much of the material in chapter 6 appeared in somewhat different form in my article "Civil War: Forerunner of Total Warfare" in *Civil War Times,* I (December, 1959), and much of chapter 10 appeared in modified form as "The Military Thought of John M. Schofield" in *Military Affairs,* XXIII (1959). To the editors of those journals I wish to express my appreciation for permission to reprint that material here.

I wish also to acknowledge permission from Appleton-Century-Crofts to quote from R. M. Johnston's *Arms and the Race,* copyright 1915 by the Century Company; from Holt, Rinehart and Winston, Inc., to quote from Johnston's *Leading American Soldiers,* copyright 1907 by Henry Holt; from *The Twentieth Century,* to quote from Johnston's article "What Could Napoleon Accomplish To-Day?", which appeared in *The Nineteenth Century,* LXXVI (1914), 1271–82, before being reprinted in part in *Arms and the Race;* from Henry Regnery Co., to quote from Leonard Wood's *Our Military History,* copyright 1916 by Reilly and Britton.

June, 1962   RUSSELL F. WEIGLEY
                                                Drexel Institute of Technology
                                                Philadelphia

Contents

I. The Dual Military Legacy of the Revolution   1

II. George Washington and Alexander Hamilton: Military Professionalism in Early Republican Style   10

III. John C. Calhoun: The Expansible Army Plan   30

IV. Dennis Hart Mahan: The Professionalism of West Point   38

V. Henry W. Halleck and George B. McClellan: The Disciples of Dennis Mahan   54

VI. William T. Sherman and Ulysses S. Grant: The Rise of Total War   79

VII. Emory Upton: The Major Prophet of Professionalism   100

VIII. John A. Logan: The Rebuttal for a Citizen Army   127

IX. The Disciples of Emory Upton   137

X. John M. Schofield: An American Plan of Command   162

XI. R. M. Johnston: The Search for an Escape from Uptonian Despair   177

XII. Leonard Wood: The Inevitability of a Citizen Army   199

XIII. John McAuley Palmer and George C. Marshall: Universal Military Training   223

Epilogue   250

Notes   255

Bibliography   277

Index   287

TOWARDS AN AMERICAN ARMY

Military Thought from

Washington to Marshall

The Dual Military Legacy of the Revolution

A well-regulated Militia, being necessary to the security of a free State, the right of the people to keep and bear Arms, shall not be infringed. The Constitution of the United States

The Jealousies of a standing Army, and the Evils to be apprehended from one, are remote; and in my judgment, situated and circumstanced as we are, not at all to be dreaded; but the consequence of wanting one, according to my Ideas, . . . is certain, and inevitable Ruin. GEORGE WASHINGTON

ON March 15, 1781, the militiamen of General Nathanael Greene's first and second defensive lines had broken before the disciplined onslaught of British regulars, and a raw Continental regiment in the third and main American line had broken also. At this critical moment in the battle of Guilford Court House, when the American army in the South seemed on the verge of final ruin, the Continental regulars of the 1st Maryland Regiment with their attached Delaware Continentals attacked in flank the British assault column consisting of the 2nd Battalion and the Grenadiers of the Guards. The Americans halted them, and stood up to them and supporting British troops so stoutly in an open field fight that General Cornwallis in desperation ordered his artillery to fire indiscriminately on the mixed mass of his own troops and the Americans. Even then, the Maryland and Delaware Continentals did not break. They held their positions until Greene withdrew them from the field so that with better support they might fight another day.[1]

This action is much different from the popular American conception which has the War of the Revolution fought on the American side by an armed and aroused citizenry. The British Guards were stopped at Guilford Court House by American regular soldiers who had become as professional in the art of war as were their adversaries. And whatever the popular American prejudices of the Revolutionary era against professional soldiers, the commanding general of the Continental Army had long since come to believe that it was on such thorough professionals, cut from the same military mold as the troops of the European powers, that the United States had to rely for its security. The combat of the Maryland and Delaware lines at Guilford Court House confirmed George Washington's judgment of what only regulars could do, and it helped establish proudly beside the American tradition of the citizen army a rival tradition of the prowess in arms of the American regular army.

The American Revolution was probably the most conservative of the great revolutions of the modern world. Many of the American revolutionists fought to preserve the values of a cherished past rather than to force the coming of an uncertain future. This was as true of the American revolutionists' approach to war as of their approach to other things. At first, the American approach to war was remarkably conservative, considering that it was an approach born in a new world and in revolution.

The War of the American Revolution occurred in an age of marked stability in European military methods. Army organization and tactics had changed little in more than a century. Frederick the Great was the premier military figure of the age, but Frederick's mode of war consisted of the perfecting of old tactical methods rather than the introduction of new ones. For the better part of two centuries, since the emergence of the modern dynastic state, the armies of Europe had been armies of well-drilled professional soldiers. Much of Frederick's success lay simply in his carrying the drill and discipline of such professionals to a new intensity.[2] His famous oblique order of battlefield tactics stemmed from an even older source, for it had been a principal reliance of Epaminondas of Thebes. With Frederick's Prussian forces as their outstanding model, the armies of Europe in the late eighteenth century made war by means of ponderous marches and ritualistic maneuvers. The highest degree of machinelike precision of movement was regarded as the essential of a good army.[3]

Such precision could be attained only by armies of long-term military careerists, preferably of a sort not much addicted to thinking. Since European wars were principally dynastic quarrels, of concern mainly to kings and their advisers, professional armies fought out the disputes of kings without calling forth much interest or participation from the masses of European humanity. Populations did not war against populations. War was a game for the amusement and aggrandizement of kings, played by teams of the kings' hired men.

Because the European wars of the eighteenth century only slightly touched the affairs of most people, they have won much praise in our time as embodiments of a more civilized approach to intergovernmental politics than the contemporary world has been able to maintain.[4] In the late nineteenth and early twentieth centuries, fashionable military thinking tended to regard the wars of Frederick the Great and his contemporaries as absurd in their transformation of a deadly serious business into a ritual and a game. Late nineteenth- and early twentieth-century disciples of the great military philosopher Karl von Clausewitz pointed to his dictum that war, in essence, is violence carried to the utmost, and that to introduce a principle of moderation into the philosophy of war is therefore ridiculous. Thus they viewed the wars of the eighteenth century with amusement.[5] But the middle twentieth century, which has seen war become violence carried to the utmost, must regard the moderate warfare of the age of the Enlightenment with nostalgia.

The French Revolution began the eclipse of the old, restrained, dynastic warfare by inaugurating the wars of national interests and passions, and the principle of the nation in arms. In the wars of the French Revolution, the issues concerned not only kings but also peoples, and the revolutionary governments of France led the other governments of Europe to rally whole peoples to fight over those issues. Lazare Carnot's *levée en masse* opened a new age of warfare. The French proved to be the radical revolutionaries of war as well as of politics.[6]

For the most part, the American Revolution was much less radical in politics and in war alike. Within the American revolutionary movement those who would have used the rupture of the British Empire to establish a new order of society in America did struggle continually for control. But the rival group, who desired only independence and self-government, not an upheaval toppling established patterns of life, generally prevailed. In the latter group was George Washington.

As commander of the Continental Army, Washington was usually grateful for any armed men he could get. Amidst the trials of the New Jersey campaign of 1776–1777 and the Valley Forge winter of 1777–1778, Washington and his generals could scarcely have afforded to govern their conduct by the thought that a general armed levy of all the people might create a force which would generate a dangerous social revolution. The Continental officers would have taken such a levy had they been able to raise it. Nevertheless, it is characteristic that Washington and the cautious men who shared military leadership with him placed their principal military reliance not on a mass rising but on the hope of building a professional army comparable to the armies of Great Britain and France. Washington hoped to fight the British and the Hessians in their own manner. In things strictly military, Washington was scarcely a revolutionary. His answer to the redcoats' invasion of North America was patiently to create a professional army of his own. He did not base his war-making primarily on a departure from orthodoxy; he accepted military orthodoxy and worked within it.[7]

In the end he succeeded. His Continental Army did become a force whose best units were comparable to the British regulars, as the Maryland and Delaware Continentals demonstrated at Guilford Court House and on many other fields. With the French professionals of Rochambeau, Washington's Continental regulars played a decisive role at Yorktown.[8] For years, it was Washington's maintenance of a body of Continental regulars that kept the Revolution alive. Finally the Continentals were not only able to preserve their own vitality and thus that of the Revolution, but to capture the British army of Lord Cornwallis and to win the war.

The British forces in America assisted Washington's strategy by fighting principally in orthodox European style. In effect their task in the American Revolution was to defeat a people, not simply an army. But they were so accustomed to fighting wars in which the enemy's army was the objective that to wage war on the American people scarcely occurred to them. Indian allies, Tory forces, and certain British detachments struck at people rather than at American troops and lines of communications, but the British never undertook the systematic and ruthless assault against the enemy's whole society and economy that later soldiers might have used against a popular rebellion. The British confined themselves mainly to the conventional tasks of seizing territory and fighting armies. To do this as the Continental Army grew in effectiveness was to play Washington's game.

Thus the War of the American Revolution was a remarkably conventional war. Washington's campaigns were not essentially different in style from European campaigns of the day. Even tactical innovations were slight, despite the experience of the Americans in Indian warfare and a consequent tendency towards increasingly open battle formations. The French were to recognize in armed citizens the possibilities of a military revolution that would sweep the skillful but small professional armies of the Frederician era from the scene, but Washington saw in levies of citizenry simply that militia to depend on which was "assuredly, resting upon a broken staff." [9]

Of militia, and thus of levies raised from the citizenry, Washington wrote:

Men just dragged from the tender Scenes of domestick life; unaccustomed to the din of Arms; totally unacquainted with every kind of Military skill, . . . when opposed to Troops regularly train'd, disciplined, and appointed, superior in knowledge, and superior in Arms, makes them timid, and ready to fly from their own shadows. . . . Again, Men accustomed to unbounded freedom, and no controul, cannot brook the Restraint which is indispensably necessary to the good order and Government of an Army. . . . To bring Men to a proper degree of Subordination, is not the work of a day, a Month or even a year.[10]

So great was Washington's disgust with such armed citizens' militia as he had had to command by December, 1776, that he hoped then "that no reliance, except such as may arise from necessity, should ever be had in them again." [11] For these reasons Washington placed his confidence in regulars:

The Jealousies of a standing Army, and the Evils to be apprehended from one, are remote; and in my judgment, situated and circumstanced as we are, not at all to be dreaded; but the consequence of wanting one, according to my Ideas, . . . is certain, and inevitable Ruin.[12]

From early in the Revolutionary War, Washington believed that his cause needed a trained regular army, and that he could build one. He needed good officers for that purpose. Substantially he would have agreed with Nathanael Greene, who wrote: "We want nothing but good officers to constitute as good an army as ever marched into the field. Our men are better than the officers." [13] But Washington believed that good officers could be secured only by offering them a permanent career in a regular army, so that again he returned to his original goal. Viewed from any perspective, the creation of a regular army seemed to him essential to the American cause. By the end of 1776 all Washington's experience as military commander of the Revolution had led him to a single conclusion, in which he persisted thereafter: "Let us have a respectable Army, and such as will be competent to every exigency." [14]

Of course, even the most professional regiments of Washington's Continental Army were not carbon copies of European regiments. The Continental Army was a product of a middle-class society, while the European armies of the era remained largely the products of a feudal age, and this distinction made for profound differences of spirit, discipline, and organization. The American officer corps came from the same general social strata as the American soldiery, while European officer corps were composed overwhelmingly of noblemen, or among the British at least of members of the gentry. The American officers may eventually have developed pretensions toward forming a new nobility, climaxing in the establishment of the Society of the Cincinnati, but they knew that the men they commanded were of the same stuff as themselves, and the comparatively easygoing discipline even of Continental regulars was a result. In Europe holding a commission was virtually a prerogative of noble birth, an almost unbridgeable gulf separated officers and men, and the whiplash discipline of Frederick the Great's army resulted. But if the Europeans could achieve a severer discipline, in a sense the American officers could become more professional than their European counterparts, for their advancement depended less on connections and more on merit.[15]

Certain qualities of American militiamen were of military value and remained features of the Continental Army, often to become permanent aspects of the American approach to war. Militiamen fought, not in the ordered lines of European regulars but in loose formations and with an eye to any cover afforded by terrain. Such tactics were valuable in skirmishing in advance of a main attack, to reconnoiter and to soften the enemy; the professionalized Continental Army continued to use them. To some extent they may have contributed also to the light infantry tactics of the *tirailleurs* in Europe. Whether fighting in open order or in formal lines, Americans employed their hunting and Indian-fighting traditions and shot to kill. They had received training in marksmanship, and they aimed their weapons. Europeans, in contrast, fired mechanically in the general direction of the enemy. Thus from the beginning, a special skill in marksmanship became characteristic of the American army. These instances are among the most important of their kind. Together, they demonstrate that the American army remained *sui generis*. But what is most remarkable is not the Continental Army's uniqueness, but how little it differed from European armies. When Washington wrote of "a respectable Army," he was thinking in European terms, and by 1781 he had largely achieved what he sought.[16]

One military legacy of the War for Independence was an American military professionalism in the European tradition. But if the Americans were moderate revolutionaries, they were revolutionaries nevertheless. On the one hand, Washington fought the campaigns of New York, Brandywine–Germantown, Monmouth, and York-town with a force that was as close an approximation of European regulars as he could muster, and Greene fought at Guilford Court House, Hobkirk's Hill, and Eutaw Springs with an army whose core was of much the same sort. On the other hand, Burgoyne's invasion of the rebellious colonies by the Lake Champlain–Hudson River route came to grief largely because the farther he advanced, the more unexpected armed enemies he encountered. The American Revolution was not simply a European dynastic war. On the American side it was a national war. People in large numbers cared about its issues, as they did not care about the quarrels of kings. A logical corollary was for the American leaders to mobilize the concern of the people, to call on them to fight in battles where the stakes were their own. And in part this was done. Burgoyne was defeated by a miniature of the nation in arms. His opponents seemed to him to spring from the very trees.

The repulse of Burgoyne's supply-hunting detachment at Bennington offered a good example of the deadly work an armed population could do. Burgoyne sent Baron von Riedesel to gather from Bennington stores that he supposed were to be had for the taking. But the armed farmers of Vermont utterly ruined Riedesel's column and the reinforcements that Burgoyne sent following it. Here, as at Concord earlier and at King's Mountain later, conventional European professionals met an armed and angry people, and the results to the professionals were murderous.[17]

At Concord, Bennington, King's Mountain, and a host of similar engagements began a military revolution to go with the political one. The Indian wars already had created an armed citizenry. If the fighting strength of the American population could be properly harnessed, possible results were unlimited. Popular legend came to recognize this fact, and thereafter many Americans long inclined to the belief that their country needed no professional army, because American citizens could whip any professional soldiers on earth. In America there were no kings. American wars would be people's wars, and in them the people would do their own fighting and win their own triumphs. Out of America would come a new style of war.[18]

But Washington and other more serious military observers remembered not only the occasional spectacular successes of an armed populace but also remembered the more frequent failures. The militia Washington saw break and flee before the British again and again, who did not cross the Delaware to assist in the raid on Trenton, and who failed to carry out their assignment at Germantown also were the nation in arms, and their performance led Washington to hope he would never have to rely on them again.

The result was that the United States drew from the War of the Revolution two different military traditions, a conservative tradition and a revolutionary one. The British had attempted to subdue their rebellious colonies principally by means of an orthodox war in which professional soldiers seized strategic territories and defeated the enemy's armed forces. The Americans had replied in two ways. Often they had attempted to create an orthodox professional force of their own, but sometimes they had drawn a logical conclusion from the fact that they were fighting a national war, and then they had moved toward raising the nation in arms. The War of the American Revolution had been fought by a mixture of both methods, but those who especially favored one method often saw little merit in the other. Therefore the two military traditions born of the American Revolution came to be regarded as contradictory and rival traditions, and the struggle between their adherents was to become a dominant theme in the history of American military thought.

Which should be regarded as the primary approach to war, Americans came to argue, the conventional approach, with its reliance on regulars and its emphasis on battle with other regulars, or the revolutionary approach, with its reliance on the nation in arms and the still further revolutionary implications which that principle gradually revealed? Should America be an orthodox military power, or a revolutionary one?

ALEXANDER HAMILTON

Military Professionalism in Early Republican Style

> When the perfect order and exact discipline which are essential
> to regular troops are contemplated, and with what ease and pre-
> cision they execute the difficult maneuvers indispensable to the suc-
> cess of offensive or defensive operations, the conviction cannot be
> resisted that such troops will always have a decided advantage over
> more numerous forces composed of uninstructed militia or undis-
> ciplined recruits. ALEXANDER HAMILTON

IN 1783, with the War of the Revolution won, the Congress of the
Confederation undertook to consider a permanent military establishment for the United States. It organized a committee for that purpose under Alexander Hamilton, and the committee solicited the
opinions of the leading generals of the war. First among them was
Washington, and his response to the committee's request was his
famous "Sentiments on a Peace Establishment." [1]

Washington's wartime views had identified him as a military
conservative, a champion of reliance on regulars. But the "Sentiments" which he now wrote, destined to be virtually forgotten in
the nineteenth century and then resurrected by twentieth-century
champions of the nation in arms, eventually made him the patron
saint of the opposite camp, the military revolutionists. For in his
"Sentiments," Washington felt compelled by American realities to
modify his wartime position and to endorse a popular militia and
the principle of the nation in arms.

Washington had relied as much as possible on Continental regulars to win the war, but he recognized that a large regular establishment in peacetime, and especially under the government of the

Confederation, was unattainable. Americans had inherited from England a profound fear of a standing army, and the events preceding the Revolution, revolving as they did around the stationing of British garrisons in America, had intensified that fear. Even if the traditional repugnance to a standing army could be overcome, Washington had to recognize that the infant United States was an agricultural nation of limited means, and that for the present any considerable standing army would involve insupportable expense. Therefore, the general in chief's scheme of a peace organization had to depart from his wartime reliance on regulars.

Washington called for a small regular army of 2,631 officers and men, forming four regiments of infantry and a regiment of artillery and artificers. He regarded this force as the minimum necessary to guard the western frontier and the Canadian and Florida borders, to secure the national magazines, and in general to form a first line of defense against surprises. The restless Indians to the west, and the dubiously friendly British and Spanish seemed to him to make such a regular army indispensable.

Washington believed that, as soon as possible, the United States should build a respectable navy to patrol its coasts against invasion and thus to lighten the potential burden on its army.

But even with a navy as an outer defense, a regular army of 2,631 would not provide adequate security. There was no choice but to rely on militia, an armed citizenry to supplement the regular army, despite Washington's despair of them in the past. Unable to afford a professional army comparable to the armies of Europe, the United States could at least take advantage of being a republican government to rally to its support the people it represented. The troops might not be the best, but the armies of European kings would be hard put to match them in numbers.

Washington's arguments in later years became the stock in trade of those who would claim his support for the principle of the nation in arms, including in the twentieth century, the imposition of conscription. Indeed, he advanced the basic rationalization which has supported conscription in democratic countries everywhere from revolutionary France to the modern United States, the idea which historically has tied democratic political revolution to military revolution culminating in total war:

It may be laid down as a primary position, and the basis of our system, that every Citizen who enjoys the protection of a free Government, owes not only a proportion of his property, but even of his personal services to the defence of it.

This idea, proclaiming a universal military obligation as the concomitant of the ballot, is the foundation of the modern mass army.

The implications of a universal obligation to arms were revolutionary, but Washington was sufficiently a product of eighteenth-century training in the classics and in English history to know that he was not proposing a complete innovation:

We might have recourse to the Histories of Greece and Rome in their most virtuous and Patriotic ages to demonstrate the Utility of such Establishments. Then passing by the Mercinary Armies, which have at one time or another subverted the liberties of allmost [sic] all the Countries they have been raised to defend, we might see, with admiration, the Freedom and Independence of Switzerland supported for Centuries, in the midst of powerful and jealous neighbors, by means of a hardy and well organized Militia.

Therefore Washington called for an enrollment of all citizens of the United States from eighteen to fifty years of age into a nationally established militia, all to be provided with uniform arms.

But Washington had pointed to the Swiss militia as an example of the sort of formations desired, a "hardy and well organized Militia." He stressed this point, that it was not the militia of the Revolution that he wanted to see again, but "A well organized Militia; upon a Plan that will pervade all the States, and introduce similarity in their Establishment Manœuvres, Exercise and Arms." Indeed, Washington desired a militia in which some men, at least, would be much like regulars. He proposed that there be a special force of carefully trained men, capable of immediate resistance to European regulars, within the general militia. All the militia, he held, should be organized to be available for immediate call "on any very interesting Emergency" and regularly mustered, trained, and inspected. But it would be impossible to make anything resembling finished soldiers of the militia at large, and Washington's experience warned him that only soldiers who at least approximated that type would be able to resist European regulars. Therefore he urged that a special group should be recruited from among the able-bodied young men between eighteen and twenty-five who had a special "fondness for military Parade (which passion is almost ever prevalent at that period of life)." Given the prevalence of the passion, the numbers that could be recruited would be substantial. These men would then constitute a ready reserve who, while part of the militia system, would nevertheless possess a military skill at least somewhat comparable to that of professionals.

The specially recruited young men were to be exercised *at least* twelve to twenty-five days a year. They were to train partly in their own companies, but part of their annual training was also to be in battalions and brigades. As brigades, they should form camps, whereby "their Discipline would be greatly promoted, and their Ideas raised, as near as possible, to real service." Their organization should follow that of the Continental Army, and their officers should be commissioned on the Continental plan, not by states. The officers of all militia should be as much as possible veterans of regular service.[2]

But would the training period stipulated for the ready reserve be adequate to permit the reserve to combat European soldiers? Washington clearly developed doubts, and came to lean towards a longer training. He later acknowledged not only that his "Sentiments" had been hastily drawn upon a sudden call but also that in preparing them he had "glided almost insensibly into what I thought *would,* rather than what I conceived *ought* to be a proper peace Establishment for this Country." [3] As he reflected further, he came to prefer the proposals of Baron von Steuben, who also recommended to Congress an improved militia system, but who would have established within the militia a ready force slightly better prepared for war than Washington's, a group of three-year volunteers who would train for thirty days each year and who would be organized into regional defense commands to facilitate their mobilization.[4]

In any case, it was a special militia force of the maximum possible training, not the armed citizenry in general, that Washington preferred as support for the regular army in war:

I am fully persuaded [he wrote], that the Fensible, Fusileers, or Train Bands formed of the Inhabitants of Cities and Incorporated Towns will not afford that prompt and efficacious resistance to an Enemy, which might be expected from regularly established Light Infantry Companies, or a general selection of the ablest Men from every Regt. or Brigade of Militia . . . ; the number being fixed to any proportion from $\frac{1}{8}$ to $\frac{1}{50}$ of the whole Militia, that number of disciplined effective Men may always be relied on in case of war, as an effective Barrier to stop the torrent of Hostility, until a regular and permanent force could be levied; And in order to make this Corps the more respectable, I should heartily concur in giving them a superiority of rank, immunities or emoluments over the rest of the Militia.[5]

At bottom, Washington's "Sentiments" of 1783 were not so different from the conservative, professionalist military views he set forth during the war. The *levée en masse* had not yet appeared, and Washington was not engaged in inventing it. His emphasis was on a small regular army, on a ready reserve chosen from among the militia and trained to as close an approximation of professional standards as possible, and finally on "a regular and permanent force" raised when war had swept away objections to such a force.

The committee chairman to whom Washington and Steuben submitted their recommendations liked their views, and reflections of them appeared in his report to Congress. Alexander Hamilton, with his realistic appreciation of the role of force in world affairs and of the insecurity of the United States, was to be a champion of military preparedness throughout his career, but he was not inclined to suggest a revolutionary means of achieving it. Now he felt obliged to devote much of his report on military affairs to defending the establishment of any national army whatever, arguing that points of strategic importance to the whole Confederation ought to be guarded by Continental troops. He had to strain himself to seek ideas that would pay some regard to the jealousies of state sovereignties but would not hamstring national programs for defense. In the Congress of the Confederation skepticism about any national military force was likely to prove overwhelming. But once Hamilton had offered all the arguments he knew to overcome that skepticism, his specific recommendations hewed closely to the Washington-Steuben line.

Like Washington, Hamilton suggested a regular military establishment of four regiments of infantry plus one regiment of artillery and engineers, although he added also a regiment of dragoons. Like Washington and Steuben, he proposed in the absence of a substantial regular army a reliance upon "a well-regulated militia," under congressional as well as state supervision in order to ensure uniformity of organization and equipment. Like the two elder military statesmen, Hamilton urged that a special and as much as possible a professionalized force be established within the militia.

Hamilton would have divided the militia, composed of all free male inhabitants between twenty and fifty, into one class of married men, one of single men. The single men were to assemble in companies once a month, in regiments once every three months, for exercises and inspection. The married men were to assemble in companies once every three months, in regiments once every six months, for the same purposes. When a state was invaded, its troops of either class were to take the field, to remain in active service for a maximum of one year. When another state was attacked and needed aid, half the corps of single men from its sister states were to go to its defense for a maximum of one year, to be relieved in time by other militiamen.

Beyond the two general classes of militia, Hamilton called for a third class, to be trained to a high degree of military skill. Volunteers were to be enlisted in the third class for eight years, binding themselves to serve three years in war wherever they might be sent. They were to number not more than one-fiftieth of the total militia. They were to receive from the Confederation government musket, bayonet, cartouchbox, and twenty-four rounds of powder and ball, together with a new uniform every two years. Most important, they were to assemble by companies once a week and by regiments every month, and for twenty additional days each year they were to go into camp. They were to be, in fact, a reserve possessing virtually the full training of regulars, lacking only the constant day by day practice of regulars.[6]

None of these plans won the approval of the Confederation Congress. Lacking adequate powers as well as inclination, that body contented itself with providing a handful of regulars—immediately after the close of the Revolutionary War, fewer than a hundred of them—to guard the military stores at West Point and Pittsburgh; otherwise it left military activity to the states.[7] But the trend of thinking among the leading military figures of the country was clear. Because the United States had emerged from a popular revolution, because there was a deep popular suspicion of standing armies and conversely a regard for the militia as a bulwark of liberties, and because the nation could not afford a full European-type regular army, the leading American military spokesmen called for some reliance on a popular militia. But they minimized the revolutionary possibilities of such a force. They continued to envision war in orthodox European terms, and to prepare for possible war against a European military power they did not rely mainly on any mass levies but on a picked force that would be trained to the highest military skills that American conditions would permit. If a larger force were needed to win a war, "a regular and permanent force" would be mustered while the ready militia held the line.

In his hope for a conventionally powerful American army capable of combatting the armies of Europe on their own terms, Washington contemplated the establishment of a United States military academy. Hamilton's committee called for three professors to be attached to the Corps of Engineers, while otherwise professing skepticisim about an academy, saying the subject must be postponed to the future. Probably his committee colleagues and the circumstances of the time restrained Hamilton from taking the views he later endorsed.[8] But Washington advocated a full-fledged academy to be organized as soon as possible. For the present, he thought it would be necessary to be content with instruction of young artillerists and engineers in their camps. But more would soon be needed:

Of so great importance is it to preserve the knowledge which has been acquired thro' the various Stages of a long and arduous service, that I cannot conclude without repeating the necessity of the proposed Institution, unless we intend to let the Science [of war] become extinct, and to depend entirely upon the Foreigners for their friendly aid, if ever we should again be involved in Hostility.[9]

Here is the essence of Washington's view. Thinking in terms of European warfare, he regarded warmaking as a science, not a subject for amateurs but a matter for careful schooling. All his other observations on armies and warfare followed from this premise.

There were many reasons why the recommendations of Washington, Steuben, and Hamilton came to nothing. The Congress of the Confederation could barely manage to mobilize sufficient revenues to keep the Confederation alive. Even the states'-rightists came to admit that the revenue system of the Confederation needed overhauling if the Union were to survive, and in these circumstances even a moderately strong standing army of the sort that Washington proposed was beyond the means of Congress. As for the recommendations for a well-organized militia, the burden of paying off state war debts in a period of postwar business readjustment was itself enough to excite a rebellious spirit among the populace of the states, and there was no likelihood of the states' taking on high military expenses. Beyond inadequate finances, furthermore, party strife within many states created a distrust of state armies, lest they be used to further the political interests of the dominant factions.[10]

Such considerations helped lead Washington and Hamilton to propose a drastic reformation of the national government. But the inauguration of the new government of the Constitution of 1787 under the presidency of Washington brought little change to the military situation at first. The weakness of the Confederation government had provided some of the causes for the neglect of Washington's proposals of 1783, but more fundamental causes still persisted. The traditional distrust of a standing army remained, intensified by experiences with British troops before and during the Revolution. Having expelled the redcoats from their soil, the Americans felt no inclination to throw up a new force essentially the same though it might wear coats of buff and blue; for the United States to have established any formidable regular army in the 1790s would have seemed like nullifying the victory of the Revolution. More than that, either a good regular army or a well-organized militia on the Washington-Steuben-Hamilton plan would have cost money, and although the government of the Constitution could command revenues beyond those of the Confederation, it still had to proceed cautiously. Events were to prove that even a tax designed to meet necessary expenses and help pay off war debts could provoke fresh rebellion. As John Adams observed, Americans were not accustomed to much taxation, and they objected to it whatever the source.

Regarding military establishments as instruments of tyranny, hostile to taxation of any kind, Americans easily persuaded them-

selves that the War of Independence had demonstrated the need-
lessness of expensive military establishments, federal or state. They
had possessed no such establishments at the beginning of the war,
yet they had defeated the foremost power of the globe. They for-
got the rout at Long Island and Washington's disastrous retreat
across the Jerseys, and they remembered Concord, Bunker Hill,
and Saratoga. They proposed as the military policy of the United
States a version of the nation in arms. Indeed, they not only believed that every citizen should bear arms, but they regarded arms-
bearing as not so much a duty as a right. They described it as
such in the second amendment to the Constitution. An armed
citizenry, Americans believed, constituted the best foundation of
military policy, for it ensured safety against foreign attack and
defense against any possible tyrannical pretensions of the government at home. And with the record of Bennington and King's Mountain to its credit, why should the armed citizenry be burdened with
costly, unpleasant, and time-consuming military training? [11]

The new government of the Constitution did augment the regular army. By 1789, requirements of frontier defense had compelled
an increase of the Confederation army to an eight-company regiment of infantry and a four-company battalion of artillery. In 1790
the new Congress raised the infantry regiment to twelve-company
strength. When this force under Colonel Josiah Harmer proved
only large enough to provoke an Indian concentration which decisively defeated it, Congress acted in 1791, to add a second infantry regiment and to authorize federal emergency volunteers to
serve for six-months periods. When General Arthur St. Clair led
both regular infantry regiments, 300 men in each, and also 1,500
volunteers on another campaign against the Indians who had
whipped Harmar, the result was another defeat. Thereupon in
1792 Congress authorized five regiments of infantry with appropriate cavalry and artillery support, 5,000 men in all, the force
which became General Anthony Wayne's Legion of the United
States and won the battle of Fallen Timbers.[12]

But the regular army of 1792 did not grow because of any inclination of Congress to abandon the armed-citizenry theory for a
professional-army policy; it was a pragmatic response to Indian
hostility in the Northwest Territory. Once the Indians were some-

what quieted, Congress proceeded with a gradual reduction of the army. The regular army of the United States was conceived in the beginning less as a defense against foreign enemies, for which purpose it was plainly inadequate, than as a police force to maintain order in the Indian country. There was no intention among congressional leaders to place major reliance for foreign defense on the regular army. If a defense against foreign enemies were to be established, it would be through the militia.[13]

Recognizing this fact, President Washington's secretary of war, Henry Knox, hoped at least to establish a "well-regulated" militia. At the beginning of 1790, Knox presented to Washington for submission to Congress an elaborate plan for the organization and training of a militia under substantial federal control. He suggested that all able-bodied men between the ages of eighteen and sixty be enrolled in the militia, pleading again the universal obligation of military service to a popular government. Mariners were to enroll in a naval militia. Apparently Knox was drawing as much as seemed feasible on the Washington-Steuben-Hamilton plans of the Confederation period, although without the suggestion of a specially trained force of volunteers within the militia. He hoped to assure adequate training by dividing the militia into three categories by age. Youths of eighteen to twenty would form the Advanced Corps, with the members aged eighteen and nineteen to train thirty consecutive days each year and those aged twenty to train ten consecutive days. Thus the elements of military drill might be learned with a fair degree of thoroughness. On becoming twenty-one, the militiamen would pass from the Advanced Corps to the Main Corps, on which first reliance would be placed to mobilize an army in an emergency. The Main Corps was to be organized fully into legions, which would combine elements of all arms to form miniature armies. The members of the Main Corps were to drill four days each year, with the regiments assembling once annually and the legions assembling once every three years. On reaching the age of forty-six, militiamen would pass into the Reserved Corps, there to be eligible until age sixty for call to duty in garrisons and behind the lines.[14]

Significantly, Knox's plan prescribed day by day the type of training that the militia were to receive in their annual encampments, from elementary drill for the new members of the Advanced Corps to maneuvers of regiments or legions when all had assembled; the pattern of activity was thus to be prescribed by federal authority. Furthermore, the militia were to be clothed, armed, and subsisted at the expense of the United States and according to federal standards. All arms and accoutrements were to be marked in a conspicuous place with the letters "M. U. S.". Knox's militia was to be emphatically a United States militia, not simply a congeries of state forces.[15]

Henry Knox was a citizen soldier, but one who had trained himself thoroughly with his books and then through experience. He believed there were high military possibilities in an armed citizenry, if the citizenry were well trained. Indeed, as a political conservative he hoped the militia might create a disciplined and readily governable populace, and he apparently felt real enthusiasm for his militia plan.[16] But neither he nor Washington could persuade Congress to accept the plan. The popular faith was in armed citizens ready to spring into action without formal military training, as they had done against the Indians and against the British. Washington presented Knox's views to Congress in January, 1790, but it was not until July that a militia bill was introduced into the House, and then it was a far weaker bill than Knox desired. Even a weak militia measure, however, was reported from committee to the House repeatedly without winning passage, and a still more diluted bill at last received approval as the Militia Act of May 8, 1792.[17]

This act became the foundation of the permanent military policy of the United States, proclaiming the reliance of the nation not on the regulars of traditional European warfare but on an armed mass of able-bodied men between eighteen and forty-five. The year 1792 was also the year in which untrained masses of Frenchmen first sprang to arms to defend their revolution against the foreign kings, foreshadowing the *levée en masse* of the following year. But the Militia Act of 1792 declared a policy without offering the means to realize it. It gave no assurance that the militia would be well organized and well regulated. Leaving training and organization to the states, it put those matters in the hands of political functionaries who would find it expedient to minimize them. It failed to provide means of enforcing its own requirement of a universal obligation to service; it offered no means of assuring that citizens would comply with its requirement that they furnish their own arms and accoutrements at personal expense.[18]

To such men as Washington, Hamilton, and Knox its weaknesses were immediately apparent, and they became increasingly evident with each feeble attempt to apply the law. In March, 1794, the House appointed a committee to report what alterations and amendments were necessary to make the Militia Act effective. In December, Knox made a special report to Congress on the difficulties of enforcing the act. On December 29, even the Jeffersonian James Branch Giles of Virginia reported as chairman of another House committee that the Militia Act ought to be amended to provide for arming the militia at public expense and for enforcing the provisions of law by adequate penalties.[19] But nothing substantial came of the proposals for improvement. The general view of Congress continued in accord with the report of the March, 1794, committee, which held that to strengthen the militia through further federal legislation would violate the constitutional powers of the states, and that persuading the states to be more diligent would doubtless create an efficient militia without the need of congressional legislation.[20] An act of July 6, 1798, passed during the crisis with France, provided for arming the militia at government expense, but no other important change was made in the Militia Act of 1792.[21]

The militia continued to enjoy their occasional muster days of parades and frolics and sometimes serious training. A few companies became respectable military units, but most of them remained no better than the militia of the War of Independence. The Militia Act of 1792 had as one of its principal results strengthening the zeal of the advocates of a professional army. Knowing that no adequate popular defense force existed, they seized such new opportunities as developed to call again for an American approximation of the regular armies of Europe. Through its weakness, the Militia Act of 1792 played into their hands.

When war with France threatened after the XYZ Affair, for example, Washington and Hamilton returned to the effort to secure a good professional force. Only an augmented professional army, they and their party urged, could prepare the nation for the conflict which might erupt against the foremost military power of the globe. The Federalists pushed through Congress an authorization for raising 40,000 regulars and 75,000 federal volunteers.[22]

The John Adams administration never saw fit to create this force, but Washington, recalled to military service as commanding general of the new army with the grade of lieutenant general, and Hamilton, inspector general and active commander, drew their plans against the possibility of battle with the French around an increased number of regulars. Under the threat of a French war, the purpose of the regular army underwent a change in emphasis. Congress had created it mainly as a police force for the Indian frontier. Now many came to regard it as the principal instrument for waging foreign war.

There now emerged from Hamilton's pen and over Washington's name an idea important in the future thought of American champions of a primarily professional army. Hamilton suggested that the peacetime standing army should be so organized as to be readily expansible at the first call of war, with wartime recruits simply adding flesh to an already existing skeleton. Reliance on militia could be minimized and new recruits could come immediately under the influence of veteran regulars. Advocacy of such an expansible army or cadre system became the main reliance of those who believed that only a professional army resembling the conventional European type offered real military security.[23]

The germ of the expansible army idea had appeared as early as Washington's military proposals of 1783, in which the Virginian had called for regular regiments smaller than those of the Continental Army in that they would exclude the light company of the Continental regiments and reduce each of the battalion companies by a sergeant and eighteen privates. Meanwhile the regimental complement of commissioned officers would remain the same as in the Continental Army. Then in case of war the regiment could be strengthened readily, simply by giving it its flank company and adding eighteen men to each other company.[24]

Hamilton and Washington developed the idea further. In 1798, they suggested standards for infantry, cavalry, and artillery regiments which would provide considerably more men in proportion to officers than the existing tables of organization. However they proposed that the new standards not be realized until wartime. Meanwhile the regiments would have a surplus of officers, whose companies could be filled and the regular army thus increased immediately on the outbreak of war, with no need for the confusion of creating new formations. In case new formations eventually should be required, however, and in order to assure a more than adequate supply of leaders, Hamilton also proposed a special regiment made up entirely of men training for higher ranks, even with its privates prepared to become sergeants at the outbreak of war.[25]

If the nation were to rely primarily on its regular army for defense against foreign enemies, the regular army would have to possess a capacity for rapid growth. The Washington-Hamilton suggestion of skeleton cadres to be filled out in war and a surplus of peacetime officers, commissioned and non-commissioned, made such growth seem feasible.

Meanwhile Hamilton advanced other suggestions for creating an army both respectably large and professional. With a view to the congressionally authorized 75,000 volunteers, he proposed to substitute for the militia a more professional "provisional or auxiliary army" as a second line. This force might guard the frontier, freeing much of the regular army for duty along the Eastern seaboard, and sharply underlining the departure from the original purpose of the post-Revolutionary regular army. As a frontier guard, the auxiliary force might be recruited in western Pennsylvania and Virginia, the Northwest and Southwest territories, Kentucky, South Carolina, and Georgia. Its men would not need to serve continuously in peacetime, but they were to be no mere militia, for they were to take the field for at least several months every year.[26]

As for the militia, Hamilton once again urged dividing them into various classes, with a class of young, active, and unmarried men to receive more thorough training than the rest, thus creating as professional as possible a force within the militia.[27]

To professionalize the command of the whole military establishment he proposed a full-fledged military university, with a basic school to be supplemented by schools for advanced training and thought in the military art.[28] If such a university had been established, it might have anticipated the Prussian *Kriegsakademie* of the Scharnhorst-Gneisenau period as a nursery of military science, but its establishment was beyond the range of American possibilities.

Early in 1800, even though the French crisis was by then fading, Hamilton renewed his effort to establish a good professional American army. Washington was dead now, and Hamilton could no longer rely on his prestigious signature to give weight to his own arguments. He had to content himself with utilizing Secretary of War James McHenry's special report to Congress on "various matters in which the honor and safety of the nation are deeply interested"; that is, Hamilton spoke through McHenry to argue at length to the nation the necessity for a sound military defense, the folly of relying upon any but professional soldiers to ensure such defense, and the need for a military academy to crown the military establishment. The very reluctance of the United States to create a large military force, he urged, demanded that the country create an excellent force:

> No sentiment is more just than this, that in proportion as the circumstances and policy of a people are opposed to the maintenance of a large military force, it is important that as much perfection as possible be given to that which may at any time exist.
> It is not, however, enough that the troops that it may be deemed proper to maintain be rendered as perfect as possible in form, organization, and discipline: the dignity, the character to be supported, and the safety of the country further require that it should have military institutions, should be capable of perpetuating the art of war, and of furnishing the means for forming a new and enlarged army, fit for service in the shortest time possible, and at the least practicable expense to the state.[29]

Again Hamilton urged upon Congress as a military institution to perpetuate the art of war, a military university or academy.[30] But in a succeeding report he emphasized that such institutions, though essential, could only be supplements to the prime necessity, a strong regular army. The American army might have to be small by European standards, but surely it must be as large as possible. In a report transmitted from Secretary McHenry to Congress in February, 1800, Hamilton gave his clearest statement of his belief in the superiority of regulars over militia. He rejected utterly the revolutionary theme implicit in the original military legislation of

Congress, under which the regular army was to have been a border police force and the militia the chief reliance in war.

It is not conceived [he hoped] that the United States will ever think it expedient . . . to place their reliance, for defense against a foreign invading enemy, upon militia alone, but that they will, at all times, maintain a body of regular troops, commensurate with their ability to maintain them, and the necessity or policy that may demand such an establishment.

To qualify and keep our citizens in general . . . prepared to take the field against regular forces, would demand . . . such uninterrupted series of training, discipline, and instruction . . . as comports with regular troops only. . . .

Practically considered, may we not as well calculate to be commodiously lodged, and have the science of building improved, by employing every man in the community in the construction of houses, and by excluding from society as useless, architects, masons, and carpenters, as expect to be defended efficiently from an invading enemy by causing every citizen to endeavor to make himself master of the several branches of the art of war, and excluding engineers, scientific officers, and regular troops. . . .

When the perfect order and exact discipline which are essential to regular troops are contemplated, and with what ease and precision they execute the different maneuvers indispensable to the success of offensive or defensive operations, the conviction cannot be resisted that such troops will always have a decided advantage over more numerous forces composed of uninstructed militia or undisciplined recruits.

It cannot yet be forgotten that in our Revolutionary War it was not until after several years' practice in arms, and the extension of the periods for which our soldiers were first enlisted, that we found them at all qualified to meet in the field of battle those to whom they were opposed. The occasional brilliant and justly celebrated acts of some of our militia during that eventful period detract nothing from this dear-bought truth. With all the enthusiasm which marked those days, it was perceived and universally felt that regular and disciplined troops were indispensable, and that it was utterly unsafe for us to trust to our militia alone the issue of the war. The position, therefore, is illustrated that even in times of greatest danger we cannot give to our militia that degree of discipline or to their officers that degree of military science upon which a nation may safely hazard its fate.[31]

The point could not have received a more categoric statement. Contrary to legend, said Hamilton, the nation in arms had not won the War of the Revolution; disciplined regulars had won it. In them alone could the nation place its trust. The new, democratic ideas of warfare were unrealistic. The professional military tradition was the only viable one.

By the time Washington and Hamilton prepared for renewed military careers under the threat of war with France, the potential enemy had thrown over the professional army of the eighteenth century for the principle of the nation in arms. Even as Washington and Hamilton planned another professional army, General Bonaparte in France was rising toward dictatorship on the strength of what he could accomplish with the new *levée en masse*. Victory after victory had flown to the hosts of the French Republic. Their numbers and their élan had proven more than enough to compensate for their lack of military polish. But characteristically, Washington and Hamilton continued to prepare for war in the old style. They may have done so partly because they intended, Hamilton especially, that the army should put down not only foreign enemies but also the enemies of Federalism at home; for that purpose a popular force could not serve.[32] But beyond such a consideration, the persistence of Washington and Hamilton in preparing for old-fashioned war demonstrated the strength of the conservative one of the two military traditions which had emerged with American independence. In fact, that strength was just beginning to appear. The American professional military tradition was to survive not only the impact of the wars of the French Revolution and Napoleon but also that of Jeffersonian liberalism.

The advent of Thomas Jefferson to the Presidency seemed at first to promise the eclipse of Hamilton's doctrine of the professional army as the primary means of defense. Jefferson's eighteenth-century liberalism was hostile to standing armies as the natural foes of liberty, and the new President's devotion to public economy made him take an all the more jaundiced view of the regulars. He regarded the sturdy yeomanry of the American farms as the backbone of the nation in every respect, including military defense, and freedom and military security alike seemed to him to demand that the defense of the country rest on the strong arms and stubborn self-reliance of the farmers, not on hired and thus corruptible mercenaries. As for the distinction between the civil and the military, he said, "it is for the happiness of both to obliterate it." Beyond these permanent considerations, the existing standing army was identified with Federalism and with the reputed intention of the Hamiltonian Federalists to quash their political rivals by force. Fear of its augmentation and its purposes had done much to ensure the Jeffersonian victory in the election of 1800. For all these reasons, Jefferson entered the executive mansion prepared to reduce the regular army, and he did so.[33]

The authorized strength of the army was 5,438, but vacancies appeared without being filled, and the actual strength soon fell to 3,794 and continued to decrease. "A well-disciplined militia, our best reliance in peace, and for the first moments of war," Jefferson said in his first inaugural address. Although he added the words, "till regulars may relieve them," he obviously was not thinking of Hamilton's type of regulars.[34]

Despite such initial auguries, the Jeffersonian era proved to be one of rising official belief that the true reliance for the defense of the United States must be first upon a substantial force of regulars, not upon militia. The rise was in official belief, not in popular thought. But the result was an increasing reliance in fact on a professional army.

Jefferson himself acknowledged that if the regular army were to be very small it ought at the same time to be very good. Therefore in 1802, the President was instrumental in founding the United States Military Academy at West Point; Jefferson brought this dream of the professionalists Washington and Hamilton to realization. At first the academy was merely an adjunct of the newly organized Corps of Engineers, which was only now separated from the artillerists. As a branch of the military engineers, the school might have peaceful as well as military uses. This proved true when the academy became and long continued to be the first and one of the foremost schools of professional engineering in the nation. The peaceful work of its engineers was often to guard the academy against the attacks of its political enemies. Under the establishing act of 1802, the superintendent was to be the commandant of the Corps of Engineers, or his next in rank when he was absent from the academy at West Point. The cadets were to be merely ten in number, attached also to the Corps of Engineers. Before the Jefferson administration ended, however, the authorized cadet strength was raised to 150, attached to infantry and artillery regiments as well as to the engineers. Thus in this Hamiltonian institution created by Jefferson there lay at least the germ of the future nursery of a professional officer corps for the regular army.[35]

Meanwhile the great revolutionary wars in Europe, which had seemed about to smolder out when Jefferson took office, flared up again in 1803 as the newly crowned Emperor Napoleon assembled his Army of the Coasts of the Ocean for the invasion of England. The British and French in their struggle for commercial supremacy threatened to pull the United States into the war just as America had entered all their struggles of the past century and a half. Although Jefferson hoped to maintain American rights at sea in the face of threatening belligerent maritime systems through peaceful coercion, he could not be sure that his embargo policy would work. Faced with a tangible threat of war with one or the other of the great military powers of the Atlantic world, Jefferson thought carefully about his military policy and grew less enamored of the militia. The French had fought so long now that their once raw levies had become professionalized; their armies won battles through military skill as well as through numbers. Military skill at least equal to the French also characterized the smaller British army, for that army remained a professional force of the eighteenth-century type. Fortunately, the troubles of Europe would ensure that neither could throw the full strength of its numbers against America in case the United States went to war. But to cope with any British or French force that might reach American shores, the United States would require men of military training and experience far beyond the attainments of militia and in greater numbers than the minuscule regular army of 1803 could offer. Therefore, by 1808 Jefferson himself had presided over an increase in the authorized standing army to nearly 10,000.[36]

Jefferson's chosen successor, James Madison, confronted not only the threat of foreign war but war itself. Under the impetus of the War Hawks of the West, themselves professedly Jeffersonians, the authorized strength of the regulars grew to 35,603 by the opening of the War of 1812. Only 6,686 of these troops were actually under arms when the war began, and the hastily mustered new regular regiments were for months not much different from militia. As the war progressed it became evident that the existing militia was likely to be so worthless in combat as to merit anew Washington's most bitter strictures against the Revolutionary militia, while the battles against the British that the United States could view without blushing were principally those fought by the regulars. Repeatedly the militia fled or refused to fight, while regular army officers and methods soon made respectable soldiers even of the newly enlisted regulars. For thoughtful men, the battle of New Orleans did not change this picture. Andrew Jackson's men fought that battle behind the entrenchments of the Rodrigues Canal; it was doubtful what they would have done in the open field. Through all the war, only Jacob Brown's and Winfield Scott's regulars at Chippewa and Lundy's Lane stood up solidly against the British when the tactical advantages were even.[37]

The United States regular army had begun its post-Revolutionary career as a frontier police force. The threat of war with France in 1798 had suggested a change of emphasis in its purpose. In the War of 1812 it became in fact the first reliance of the nation in foreign war. Not so much the arguments of Washington and Hamilton as the march of events had brought about the revival of the American professional army from its nadir of the Confederation period. Events seemed so much to confirm the wisdom of Washington and Hamilton that their arguments were now taken up from within a Jeffersonian administration.

III JOHN C. CALHOUN *The Expansible*
Army Plan

> To suppose our militia capable of meeting in the open field the regular troops of Europe, would be to resist the most obvious truth, and the whole of our experience as a nation. War is an art, to attain perfection in which, much time and experience, particularly for the officers, are necessary. JOHN C. CALHOUN

THE administration of President James Monroe was nominally a Jeffersonian one, and Secretary of War John C. Calhoun brought from his South Carolina constituency particular affinities with Jeffersonian doctrine. Under these circumstances, there could be no more dramatic evidence of the impact of the War of 1812 on the relative strength of the conservative, professionalist and the revolutionary, amateurist American military traditions than Calhoun's straightforward endorsement of military professionalism.

The experiences of the war had helped to dilute pure Jeffersonianism with a heady new nationalism in almost every area of public policy. But the new emphasis of a leading Jeffersonian Republican statesman on the professional regular army as America's necessary reliance in war, was significant whatever the circumstances.

In his first official papers issued from the War Department, Calhoun still made formal obeisance to Jeffersonian regard for the militia. Even then, however, the principal emphasis of his reports was on maintaining the regular army at what seemed to many a high peacetime strength, 12,656 men. He argued that the increased extent of the country and the growth of its resources made an army of 12,656 in 1818, no larger proportionately than an army of 3,323 had been in 1802, and the earlier strength had carried the sanction of Jefferson himself. Now that the Napoleonic wars were over, he could point to no immediate European threat to American security, although the interest of the conservative European powers in the

Latin American revolutions would presently seem to offer such a threat. Meanwhile, Calhoun's strong recommendations in the absence of an immediate threat were the more significant. Calhoun pointed to the absurdity of the idea that an army of 12,000, scattered mainly across the vastnesses of the West, might ever be a menace to American liberty. Implying that armies reflect the climate in which they exist, he pointed out that American officers and soldiers were not likely instruments for erecting a military despotism.[1]

Calhoun went much further in elevating the regular army and discounting the militia when he prepared his famous "Report on the Reduction of the Army" of December 12, 1820. In this report Calhoun turned the full power of his blunt bulldozer of a mind to the problem of American military policy, and he produced one of the pivotal documents in the history of American military thought. With characteristic brusqueness he turned his back on the tradition of his party and his region to pronounce confidence in the militia a delusion. Believing that only American professionals could fight adequately in any war against Europeans, he sought a means of affording the regular army adequate numbers in war despite its inevitable smallness in peace. The proposal to which this search led him was an elaboration of the Washington-Hamilton plan of the expansible army.

Calhoun said the militia, supported by good artillery and a small force of regular infantry, might be relied on to garrison forts and to serve in the field as scouts, skirmishers, and raiders. This was especially true when the militia were Southern or Western men, accustomed to the use of firearms. But here was the limit of the militia's usefulness.

To rely on them beyond this, to suppose our militia capable of meeting in the open field the regular troops of Europe, would be to resist the most obvious truth, and the whole of our experience as a nation. War is an art, to attain perfection in which, much time and experience, particularly for the officers, are necessary.

To resist European professionals, an American army would have to possess a military tone and habit enabling it to perform the most complex evolutions precisely and promptly even in the face of gravest danger. Such qualities could be acquired only with ex-

perience and training. The need for a substantial body of experienced officers could not be overestimated. With numerous experienced officers at hand, even a shortage of seasoned troops
could be remedied with dispatch. But without sufficient good officers, especially on the company and regimental levels, troops
would remain persistently undisciplined. Even experience or genius
itself in the highest commander would be of little avail. The establishment of a sound regular army, with emphasis on the officers,
must be the goal of American military policy. Furthermore, the
attainment of this goal demanded a strengthening of the military
academy at West Point, transforming it from an engineering school
into a thoroughgoing military academy to produce professional
captains of war.

Calhoun again denied that a good regular army would threaten
American liberty. The danger to liberty, he believed, would lie
rather in failure to create such an army until the opening of war,
for then the military emergency might compel the cession of power
to a dictator.

The regular army of the United States had two roles, Calhoun
said: guarding forts and frontiers in peacetime, and providing the
primary defense of the nation in wartime. The second of these roles
was so much more important than the first, Calhoun believed, that it
must govern the army's organization in peace as well as in war. The
primary responsibility of the regular army in peace was to be ready
for war. Despite its good showing in the War of 1812, the regular
army had not been ready for war when hostilities began. Even its
new regiments had performed remarkably in the campaign of
1814, but for nearly two years they had been preoccupied simply
with getting themselves established. The United States should profit
by the lesson. It should not again find itself at the opening of a
war merely organizing the regular regiments it needed. At the
start of a future war, Calhoun urged, the nation should possess
substantially organized, the regular regiments it needed to defend
itself.

This was the crux of Calhoun's plan. His proposal was to put
on foot in peacetime the full organization of a wartime army, both
staff and line, though not a full wartime army. All the regular regiments should be already organized and officered at the outbreak

of a war; all they would require in war was the filling of their ranks. In an adequate regular army:

the leading principles in its formation ought to be, that, at the commencement of hostilities, there should be nothing either to new model or to create. The only difference, consequently, between the peace and the war formation of the army, ought to be in the increased magnitude of the latter; and the only change in passing from the former to the latter, should consist in giving to it the augmentation which will then be necessary.

Specifically, Calhoun recommended that the companies of artillery and infantry be established at a peacetime standard of 64 and 37 men respectively. If the peacetime strength of the army in enlisted men were then set at 6,316 (Congress was proposing 6,000 at the time), there would be sufficient numbers to organize nine regiments of infantry and five battalions of artillery. Then, merely by raising the companies to a war strength almost double the peace strength, to a point where each battalion would attain its maximum maneuverable size, it would be possible to mobilize an army of 11,558 without adding a single officer or a single company.

Furthermore, Calhoun proposed a plan whereby war strength having been achieved, the addition of 288 officers to the existing regiments would raise the total strength of the army, officers and men, to 19,035. Again there were to be no new regimental formations. Each company was to be split into two companies and then filled up again, meanwhile doubling the strength of the regiment, whose colonel would then command a small brigade, assisted by two lieutenant colonels.

Thus, with "nothing either to new model or to create," the United States would be able immediately to put into the field a regular army capable of resisting the first wave of any hostile invasion in any strength likely to be met. Calhoun reiterated that the surplus of officers to be gathered in peacetime was central in his thinking, for while "The progress of military science has not added much to the difficulty of performing the duty of a soldier or of training him, . . . it has greatly to that of an officer."

That the surplus might be gathered, it was necessary that men of ability be persuaded to make arms their career. Therefore Calhoun urged that the pay of officers and enlisted men, but especially

of officers, ought to be maintained at levels comparable to those of
civilian life. To do otherwise would be false economy. More than
that, he urged that even the small peacetime army retain two major
generals and two brigadiers, for the hope of attaining such posts
would be likely to attract valuable men to the officer corps. Few
could win the posts; but neither do many persons win lotteries,
although many are persuaded to enter.[2]

Until the years of Calhoun's duty at the War Department, the
United States had rarely seemed free of a more or less immediate
danger of foreign war. The founding of the new government of
the Constitution had coincided with the outbreak of the French
Revolution, and the incessant European wars which followed had
provoked continual collisions between the warring powers and
the American Republic. Advocates of a larger American military
strength had never had to look far to point out danger. But now
the European wars were ended, an exhausted Europe was unlikely
to seek martial adventures for some time, and Calhoun accordingly
could not warn of a pressing need for new military preparations in
support of his expansible army plan. He could resort only to vague
enough warnings that preparation for war is always necessary because history demonstrates that mankind is always addicted to war:

However remote our situation from the great powers of the world, and
however pacific our policy, we are, notwithstanding, liable to be involved
in war; and, to resist, with success, its calamities and dangers, a standing
army in peace, in the present improved state of military science, is an
indispensable preparation.[3]

Congress and the voters chose to ignore such uncertain warnings.
By the time Calhoun called for an expansible regular army, the
memories of real war were again fading, and in their place rose
fantasies of war as Americans wished it to be. The forces which
after the Revolution had won popular acceptance for the militia
tradition and rejection for the professional military tradition were
still at work, despite the wartime failures of the militia. Americans
did not want to pay the bill for a strong regular army, and they
distrusted a regular army and a professional officer corps. Therefore
they suppressed remembrance that only regulars had been able
to stand against the British in the open field in 1812–1814 as in the
Revolution—if they had ever noticed the fact. Forgetting the re-

peated failures of the militia, they apotheosized the battle of New Orleans as the great battle of the war and the vindication of the armed citizenry. They convinced themselves again that an armed citizenry can win victory in war while best preserving liberty in peace.

By 1820 it was questionable how much Calhoun spoke for the administration when he called for a stronger regular force. His military ideas were in fact one indication of his impending departure from Jeffersonian thought for his later career as a spokesman of Southernism and conservatism. It is significant that Calhoun's expansible army plan was an elaboration of ideas which had been suggested earlier by Hamilton, for Calhoun's political philosophy in general was now about to place him beside Hamilton as one of the two preeminent conservative statesmen of America. In any case, whatever Calhoun's colleagues in the Monroe administration thought of his military proposals, Congress would have nothing to do with them. Reinforcing the standard obstacles to military professionalism, the emerging Jacksonian movement in politics was to exalt the abilities of the amateur citizen in every area of public affairs. In the emerging Jacksonian era, furthermore, matters more pressing than military problems were soon to absorb all the national energies and to call for more: expansion across the continent, democratization of American life, slavery, the beginnings of industrialism. The potential defensive military strength of the United States was obvious and seemed to most Americans to be military strength enough.[4]

On March 2, 1821, Congress struck one regiment of infantry and the Rifle Regiment from the army lists, leaving seven regiments of infantry and four of artillery. General officers were cut to one major general and two brigadiers. The idea of the expansible army was ignored.[5]

Yet despite all the reductions and the failure of Calhoun to secure the cadre system, one salient fact about the regular army remained. The vague popular and congressional reliance on an armed citizenry notwithstanding, in practice the regular army continued in its new role as the center of official military planning, the first reliance for national defense. Political praise of the militia still resounded at every muster day, but without a genuinely effective militia, the nation in fact was basing its military policy upon professionals. If war did come, not only would the professional army fight first, but its officers would probably exercise the principal commands over troops of all kinds. In that sense, the conservative military tradition had prevailed.

The Mexican War demonstrated the point. At the outbreak of war, Congress quickly authorized a force of 50,000 volunteers. But it also raised the strength of the regular army from 8,613 to an authorized enrollment of 15,000 (although this strength was not attained), and the James K. Polk administration proceeded to fight the war in a thoroughly conventional manner which regarded the regular army as the principal instrument of American power.

When the war erupted on the Rio Grande, the bulk of the regular army promptly moved to reinforce Zachary Taylor there. When the Rio Grande ceased to be the main front, Taylor had to make do with volunteers, while the regulars sailed away to become the spearhead of the decisive campaign, Winfield Scott's march to Mexico City. The regulars always went to the decisive front; the volunteers were used as though they were auxiliaries. The relatively limited numbers of the enemy, of course, made such a policy feasible. But the fact remained that in a military sense the United States of 1846 was not a revolutionary power, an exemplar of the nation in arms theory, but a conventional power.

This was true despite the appearance of nonprofessional officers against Mexico. It is less significant that President Polk contemplated appointing Democratic Senator Thomas Hart Benton a lieutenant general to take over chief command from the Whig professional Winfield Scott, and thus to keep the glory of the war in Polk's party, than that in the end Polk felt obliged to go along with Scott the professional. Of Scott's four division commanders, three were professionals. If politics demanded the appointment of political brigadiers such as Franklin Pierce, nevertheless the tone of Winfield Scott's army in Mexico was set by the commander and his professional lieutenants, and especially by the West Pointers, whose contribution to Scott's victory is famous.[6]

It is true that in the Mexican War and throughout the early nineteenth century many of the professional officers themselves lacked formal military training. Under the Jacksonian faith that all men are equal in their capacity for government service, including military service, appointments from civilian life to high military rank were common. The army had thirty-seven generals from 1802 to 1861, and only one was a West Pointer. Twenty-three received their stars with practically no military experience, and eleven others received appointments from civil life to the rank of captain or higher. Yet many of these officers—such as Winfield Scott himself—became thoroughly professional in time, and their presence does not change the fact that it was the professionals who supplied the principal leadership in Mexico, nor the salient point that throughout the period the Military Academy influence grew within the officer corps until by the 1860s even the strongest political pressures could not prevent the armies of North and South from being led primarily by the gentlemen from West Point.[7]

John C. Calhoun's emphasis on professionalism, then, prevailed in the military establishment itself if not in Congress, and his expansible arm plan for a stronger professional force in wartime was not so fully forgotten as it had seemed at the death of its author in 1850.

Professionalism of West Point

Of all the civilized states of Christendom, we are perhaps the least military, though not behind the foremost as a warlike one. A sounder era, however, is dawning upon us. . . . What are the military resources of this great Republic is no longer a question; a more thorough organization is alone wanting for their complete development. DENNIS HART MAHAN

THE triumph of Jacksonian democracy made the tradition of military amateurism stronger than ever among the American population. Jefferson at first had hoped to rely for national security on the militia and the principle of the nation in arms, but he had hoped also that the states would attend to the proper military training of the armed citizenry. He did not expect to rely on citizens utterly uneducated for war. But the Jacksonians, with their confidence in the natural capacities of the common man, regarded serious military drill as superfluous, and the era following the War of 1812 witnessed a decline even of such militia training as previously had existed.

Part of the cause also lay in Jacksonian hostility against even the militia as an aristocratic organization. The custom of the time was to punish absences from militia muster days with a fine. The well-to-do could readily pay the fine and thus, in effect, they could purchase exemption from military service; the ordinary citizen who could not afford the fine either sweated through his drill or languished periodically in jail. Therefore the Jacksonians took up an attack on compulsory militia duty for the yeoman and working-man as one of their democratic reforms, and theoretical obligation of universal military service was reduced to a fiction. In most localities militia musters ceased to be enforced. The militia came to be divided into the unorganized and the organized militia, the former including every able-bodied male of military age but existing only in theory, the latter comprising active companies of volunteers but mustering limited numbers. Such volunteering as developed did so partly because the active companies were generally less military than social.[1]

Thus a militia which had never been militarily impressive gradually faded to a still less substantial state. While most Americans yet found it possible to remain committed to the militia as the principal instrument of national defense, those who thought seriously about national defense had little choice but to commit themselves increasingly to defense by professional soldiers. With no militia save a few more or less fancily uniformed drill companies, there was no alternative to reliance on the regular army.

The regular army officer corps became committed to reliance on their own regulars, since to speak of Americans who from the Jacksonian era until the Civil War thought seriously about national defense is to speak virtually of the regular officers alone. Unfortunately for them, those gentlemen did not have much of a regular army on which to rely. In 1849, General Scott reported to the Secretary of War that the enlisted strength of the army was nominally 9,438, which was 2,499 less than the peace establishment of 1815. By late 1860, the authorized strength had grown only to 18,114, the actual strength to 14,072.[2]

Yet the tendency of the officer corps to regard the small professional army as the only sure military reliance was all the greater. This was so because the Jacksonian era, in which the citizenry became increasingly wedded to military amateurism, found the regular army becoming, paradoxically, more professional. For now the officer corps emerged as professionals not only in the sense of being full-time soldiers but, for the first time, in the sense that they possessed the career standards of a profession rather than of a trade. They came to develop a professional sense of corporateness, based on the knowledge that the gap between them and the military amateurs was widening. They came to develop a professional sense of responsibility, a corollary to the belief that they alone could offer the nation sound military defense. Principally, they began to emerge as professionals in their mastery of a body of specialized knowledge, not simply of techniques, but of a written literature which sought inductively to establish a theory of war.[3]

The American roots of all these developments, converging to

make the officer corps a body of genuine professionals and not simply craftsmen, lay in the Military Academy at West Point. In the Jacksonian era, despite the hostility of politicians (though not of Andrew Jackson himself) who recognized that the academy fitted ill with Jacksonian disregard for learning, the Military Academy first became the guiding center of army thought. Not surprisingly, however, the source of the new professional standards of officership lay in Europe, not in the academy itself nor anywhere in Jacksonian America.

War Secretary Calhoun in his message of December 18, 1820, had noted that "The progress of military science has not added much to the difficulty of performing the duty of a soldier or of training him, but it has greatly to that of the officer." Calhoun probably had reference to advances in military technology, making more exacting the military sciences of engineering, fortification, and artillery. But while a rising technology already was revolutionizing industry, warfare as yet had felt little of its impact. It was not so much technological change that justified Calhoun's remark as the increasing refinement of European military thought, training, and preparation.

This refinement had begun principally in Prussia after the catastrophic campaign of Jena. Despite the tactical finesse of eighteenth-century warfare, eighteenth-century methods of waging war had rested on the slightest of theoretical bases. The eighteenth century had done relatively little toward the systematic study of war in an effort to establish general principles and rules of war. The distinction between strategy and tactics was almost unrecognized. Such military writers of the period as won prominence and retained it, including Marshal Saxe, Guibert, Bourcet, and Henry Lloyd, were hampered by the necessity of building anew the most elementary foundations of military thought, and of working as individuals without the support and criticism of schools. The eighteenth-century officer was the master not so much of a wide body of theoretical knowledge capable of practical applications, as of a set of techniques, analogous to those of a skilled craft but simply of a craft. Napoleon himself did not carry military *thought* much further, though his campaigns were to furnish the foundation for the theories of others.[4]

The change began in Prussia after 1806, where the immediate goal was to find a means of countering Napoleon's military genius. Lacking their own leader of comparable genius, the Prussian military reformers, led by Scharnhorst, Gneisenau, Grolman, and Boyen, sought to offset the brilliance of Napoleon through military education in the Prussian officer corps. They hoped that men of average ability working in harmony, with their ability finely honed by rigorous education, would prove superior in warfare to the individual genius, however brilliant. The sequel vindicated them. Establishing the rudiments of the Prussian general staff, and more than that ensuring uncommonly high educational standards among Prussian officers by requiring a liberal education of officer candidates, establishing division schools for military education, and capping the structure with an unprecedented higher school of war, the *Kriegsakademie*, they made military officership a profession in the full sense of the word for the first time. There came, especially from the *Kriegsakademie*, the first modern systematic studies of war, to supply the new profession with its core of theoretical knowledge. These studies culminated in the posthumous publication in 1831 of *Vom Kriege*, the classic nineteenth-century formulation of military thought by the *Kriegsakademie* director, Karl von Clausewitz.[5]

Eventually Clausewitz's work would stand at the center of nearly all military thought in Western civilization. At first, however, *Vom Kriege* remained untranslated into French or English, and the states west of Germany remained relatively little influenced by it. But the Prussian establishment of professional standards in the officer corps compelled the other European powers to attempt to follow suit. Although none at first equalled Prussian standards, France at least went far in that direction. She established no true equivalent of the *Kriegsakademie*, which was a school of advanced studies of war, but in St. Cyr for cavalry and infantry officers and the *École Polytechnique* for her engineers, she did create excellent professional schools for officers.[6]

The War for Independence had given American soldiers a close association with the French army. The glamor of French triumphs in the wars of the French Revolution and Napoleon obscured both Napoleon's final defeat and the painstaking methods by which the

Prussian military leaders had helped accomplish that defeat. Americans of the revolutionary military tradition admired France for the successes she had won with the bayonets of her armed citizens. Americans of the conservative military tradition noted that after her wars France reverted to an army of regulars, presumably retaining, however, the high standards which Napoleon had bequeathed to the officer corps. For these reasons all parties in the United States looked to France as the foremost military state of Europe, and the United States turned to her to seek guidance and models for its own military system.

In the years immediately following the War of 1812, the United States Military Academy nearly foundered. It was troubled by public suspicion grown stronger with the disappearance of military threats from abroad and the rise of democratic aspirations at home, and wracked too by its own intramural quarrels and a weak leadership which encouraged their proliferation. Fortunately for the academy, in 1819 President Monroe appointed to the superintendency a man with the ability and the strength of character to save the institution and a plan for going on to improve it. He was Colonel Sylvanus Thayer, a handsome, commanding, and intelligent engineer officer from Connecticut. Thayer had recently visited France. He shared the usual American respect for French military skill, and he knew something of the rise of professionalism in the French officer corps. He proposed to model West Point on the new French military schools. Despite the admission of officer candidates from all branches of the army since 1808, West Point was still an adjunct of the Corps of Engineers. Thayer proposed to model it primarily upon the French schools of engineering and fortification. By doing so he would make West Point more than ever a nursery of civil engineers and thus mitigate popular criticism by enhancing the usefulness of academy graduates in peacetime. But this qualification did not alter the central purpose of Thayer to transplant French standards of officer professionalism to the United States.[7]

Thayer's purpose demanded a stronger faculty, some of whose members shared or improved on Thayer's knowledge of the French military system. Therefore Thayer's eye soon fell on one of the most able students the academy had yet attracted, Dennis Hart Mahan of Virginia.

Mahan was a shy, retiring, and somewhat frail youth, unsoldierly in appearance except for his quiet dignity. He was a contrast indeed to the sturdy, tough warriors whom his father's native Ireland would send for so many years to fill the enlisted ranks of the United States Army. He had come to West Point because he wanted to be an artist, and he knew the academy offered instruction in drawing as part of its engineering program. Once enrolled, however, Mahan became the sort of cadet on whom Thayer believed the future of the army depended. He found increasing fascination in engineering and in the little that the academy then taught of things strictly military. He led the graduating class of 1822, and Thayer immediately seized on his ability and enthusiasm to appoint him an instructor.

When two years later Mahan's somewhat precarious health demanded a respite from his duties, Thayer used the opportunity to secure for him an assignment to study the military schools and institutions of Europe and especially of France. Mahan delightedly made the trip, in the course of which he enrolled in the French School of Application for Engineers and Artillery at Metz, probably the leading school of the world in those areas of knowledge in which West Point itself was to specialize. Furthermore, Mahan's zeal and good will reportedly won him the privilege of examining the confidential plans of certain of the French border fortresses.[8]

Thus Mahan became the principal agent in Thayer's program of transplanting French military standards to the United States. When he returned to West Point as an assistant professor in 1832, Mahan began teaching a course in engineering and tactics for first classmen which soon took rank as the unquestioned capstone of the West Point curriculum and which remained so for more than a generation. In the era when West Point assumed clear leadership of American military thought, Dennis Mahan was the principal molder of military thought at West Point. Eventually he became chairman of the academic board of the academy. All that the cadets learned of the theory and rules of warfare they learned from Mahan, and the cadets so taught included nearly all the professional soldiers who became top commanders in the Civil War save R. E. Lee, whose graduation had preceded Mahan's own.[9]

Specifically, Mahan's course treated of military engineering, fortification, grand tactics, and minor tactics. In the West Point manner, the course was given in small recitation sections by junior faculty members, with Mahan planning, supervising, and frequently visiting the sections. Mahan found himself dealing with materials which had never been systematically presented in the United States or even presented in writing in the English language. He was compelled to work from his own translations of the standard French works on military science and engineering and to synthesize those works in his own lectures. He had his lectures lithographed on a small press that he had brought back from France for the purpose, and then distributed them among the cadets.

Out of his lectures grew his published works on civil and military engineering: *Complete Treatise on Field Fortification* (1836), *Elementary Course of Civil Engineering* (1837), *Summary of the Course of Permanent Fortification and of the Attack and Defence of Permanent Works* (1850), *Industrial Drawing* (1852), *Descriptive Geometry as Applied to the Drawing of Fortification and Stereotomy* (1864), and *An Elementary Course of Military Engineering* (1866–1867). The books on civil engineering became the cornerstone of engineering literature in the United States, just as the West Point curriculum nourished every American engineering school which followed until after the Civil War. But Mahan's most important volume for the development of the American military profession was the book he first published in 1847 and which went through numerous printings, especially for the Civil War. The first systematic American study of warfare, its title announced it with the equivalent of a flourish of trumpets: *An Elementary Treatise on Advanced-Guard, Out-Post, and Detachment Service of Troops, and the Manner of Posting and Handling Them in Presence of an Enemy. With a Historical Sketch of the Rise and Progress of Tactics, &c., &c.*

From this book military science can be studied as the generation of American officers that fought the Civil War studied it. Much of the content of American military thought at the time when that thought became primarily the property of a professionalized officer corps can be found here. Most important for our present purposes, here can be found military precepts most suitable for performance by a regular army.

Dennis Mahan's *Out-Post* contributed to the growth of American military professionalism in several ways. In the first place, it offered a rationale for the academic type of training that Mahan and his colleagues were presenting at West Point. It argued, in effect, that the career of a military officer is in the full sense a professional career requiring mastery of a body of specific knowledge set in a context of a broad historical knowledge. It argued that the officer needs to know not merely a set of techniques but a series of principles derived from historical experience, for Mahan followed the new French military leaders in the conviction that there exist universally valid principles of strategy and, to a lesser extent, of tactics.

Most importantly Mahan's book indicated that professional study is essential to sound military leadership because the professional officer must have a thorough grasp of military history, in which all principles of strategy are rooted. The Prussian *Kriegsakademie* had inaugurated an emphasis on the teaching of military history, and Mahan's pages reflect the passage through France to the United States of that new military regard for the study of the past.

No one [Mahan believed] can be said to have thoroughly mastered his art, who has neglected to make himself conversant with its early history; nor, indeed, can any tolerably clear elementary notions, even, be formed of an art, beyond those furnished by the mere technical language, without some historical knowledge of its rise and progress; for this alone can give to the mind those means of comparison, without which everything has to be painfully created anew, to reach perfection only after many cycles of misdirected mental toil.[10]

It is in military history that we are to look for the source of all military science. In it we shall find those exemplifications of failure and success by which alone the truth and value of the rules of strategy can be tested.[11]

Of course it was from French military experience and French military methods and organization that Mahan believed most was to be learned.[12] But above all Mahan believed that the good military officer was not the gifted or inspired amateur but the military student, and thus the professional.

It is true he recognized that the study of military history might become a prison in which the military methods of the past could form a straitjacket against flexible action. While principles of strategy are universally valid, he emphasized, methods of applying them must change. The officer must not allow his history books to foist a single tactical system upon him, but must be flexible in the methods by which he carries out his strategic designs. He must not allow history to determine his tactics beforehand, but must be ready to do whatever each new situation requires, whether "throwing a deployed line, with the bayonet advanced, upon his enemy, . . . or charging impetuously, with his horse in column." But the professional officer who has devoted his lifetime to the study of war, conversant through study and experience with the varieties of military methods, is more likely than the amateur to recognize the multiple possibilities of a situation and to choose freely the appropriate method of dealing with it. An amateur is limited in his military activities by his limited knowledge; but "no soldier, who has made himself conversant with the resources of his art, will allow himself to be trammelled by any exclusive system." [13]

On the title page of *Out-Post*, Mahan stated that the book was intended "especially for the use of officers of militia and volunteers." But the emphasis on professional study in the content of the book indicates that Mahan expected his readers to meet professional standards, and similarly he went on to offer precepts that suggested a professional level of performance from the troops. West Point graduates schooled under Mahan would have been instructed in methods of warfare that were best adapted to the reliable campaigning of regulars. West Point graduates schooled under Mahan would have wanted to lead regulars, because only regular troops would be able to carry on dependably Mahan's methods of war. Thus despite the title page, *Out-Post* tended to strengthen the professionalist rather than the amateur military tradition. At the same time that Mahan helped to make the American officer corps professional by developing for them a professional education, he strengthened professionalism by offering a manual on the conduct of war which, its dedication to the contrary notwithstanding, demanded well trained troops.

Out-Post demanded well trained troops because it emphasized that successful warfare is almost always offensive warfare. Few of the advocates of a national security policy based on militia had ever claimed much for the quality of militia in taking the offensive against European troops; the famous victories of American amateurs in arms were victories largely won from behind entrenchments. A military doctrine which emphasized the offensive surely entailed the use of troops who could face the armies of Europe in the open field. Therefore such a military doctrine implied that the American army must be in large part a strong professional army.

Some of Mahan's detailed tactical prescriptions were already obsolete when *Out-Post* was reissued for the Civil War. His Napoleonic artillery tactics calling for the guns to batter the enemy's line from close range, for example, could not be followed in the face of a general distribution of rifled muskets. His close-order infantry formations, standard for the 1840s, proved futile against the weapons of the 1860s.[14] But even after many more details became inapplicable, the doctrine of the attack set forth in the first American book on the military art continued to be the doctrine of the American army under Mahan's students and their successors. From Mahan's *Out-Post,* American professional military thought was to maintain a persistent preference for the offensive mode of warfare; but that preference in turn strengthened the commitment of professional officers to regular troops, since no other could with assurance be turned to their purpose.

Mahan was a military engineer, and legend has it that military engineers are incorrigibly addicted to caution as the rule for all military activity. If the addiction is real, Mahan did not share it. His education was not only an engineering education but a military education secured in France and under French influences, in an era when the spirit of Napoleon still dominated French military thought despite the political return of the Bourbons. Mahan's hero was Napoleon. The mention of Napoleon's name and of Napoleonic methods made the pages of *Out-Post* glow. And the great lesson of Mahan's hero was the value of audacity, of the offensive, and of the initiative in military affairs. A temporary defensive might help exhaust the enemy. To do this and to offer points of departure and support for the attack the fortifications of the engineer were valuable. But an Austerlitz was to be won in the end by nothing less than a smashing, irresistible offensive. Under the influence of Napoleon, Mahan called for the offensive as the true mode of victorious war: "Vigor on the field and rapidity of pursuit should go hand in hand for great success." "If Fortune is on the side of the heavy battalions, she also frequently grants her favors to superior activity and audacity." "Carrying the war into the heart of the assailant's country, or that of his allies, is the surest plan of making him share its burdens and foiling his plans." "In looking back on military history, it may with truth be said that nothing is impossible to a determined will." [15]

Even for the army standing on the strategic defensive, the most potent method of war remained the tactical offensive. This was true whether the army held good man-made fortifications or whether it stood on a strong natural defensive line. As a specialist in fortification, Mahan told his students that the spade is as important a weapon as the musket; [16] but he believed that even fortifications have as one of their principal purposes that of being a mustering place and springboard for attack.

In even the strongest positions, Mahan believed, the mere passive defensive is eventually doomed. Yet the passive defensive is the only course for which amateur soldiers are fit. Therefore in the long run it is only well trained troops who can hold any line, for the security of the line demands that its guardians seize the initiative.[17]

Mahan's stress on the offensive was one of emotional zest as well as of military reason. He enjoyed using such words as "vigor," "activity," and "audacity," and in a passage illuminated by enthusiasm he described the stout regular soldier types on whom a commander could rely to strike his aggressive blows:

The *cuirassier sans peur* . . . careless and indifferent to the maddening strife around . . . with sabre raised, he rushes on his foe . . . like the tornado, [to] level all before him, and leave nothing of his task unfinished but the gathering of the wreck he leaves in his track.

The dragoon. . . . Apt for attacks. . . .

The dashing bold hussar, that epitome of military impudence and insolence at the tavern, should present those qualities in a sublimated form on the field. . . . careering with a falcon's speed and glance upon his quarry. . . .

The artillery . . . of late years begun to infuse a dash of the dare-devil spirit of the cavalry into its ranks. . . . a well-considered recklessness of obstacles and dangers, fully borne out by a justly deserved success.[18]

And always Mahan returned to Napoleon as the greatest champion of the smashing use of the attack:

To him we owe those grand features of the art, by which an enemy is broken and utterly dispersed by one and the same blow. No futilities of preparation; no uncertain feeling about in search of the key-point; no hesitancy upon the decisive moment; the whole field of view taken in by one eagle glance; what could not be seen divined by an unerring military instinct; clouds of light troops thrown forward to bewilder his foe; a crashing fire of cannon in mass opened upon him; the rush of the impetuous column into the gap made by the artillery; the overwhelming charge of the resistless cuirassier; followed by the lancer and hussar to sweep up the broken dispersed bands; such were the tactical lessons taught in almost every battle of this great military period.[19]

For all his emphasis on the offensive and his infatuation with language describing assault, Mahan did not recommend impetuous, headlong efforts when he turned from rhetoric to prescription. It was the offensive by indirect approach, the offensive based on maneuver, that he then favored. Victories ought to be won, he believed, at the lowest possible cost, and this criterion demanded maneuver and indirection. Napoleon himself had erred in this respect and perhaps (Mahan would not permit a more categoric criticism of his hero) had purchased his victories at too high a cost. *"To do the greatest damage to our enemy with the least exposure to ourselves,* is a military axiom lost sight of only by ignorance to the true ends of victory."[20]

But if the offensive were to be pursued by maneuver and indirection, then Mahan's teachings suggested all the more the need for well trained troops, since skillful, well coordinated maneuver had never been the forte of militia. In his detailed prescriptions for the conduct of war the Mahan of the eloquent paeans to the dashing, bold hussar gave way to the mundane Mahan who cautiously carried an umbrella with him every day of his life. Warnings that prudence must mark every step of the offensive, that the offensive demands the greatest of watchful care, followed one another closely through his pages. Flanking movements rather than direct assaults were the proper means to offensive success, but flanking movements exposed themselves perilously to being flanked in turn, as the Austrians learned against Napoleon at Rivoli. By implication, only soldiers wise in warfare could guard a flanking march against the counter-surprise to which such a march was susceptible. Only experienced troops, it is clear, could follow Mahan's instructions for dealing with such a counter-surprise if despite caution it did occur:

Great prudence must be shown in advancing; as the troops engaged are liable at any moment to an attack on their flank. If the assailed attempts this manœuvre, the line of skirmishers must hold on pertinaciously to the ground gained, whilst the supports display and keep the enemy in check, until the reserves can be brought up to repel the attack with the bayonet.[21]

The student of Mahan planning to follow these instructions did not envision himself as commanding military amateurs.

It was his emphasis upon skillful maneuver and deception that led Mahan to devote his manual of military science in great part to the operations of advanced guards, outposts, and reconnaissances, the operations that must screen maneuver. There could be no successful maneuver without such screening, and there could be no successful reconnaissance and screening except by officers and men highly adept at their work.

To gain information of the enemy and to deprive him of information in turn, Mahan recommended that one-fifth to one-third of any force be detailed as reconnaissance parties, advanced guards, and outposts. A full army or a large army corps should so detail one-third of its men, so that one-third at least of any army ought to consist of soldiers proficient even beyond the usual demands of a successful offensive. The officers of reconnaissance and screening parties needed to be men of the highest professional attainments, of "great circumspection," "capable of untiring vigilance and activity," cool headed, and able to deliver reports of the highest precision. Washington had lamented of inaccurate reconnaissance reports that "these things, not being delivered with certainty, rather perplex than form the judgment." But even reportorial precision was useless if the reconnaissance officer did not combine it with "*a good coup d'œil militaire*," a discerning eye for topographical detail and for every hint of the movements and intentions of the enemy. Such an eye had to be trained.

There are no more important duties, which an officer may be called upon to perform, than those of collecting and arranging the information upon which the . . . operations of a campaign must be based.

From the services demanded of a reconnaissance officer, it is . . . evident, that he should possess acquirements of no ordinary character.[22]

As for the soldiers of the reconnaissance and screening forces, they ought to be the most efficient and active light troops available. Unskillful troops would not do, but if active and audacious light troops were used, numbering one-third of the field army, then:

Such troops, in the hands of a bold, energetic, but prudent leader, will be the right arm of an army. Prompt on all occasions; never taken at fault, they keep the enemy constantly occupied; harass him with fatiguing operations, to secure his flanks and rear; whilst their own force is kept relieved from these annoyances, and always fresh for any great emergency.[23]

Again, the student of Mahan trained to expect such qualities in reconnaissance and screening troops was by no means being taught to expect reconnaissance and screening work from military amateurs.

Beyond skillful performance by advanced guard and reconnaissance forces, Mahan's offensive of indirection and maneuver also demanded an army capable of speed. Without it the initiative was likely to pass to the enemy and his counter strokes; with it the indirect advance upon the enemy became more deceptive, the eventual descent upon him more terrible, and the pursuit of his unhappy forces more destructive. "In this one quality," speed, said Mahan, "reside all the advantages that a fortunate initiative may have procured." "No great success can be hoped for in war in which rapid movements do not enter as an element. Even the very elements of Nature seem to array themselves against the slow and over-prudent general." Speed enables an army "to accomplish the most stupendous labors in marching and fighting," yet speed again was an attainment only of well trained soldiers, never of marching military amateurs.[24]

Mahan's explicit purpose in writing *Out-Post* was to offer a handbook on tactics and, in the later editions, on strategy, not to present a dissertation on American military policy. He suggested mainly by implication that only a skillful army of regular troops and professional officers in substantial numbers could wage victorious war, though his insistence that such war must be one of offensives by indirection and maneuver, carefully screened and carried out with speed, made the implication apparent enough.

But if Mahan left many of his suggestions on the form an effective army should take to his readers' inferences, he did state explicitly that his ultimate intention was to encourage the establishment of an effective American army. He reminded readers of *Out-Post* that in considering his strategic and tactical formulas they should bear that goal in mind. He believed that the military potential of the United States was almost boundless; for that reason the actual military weakness of the United States was the more tragic.

When Mahan turned to plead with his readers that they apply his precepts to building an army, his prose shifted again from the cool retailing of empirical maxims to the impassioned advocacy of a cause. Its manner is reminiscent of the abrupt change of mood and approach in Machiavelli's *The Prince* upon the opening of Machiavelli's plea for the unification of Italy.

Of all the civilized states of Christendom [said Mahan], we are perhaps the least military, though not behind the foremost as a warlike one. A sounder era, however, is dawning upon us. The desire for war, *as such,* is decreasing, while a feeling of the necessity of being always ready for it is becoming more general. All our battle-fields, up to the glorious feat at Buena Vista, have proved to the world that the American soldier was wanting in no military quality, but combined the vivacity of the French with the tenacity of the English. But this, however, could make but little impression upon the soldier-statesmen of Europe. To be warlike, does not render a nation formidable to its neighbors. They may dread to attack it, but have no apprehensions from its offensive demonstrations. It was reserved for the expedition to Vera-Cruz, and its sequel, the victory of Cerro-Gordo, to bring into strong relief the fact, that we were unostentatiously, and almost silently, becoming a powerful military state. The lesson will not be lost upon our neighbors, however slowly we, in the end, may profit by it. A shout has gone forth from the Rio-Grande, and the shores of the Gulf of Mexico, which, heard on the Thames and the Seine, has resounded along the far-off shores of the Baltic and Black Sea, and will reach the farther Ind, bearing with it a significance that no prudent statesman will hereafter affect to misunderstand. What are the military resources of this great Republic is no longer a question; a more thorough organization is alone wanting for their complete development.[25]

Such was the military glory that Mahan believed awaited his country; American arms properly organized (for offensive warfare, be it noted) could carry the influence of the United States beyond even the bounds of Napoleon's conquests, through the western hemisphere, across Europe, and into Asia. To an American army that might one day fulfil such visions Mahan dedicated his teaching, his writing, and in fact his life. He cloistered himself from nonmilitary concerns so that he might devote himself to his cause. He never cast a ballot in a civil election; he stood apart from civil life, the army and its advancement offering scope and purpose enough for his energies. When he could no longer serve the army, he may have chosen no longer to live; the academic board at West Point decided in 1871 that his age demanded his retirement from the faculty, and after hearing the decision he stepped from a boat into the Hudson River. Perhaps he did so by accident; perhaps, considering his career and the circumstances, he did not.[26]

Meanwhile Mahan's call for "a more thorough organization" had gone out to more than a generation of West Pointers. It impressed them with his fervor that the United States should have a good army, and assured them that a good army was a professional one, its officers students of their calling as well as men of energy and audacity, its troops capable of the swift offensive maneuver which was the only high road to successful war.

V   HENRY W. HALLECK AND

GEORGE B. MC CLELLAN *The*

Disciples of Dennis Mahan

> War is not, as some seem to suppose, a mere game of chance. Its principles constitute one of the most intricate of modern sciences; and the general who understands the art of rightly applying its rules, and possesses the means of carrying out its precepts, may be morally certain of success. HENRY W. HALLECK

> Mere individual courage cannot suffice to overcome the forces that would be brought against us were we involved in a European war, but . . . it must be rendered manageable by discipline, and directed by that consummate and mechanical military skill which can only be acquired by a course of education instituted for the special purpose, and by a long course of habit. GEORGE B. MC-CLELLAN

DENNIS MAHAN'S legacy to American military thought included three themes that would persist: professional study, especially the study of military history, as the foundation of the mastery of the art and science of war; a flexible, pragmatic temper in the military commander as necessary to adapt the rules of textbook study to specific realities; and the offensive, based on good fortifications, conducted by maneuver and with skillful use of advanced guards, outposts, and reconnaissance, but above all the offensive, as the military road to victory. Beyond these, Mahan's emphasis on professionalism in the officer corps and on reliable performance by the troops combined with his contributions to the development of West Point to assure further the grip of the European professional and conservative military tradition on the American army.

Mahan's themes would be elaborated, modified, and carried forward by a circle of his own West Point students and contemporaries. Despite the work of Sylvanus Thayer and Mahan, West Point before the Civil War was still crude and unfinished in many ways, still searching to define its role in American life and still experimenting to find methods of fulfilling a vaguely defined role. It was not the equivalent of the Prussian *Kriegsakademie* nor of the French *École Polytechnique*, and even in mathematics its offerings fell short of the standards not only of Europe but of the best American private colleges. Nevertheless, the school possessed a remarkable vigor. Its graduates produced a body of military literature respectable by any standards, in a day when systematic military study was new everywhere. The military literature created by Mahan and his West Point associates far transcended the primitive quality of existing American military institutions.[1]

During the 1840s and 1850s four noteworthy volumes came from Mahan's contemporaries and students. Henry Wager Halleck of the West Point class of 1839 continued Mahan's labor of adapting the new European thought on military policy, strategy, and tactics. George B. McClellan, class of 1836, Richard Delafield, class of 1818, and Alfred Mordecai, class of 1823, each produced an admirable volume on European military systems as a result of their inspection of European armies at the time of the Crimean War.

As the United States Military Academy was developed under French influences, the exponent of the new, post-Napoleonic European military thought to whom West Point looked as the fountain-head of military doctrine was the French-Swiss writer, Henri, Baron de Jomini. In American eyes, Jomini was nothing less than Napoleon's St. Paul.

A Swiss bank clerk by origin, Jomini had been captivated by the martial excitement of the French Revolutionary era and became an avid student of military affairs. He early composed his own analysis of military science, *Traité des grandes opérations militaires*. He placed a copy of his work in the hands of Marshal Ney. Ney found the book highly impressive and showed it to Napoleon, who is said to have reacted with anger that anyone should have committed so many of the secrets of his own methods to paper, and to have demanded that the work be suppressed. Nevertheless, Ney accepted Jomini into his staff, and the Swiss soon proved his value by quickly understanding Napoleon's plans for the encirclement of the Austrians at Ulm. Through Ney he prevented the impetuous but not especially astute Marshal Murat from making a botch of them.

Jomini graduated to Napoleon's own staff, and he played a conspicuous role in the field in helping to assure the victories of Jena and Auerstadt. But apparently he possessed a self-esteem to match his abilities. This quality plus his rapid rise to Napoleon's confidence excited jealousy and dislike for him, particularly in Murat and in the Emperor's chief of staff, Marshal Berthier. Jomini's angry departure from the French service and his ultimate participation in the 1814 campaign as a staff officer with the Russians were the result of much friction and of Berthier's deliberate snubs. After the wars he returned to the French army to serve Louis xviii, and then he returned to the Russian service until he retired. Meanwhile he wrote a series of military studies, most notably a military biography of Napoleon and his magnum opus, *Précis de l'art de la guerre.* These volumes became the most important foreign military works in their influence upon Americans.

Jomini lacked the philosophical breadth and profundity of Clausewitz. While the latter penetrated deeply into the whole relationship between war and society, Jomini confined himself mainly to the strictly military questions of strategy, logistics, and tactics. Clausewitz emphasized that war always is in potential, and sometimes approaches in fact, the complete unleashing of violence and thus the increasing triumph of chaos. Jomini described war in terms of neat geometrical relationships among rival armies, forming patterns which seemed to defy the chaos that violence in fact engenders. Clausewitz recognized that modes of conducting war must be relative to the degree of violence which a given situation has unloosed, and that the methods appropriate to a war for national survival may not be appropriate to a contest over disputed boundaries. Jomini, while recognizing that the intensity of war varies with varying purposes, tended more than Clausewitz to write in terms of universally applicable rules of military science, and indeed to offer rules of a geometric character. The tendency to make the study of strategy almost a branch of the study of geometry, encouraged by Jomini, would reach almost absurd lengths before the nineteenth century ended, not least among certain American military writers.

Clausewitz, in short, though he was in the employ of the archconservative kings of Prussia, emphasized the revolutionary implications of the warfare of the French Revolution and Napoleon. He found in wars of nations against nations ample evidence that the ultimate principle toward which war always tends is violence without limit. Jomini, in contrast, linked himself to the eighteenth-century conservative tradition of limited war and, while dedicating himself to the study of Napoleon, he sought to confine Napoleonic strategy and tactics within eighteenth-century restraints. Where Clausewitz wrote realistically of the cruelties of war, Jomini wrote nostalgically of the polite forms to which wars had adhered before the French Revolution and to which he hoped they might return. And it was Jomini, not Clausewitz, that American soldiers of the nineteenth century read as the foremost interpreter of war. The adherence of the American army to conservative notions of war thus remained assured.[2]

The principal purveyor of Jomini's doctrines to American soldiers after Mahan himself was Mahan's student Henry W. Halleck, who in 1864 published an annotated translation of Jomini's life of Napoleon and who long before that incorporated much of the thinking of Jomini's *Précis de l'art de la guerre* into his own major work, *Elements of Military Art and Science*. Halleck was the most articulate disciple of Mahan, but more than Mahan, he was also a disciple of Jomini. He freely admitted the influence of Jomini on him and commended it to others in valuable bibliographical listings and commentaries at the close of his chapters. While he praised the "great work" of Jomini, however, and termed its discussions "exceedingly valuable," he simply listed Clausewitz's *Vom Kriege* without comment, twentieth among twenty-eight books on strategy.[3]

But Henry W. Halleck was not simply the American apostle of Jomini. His *Elements of Military Art and Science* is more than a paraphrase of *Précis de l'art de la guerre*. Halleck might well be regarded as the early fruition of Mahan's West Point system in an American equivalent to Jomini. For although Halleck disclaimed originality in his *Elements*, the book has considerable originality as a distinctively American approach to the study of war. Broader in concept than Mahan's *Out-Post*, Halleck's *Elements* attempts to encompass every aspect of war. It begins, for example, with an elaborate apologia on the waging of war by a Christian community, and it explores at length issues of national military policy and of grand strategy. It can stand side by side with Jomini's *Précis* on any bookshelf. Furthermore, Halleck like Jomini was not only an accomplished military scholar and writer but also a good staff officer in practice. Even as an independent army commander he showed a competence which Ulysses Grant recognized before the feud that colors Grant's *Memoirs,* and which military students are beginning to recognize again.

For our purposes, Halleck is important as still another exponent of the conservative, professionalist tradition in American military thought. His effort to impress upon his readers the necessity for a trained soldiery, especially a trained officer corps, is implicit throughout his *Elements.*

"Technical education is necessary in every pursuit of life," wrote Halleck, and not least in warfare. He reminded his readers how often the American Revolutionary cause had depended on the labors of foreign officers, many of them adventurers, because the United States had lacked an officer corps trained in the technical branches of artillery and engineering and in the larger principles of strategy and tactics. No nation could rest secure in such a reliance on the essentially unreliable, the zeal of foreign officers for a cause not their own. The principles of military art and science constitute the body of knowledge of a profession, and it made no more sense to entrust the professional duties of a military officer to a civilian than to give over the practice of medicine to a carpenter.[4] The military art was not a trade; military art and science was a body of knowledge to be mastered from a wide acquaintance with books, both broad general histories and specifically military works such as those of Jomini and Napoleon.[5]

Halleck could not help but know that to emphasize the study of military books was to commit heresy against the dominant Jacksonian tradition of the zealous military amateur. He knew too that to emphasize the study of books suggested that he failed to recognize the element of genius in a Hannibal, a Frederick, or a Napoleon. Such a failure he denied. Military genius, and especially the *coup d'œil* which enabled the commander to seize instantly upon the essential features of a combat, were indispensable to transcendent success in war. But not all men possessed such genius, nor could a government unerringly seek out genius. Therefore the surest road to good leadership in war was that painstaking study of the principles and the history of war that would bring a ready awareness of the useful analogies of the past to the commander in combat:

War is not, as some seem to suppose, a mere game of chance. Its principles constitute one of the most intricate of modern sciences; and the general who understands the art of rightly applying its rules, and possesses the means of carrying out its precepts, may be morally certain of success.[6]

The successful generals of the American past had universally acknowledged this truth, said Halleck. He reminded his readers that Washington, with Hamilton and Knox seconding him, had repeatedly urged the establishment of a national military academy. The objections commonly cited against military education, he argued, might equally apply against any sort of professional education. The successes which military amateurs had won in the American wars and the wars of the French Revolution had been won in spite of, not because of the professional shortcomings of their authors. The successful military amateurs themselves tended to be quick to encourage military education for others, as again Washington demonstrated. In fact, the genuinely successful military amateurs were usually not so amateur as the Jacksonian version of events made it seem; history again suggested Washington himself, with his extensive French and Indian War experience and his association with British professionals, as an example.[7]

While enlisted men, unlike officers, were craftsmen rather than professional men, Halleck argued that they needed a full apprenticeship in their trade before being sent to do the work of masters:

With the Romans, six years' instruction was required to make a soldier; and so great importance did these ancient conquerors of the world attach to military education and discipline, that the very name of their army derived from the verb *to practise*.

Modern nations, learning from experience that military success depends more upon skill and discipline than upon numbers, have generally adopted the same rule as the Romans; and nearly all of the European powers have established military schools for the education of their officers and the instruction of their soldiers.[8]

There could be no more succinct statement of the professionalist position, "that military success depends more upon skill and discipline than upon numbers." It was not a mass army that Halleck thought the United States should possess to maintain its security in a warlike world, but a skilled and disciplined one. Halleck believed the United States needed such an army, for his knowledge of history convinced him that the world was indeed warlike and that only trained and ready military forces assured against disaster in war:

For any nation to postpone the making of military preparations till such time as they are actually required in defence, is to waste the public money, and endanger the public safety. The closing of an avenue of approach, the security of a single road or river, or even the strategic movement of a small body of troops, often effects, in the beginning, what afterwards cannot be accomplished by large fortifications, and the most formidable armies. Had a small army in 1812, with a well-fortified dépôt on Lake Champlain, penetrated into Canada, and cut off all reinforcements and supplies by way of Canada, that country would inevitably have fallen into our possession.[9]

History showed that trained troops could accomplish much, and Halleck drew from an imposing erudition numerous examples of their accomplishments. History also afforded evidences that untrained troops could usually accomplish little, and Halleck could also draw on those evidences, to echo Washington and to contribute to a major theme of other professionalist writers who would follow. He quoted Washington at length on the disgust which militiamen had inspired in him.[10] He argued that records indicated that two good regiments at St. Louis in 1832 could have prevented the Black Hawk War, and that two good regiments in Florida at the outset of trouble could similarly have averted the Seminole War and saved the country thirty million dollars and hundreds of lives. He believed that the history of American Indian wars was replete with such circumstances. In his later editions he added that if the United States could have sent a well organized army of 12,000 men across the Nueces to the Rio Grande in 1846, the Mexican War might have been averted; but to advance a force of only 2,000 men to Matamoras in the face of a large Mexican army was to create an almost irresistible temptation for the Mexicans.[11]

Halleck thought the lesson of history plain: moderately large armies of trained troops quickly win wars and often even prevent war; armies of untrained troops or inadequate numbers of trained troops invite wars and then lose them or make winning excessively costly.

Even in the narrowest sense, Halleck argued, the financial savings generally attributed to reliance on militia rather than a standing army were exaggerated, for once campaigning began the expenses of militia were huge. In Indian warfare such as the Black Hawk or Seminole campaigns, "the expenses of the militia," according to Secretary of War John C. Spencer, "invariably exceed those of regulars by *at least three hundred per cent*." [12]

Halleck acknowledged that mass armies of amateur soldiers had sometimes won famous victories. New levies of citizens always brought new energy and enterprise into an army——he refused to emphasize the numbers they might also bring, for he was unwilling to stress the value of big battalions. But even with their energy and enterprise, new levies won victories only with excessive expenditure of lives and money, and they did not win reliably. Energy and enterprise are much less valuable than discipline, steady courage, and perseverance, the attributes of a trained soldiery.

No people in the world ever exhibited a more general and enthusiastic patriotism than the Americans during the war of our own Revolution. And yet our army received, even at that time, but little support from irregular and militia forces in the open field. Washington's opinions on this subject furnish so striking a contrast to the congressional speeches of modern political demagogues, who, with boastful swaggers, would fain persuade us that we require no organization or discipline to meet the veteran troops of Europe in the open field, and who would hurry us, without preparation, into war with the strongest military powers of the world—so striking is the contrast between the assertions of these men and the letters and reports of Washington, that it may be well for the cool and dispassionate lover of truth to occasionally refresh his memory by reference to the writings of Washington.[13]

Halleck believed history demonstrated that, short of the intervention of extraordinary circumstances, raw troops simply could not stand against even substantially inferior numbers of disciplined soldiers in the open field. In open combat, "*science* must determine the contest." [14]

What military policy should the United States then follow?

The peaceful habits of our citizens tend but little to the cultivation of the military character. How, then, are we to oppose the hostile force?

Must human blood be substituted for skill and preparation, and the dead bodies of our citizens serve as epaulements against the inroads of the enemy? [15]

In answering, Halleck specifically acknowledged the influence upon him of Washington, Hamilton, and John C. Calhoun. He suggested reliance on an enlarged but not a huge force of well-trained regulars expansible in wartime according to the suggestions of Calhoun's "Report on the Reduction of the Army" of December 12, 1820. Once again, the expansible army plan was the central idea in the professionalist's effort to reconcile adequate American military preparation with the popular aversion to a large standing army.[16]

This formula required first, the creation of an adequate staff and command system. Halleck, like all other professional writers, found the United States especially lacking in such a system. In the 1850s the army was plagued by a conflict in authority between the secretary of war and the commanding general with no adequate staff to assist either of those functionaries. The specialized service departments such as the Corps of Engineers and the Quartermaster's Department were organized into independent bureaus over which the commanding general of the army exercised little or no authority. There was an absence of units of administration and command higher than regiments (with the latter mostly scattered by driblets of companies across the Indian frontier), and a lack of sufficient generals to permit even a semblance of a hierarchy of command. To remedy all these defects was sure to be a labor of decades, but Halleck suggested the beginnings of a reform: the revival of the grades of general and lieutenant general to give top commanders ranks commensurate with their responsibilities; the abolition of the confusing brevet system; and the creation of a general staff corps. The staff corps was to be made up of men with special training in staff duties who would alternate tours of duty between staff and line in order to prevent an unhealthy divorcement of staff from line.[17]

Beyond such organizational reforms, Halleck believed that a good expansible army system demanded an officer corps whose members met the highest professional qualifications. To that end he recommended that the Military Academy be maintained and improved and its influence extended, and that promotion by merit be sub-stituted in large part for the prevailing practice of promotion by seniority.[18] A proper system also required a disproportionately high strength of artillery and engineers, since those technical branches did not lend themselves to rapid augmentation in war.[19] The peace-time strength of the cavalry must also be disproportionately high, since, with the effectiveness of cavalry depending greatly on its moral impression, rapidity and precision of movement and boldness in the charge were especially important.[20] The infantry, though by far the strongest arm in war, did not require so high a numerical strength in peace, since men could be trained for infantry duties with comparative rapidity; but the organization of the arm must be such as to permit of the most rapid absorption of recruits.[21]

When Halleck wrote in the 1840s, before the Mexican War, the authorized strength of the United States Army was 7,590 men, and the navy consisted of 77 ships manned by 8,724 men. "This is certainly a very small military and naval force," Halleck com-mented, "for the defence of so extended and populous a country, especially one whose political institutions and rapidly increasing power expose it to the distrust and jealousy of most other nations." [22] Halleck did not specify the numerical increase in the regulars he desired, but he made it clear that a moderate increase would suffice. The demand of the expansible army system was for an extremely well trained nucleus of a wartime army, for skill and discipline, not for numbers.

The great difficulties encountered by Washington in instructing his in-experienced forces in the more difficult branches of the art, made him the more earnest, in after years, to impress upon us how important it was for us *In peace to prepare for war*. The preparation here meant is not the keeping up, in time of peace, of a large standing army ever ready to take the field; but rather the formation of a small body, edu-cated and practised in all the scientific and difficult parts of the profes-sion; a body which shall serve as the *cadre* or framework of a large army, capable of imparting to the new and inexperienced soldiers of the republic that skill and efficiency which has been acquired by prac-tice.[23]

Above all, Halleck emphasized a thoroughly professional officer corps. Large numbers of untrained troops were to be called forward in a major war, and the influence upon them of even the best cadres must necessarily be limited. Therefore an American military system must rest upon "the absolute necessity of having in this country a body of men who shall devote themselves to the cultivation of military science, so as to be able to compete with the military science of the transatlantic powers." [24]

Halleck's emphasis on professional armies of high skill and discipline sprang partly from his inheritance of Dennis Mahan's stress on the value of the aggressive approach to war. In both strategy and tactics Halleck believed that great advantages inhered in the offensive. But offensive warfare demanded high quality troops. Unlike some professionalists, Halleck was not utterly contemptuous of militia, and he paid a glowing tribute to the defensive stands of American militia at Charleston, Mobile, New Orleans, Fort McHenry, Stonington, and Plattsburg. But the usefulness of militia was in defensive war; the offensive demanded well trained troops.[25]

And offensive war remained preferable. A strategic offensive could carry war into foreign soil and thus spare the country from an attacking force, the invading army augmenting its own resources while diminishing those of the enemy. The strategic invasion also tended to raise the moral courage of the army that conducted it, while disheartening the enemy. Further, "Regarded simply as the initiative of movements, the offensive is almost always the preferable one, as it enables the general to choose his lines for moving and concentrating his masses on the decisive point." [26] Finally, like Mahan, Halleck believed that even the army faced with the necessity for a strategic defensive would succeed if it mounted a tactical offensive; passive defense, said Halleck, "is far from being the true Fabian system of defensive war." [27]

The doctrine of an audacious and well directed initiative as the heart of strategy and tactics, urged upon the American army by Dennis Mahan, thus received the approbation of Henry W. Halleck. One effect, again, was to enhance the professionals' regard for regulars. To the professionals, offensive warfare implicitly was warfare with skillful troops.

If Halleck's emphasis on the value of the offensive seems to comport ill with the cautiousness of his later military practice (a cautiousness which should not be exaggerated, since Halleck was one of the authors of the audacious Fort Henry campaign), some foretaste of the cautious Halleck of the Civil War—and a certain ambiguity of doctrine—appear in Halleck's remarks on fortification. Halleck placed a high value on the erection of fortifications as a means for the peacetime preparation for war. "In all military operations," he wrote, "*time* is of vast importance. If a single division of an army can be retarded for a few hours only, it not unfrequently decides the fate of the campaign." [28] Such was the work fortifications could do. Fortifications were especially important for the United States, with its small regular forces and large numbers of untrained soldiers:

When a country like ours is invaded, large numbers of such [raw] troops must suddenly be called into the field. Not knowing the designs of the invaders, much time will be lost in marches and countermarches; and if there be no safe places of resort the operations must be indecisive and insecure. . . .

Every government should prepare, in time of peace, its most prominent and durable means of defence. By securing in a permanent manner its important points, it will enable a small force to retain possession of these places against a greatly superior army, for a considerable length of time. This serves the same purpose as a battle gained; for, in the beginning of a war of invasion, the economy of time is of the utmost importance to the defensive party, enabling it to organize and prepare the military resources of the state.[29]

For the United States, the great seaports most notably deserved fortification, and Halleck gave particular attention to seacoast fortification. He thus participated in and contributed to an element in the tradition of American military thought which in time was to grow virtually into an obsession, the emphasis on seacoast fortifications.

This emphasis at first grew naturally out of the amphibious attacks by British sea power in the Wars of the Revolution and of 1812. The burning of Falmouth in 1775 and of Washington in 1814 by forces landed from British ships, and the naval attacks upon Charleston in 1776 and Baltimore in 1814 seemed certain to recur in future wars against European sea powers. At the time when Halleck wrote the most likely new war appeared still to be a third struggle with Great Britain. Therefore after the War of 1812, Congress ordered a renewed effort to fortify the principal cities and harbors of the American coast. Though interest lagged in the peaceful years of the twenties and thirties and the effort often faltered, the Corps of Engineers devoted much of its energy in the first half of the nineteenth century to the erection of masonry seacoast fortifications which dotted the coast from Castle William to Fort St. Philip, and of which Fort Sumter became the most famous. The emphasis of West Point on engineering now strengthened in the professional officer corps the commitment to such a mode of defense.[30]

Halleck emphatically endorsed a heavy reliance on seacoast fortifications. Beyond a chapter advocating peacetime expenditures for fortifications in general, he devoted an additional full chapter to the values of permanent coastal defenses. Painstakingly he examined history to establish that when good seacoast fortifications had surrendered to attacking naval forces it was because of unusual circumstances, and that when a good seacoast fortress was properly defended it invariably turned back attacking ships. Thus he reasserted the ancient rule of the superiority of fortresses over ships. In later editions of his *Elements* he argued that the Crimean War decisively affirmed the rule.[31]

In the 1850s Halleck did append a cautious note on the possible effects of the increased size and range of military projectiles—meaning especially rifled projectiles—on masonry works such as those the United States was building along its coasts. He thought it a moot question then whether improved artillery would require earthen works to mask the masonry walls of seacoast fortresses.[32] As the Civil War soon demonstrated, masonry fortifications were vulnerable indeed to rifled batteries from both ship and shore.

The American seacoast fortresses of the period when Halleck wrote were sure to be of value principally in fending off raids rather than in guarding against serious invasion of the United States. The landings for the latter could of course take place on unguarded stretches of the long American coast. This fact makes Halleck's lengthy treatment of seacoast fortifications seem somewhat disproportionate, a foreshadowing of greater preoccupation with seacoast defenses in the years to come as well as a reservation to the aggressive doctrines of Mahan.

Inconsistent as Halleck's concern for seacoast fortification was with his zeal for the offensive, it was nevertheless a logical corollary of professionalist thought. The professionalists valued the offensive, but they held that a well trained soldiery was essential to its success. The United States did not possess such a soldiery in adequate numbers. Therefore American reliance on the second best mode of warfare, the defensive, was inescapable.[33]

Halleck's interest in fortification, furthermore, was related to another aspect of the conservative, professionalist nature of his military thought. Like his mentor Jomini he was a product of the eighteenth century in his general approach to war. In his disquisitions on the value of the offensive, he spoke of a limited type of offensive warfare with territories or at most armies as its objectives, not a warfare of unlimited violence reaching to whole nations. An emphasis on fortified strategic points fits naturally into a discussion of war which continues to regard the conquest of territory as the usual object of war.

Although Halleck paid obeisance to the memoirs and military maxims of Napoleon as guides to military doctrine, he took a dim view of Napoleon's departures from the polite warfare of the eighteenth century, such as the effort to subsist the French army upon the country in Spain. Of that effort he wrote:

In great wars of invasion it is sometimes impracticable, at least for a time, to provide for the immense forces placed on foot, by any regular system of magazines or of ordinary requisitions: in such cases their subsistence is entirely intrusted to the troops themselves, who levy contributions wherever they pass. The inevitable consequences of this system are universal pillage and a total relaxation of discipline; the loss of private property and the violation of individual rights, are followed by the massacre of all struggling parties, and the ordinary peaceful and non-combatant inhabitants are converted into bitter and implacable enemies.[34]

Once again, it is significant that Halleck paid little regard to Clausewitz, but that his most consistently high praise was for the conservative Jomini, "the best of military judges." American professional military thought remained military thought of the conservative tradition.

Henry W. Halleck was the most prominent in the circle of Dennis Mahan's students who elaborated on Mahan's contributions to American military thought and who tightened the hold of the professionalist tradition on the command of the American army. Even before the Civil War Halleck's eminence was rivalled by the reputation of George B. McClellan of the class of 1836, the top ranking graduate of his year and one of the best students in the early history of the Military Academy. McClellan added to sharp intelligence a winning personality and a driving energy that made him early seem a likely future commanding general of the army.[35]

Unlike Halleck, McClellan received the opportunity to display gallantry and ability on the field of battle in Mexico. As a captain of cavalry in 1855 (by which time Halleck had resigned his commission and entered civil life), he was so generally accepted as a coming man that he was a natural choice to serve on a three-member American military commission to study the operations of the Crimean War. The commission arrived in the Crimea in time to witness only the closing incidents of the siege of Sevastopol, but after the end of the campaign McClellan remained in Europe to study the organization and tactics of all the armies of Europe, emphasizing cavalry, and emphasizing also the Russian and Austrian armies, with which American soldiers were least acquainted. Out of his observations came a lengthy report on the armies of Europe, first printed by order of the War Department and later reissued by a commercial publisher when McClellan in 1861 seemed about to fulfil his promise of military eminence.[36] From his European studies came also a new set of *Regulations and Instructions for the Field Service of the U.S. Cavalry in Time of War*.[37]

McClellan's report on the armies of Europe betrayed a mind of considerably less breadth and penetration than Halleck's, but it was a competent job of technical description, and thus it further enhanced McClellan's reputation in an officer corps that was laboring to extend its specialized professional knowledge. The reader seeking keen insight into European military doctrine will be disappointed; but with that painstaking care which was later to characterize his command of an army, McClellan did set forth in elaborate detail all he had learned of the formal structure of European military establishments. He did not offer analyses of relative assets and liabilities of European armies and of their methods, but he did offer careful summaries of peace and war strengths and detailed charts of corps, divisional, and regimental organization. He said little of European strategic thought, but he did instruct in minor tactics and in camp arrangements with elaborate diagrams. In short, he wrote a book which offered little on the Prussian staff system and its evolution, but which informed its readers that in the Prussian army the drums were eighteen inches in diameter and four inches deep. There was little about the Russian conscription system, but the book did reveal that soldiers of the Russian army wore no socks but instead wrapped bandages of linen about their feet.

For all that, McClellan's report was a good intelligence study, and it was not lacking in thoughtful passages. McClellan was at his best, for example, in his remarks on the lessons of European cavalry for the United States. In this connection he gave a characteristic professionalist emphasis to the American need for improved training and discipline, but he sought also to adapt European professional standards to American conditions.

Not only a thorough professionalist but one with regard for the outward manifestations of military training in smart appearance and crackling drill, McClellan found European regular cavalry immensely impressive, especially the superbly drilled Russians, with their mounted maneuvers of unparalleled precision. He could not but acknowledge that on its own terms European cavalry was far superior to any cavalry in the United States, including even the best American regulars. But McClellan also recognized that United States cavalry would probably never have to meet European cavalry on European terms. Therefore he proposed higher professional standards for the American service not to duplicate European cavalry but to make it better able to meet the demands likely to face it, incorporating appropriate features of European organization and training while maintaining a frankly American character in the arm.[38]

The proper organization of United States cavalry, McClellan maintained, must be guided by three considerations: first, the nature of the service it would perform against the Indians; second, the probable nature of its possible employment against a civilized enemy who had invaded the United States; and third, its possible service in an offensive war against a neighbor state on the American continent.

None of these prospective services, McClellan held, demanded a true heavy cavalry, equipped and trained for mass mounted action

against European cuirassiers. They demanded a light cavalry, speedy
in travel and movement. The need for light cavalry against the
Indians of the plains was obvious. A force was necessary which was
as light and quick as the Indians, to compel them to battle where
the superiority of the white man's weapons and discipline would
ensure him victory. But even for foreign wars, a light cavalry
would best serve the American purpose. No European power would
be able to transport great bodies of heavy cavalry to the American
coast, and in cavalry actions of limited numbers the superior
mobility of light cavalry always tended to prevail. McClellan rightly
regarded an American offensive against a European power in its
homeland as inconceivable at the time, and in any offensive action
against Canada, Mexico, or the West Indies European-style heavy
cavalry would be no more likely to appear in quantity than in the
United States.[39]

Nevertheless, McClellan argued in the characteristic professionalist vein that the United States cavalry might profit from the example of the superior drill and discipline of its European counterparts. He regarded "the individual instruction of man and horse"
as "the most important point of the whole system": cavalry above
all required thorough training before its commitment to the field.
He believed that the training methods he saw in Russia and Austria
might be applied in America, with a slow progression from step
to step in riding procedures, with the use of wooden horses, with
"great care . . . taken not to exact too great precision" in the first
exercises on horseback, and with "the observation of the principles
. . . insisted upon only when they [the recruits] can sit the horse
without fear of falling off, and have acquired a certain amount of
self-confidence." In short, cavalry training could not be too much
hurried, and training must follow a reasonable pace because badly
trained cavalry was often worse than none at all. The prescriptions
obviously could apply only among regulars.[40]

That cavalry training might receive the attention it deserved,
McClellan proposed a United States cavalry school and depot. The
school was to afford thorough instruction to cavalry officers in all
that applied to their service: it was to be a professional school
modeled upon the French cavalry school of application at Saumur.
It was to provide also for the instruction of recruits, that they might

be well drilled before they joined their regiments. There should also be a veterinary school and a thoroughly trained veterinary service. Again, McClellan's whole concern was to approach European standards of professionalism.[41]

McClellan believed that the Crimean War clearly implied a need for the improvement of organization and for higher professional standards among officers and men in the cavalry and in the United States Army in general. It was true, he said, that no immediate cause for war with a European power existed, and that none could be foreseen. But the Crimean War demonstrated that in the event of conflict a European invasion of the United States was more possible than ever before:

> In the day of sailing-vessels the successful siege of Sebastopol would have been impossible. It is evident that the Russians did not appreciate the advantages afforded by steamers, and were unprepared to sustain a siege.
> This same power of steam would enable European nations to disembark upon our shores even a larger force than that which finally encamped around Sebastopol.[42]

Therefore McClellan believed that the war demanded renewed consideration of the old problem of how best to prepare the United States for a large scale foreign war, and here he returned to the same emphasis which Halleck had given to seacoast fortifications. The siege of Sevastopol impressed McClellan with the power of fortifications to withstand naval attack, and consequently he believed that the United States was taking one essential step toward preparation for war by fortifying its principal harbors, and that the seacoast fortifications should be pushed energetically to completion. He noted that many observers at Sevastopol had been especially impressed with the durability of earthwork fortifications; but he recommended for the American seacoasts the completion of the masonry fortresses of the Sumter variety. Not having had an opportunity to witness the effect of modern ordnance upon masonry, he continued to believe that the impressive performance of the earthworks at Sevastopol promised even better results from permanent masonry defenses. In any case, to resist a possible European attack by a force greater than that which fell upon Sevastopol, "our cities and harbors must be fortified, and those fortifications must be provided with guns, ammunition, and instructed artillerists." [43] In a book whose great emphasis was on preparing the regular army for war, McClellan made one concession to the fact that an extensive war would demand greater numbers than the regulars could offer. He suggested that volunteer companies in the coastal area might receive artillery instruction to permit them to help garrison the coastal fortresses.[44]

Like Halleck, McClellan did not abandon the emphasis on the offensive which was so important in Mahan's West Point doctrine. More explicitly than Halleck, he acknowledged that fortifications alone would not suffice to guard the United States against foreign invasion. Like Mahan, if paradoxically in view of his own later military career, McClellan placed a premium upon aggressive strategy and tactics and upon the ability of such methods to cancel out much of the value of fortifications.

In his comments on the Crimean War, McClellan was critical of both allied and Russian commanders for their lack of celerity and aggressiveness. He regarded the long siege of Sevastopol as a needless product of the inadequate drive of the initial British and French incursions into the Crimea. If they had moved energetically enough, the allies might at first have cut off the Russian army from Sevastopol and then entered the city "at all hazards, over the bodies of its weak garrison." Or the allies might have cut off the Russian Crimean army from all aid from the north and then pushed forward "to drive them into the city, and enter it at their heels." They failed to follow either of these courses but moved instead with cumbersome slowness, and the Russians in turn failed through lack of aggressiveness to seize the opportunities presented them by the mistakes of the allies. On one occasion the British stood with precipitous heights behind them, only a single road to carry a retreat, and virtually out of touch with the French; but the Russians did nothing. McClellan the field commander was later to miss his own share of such opportunities, but as a military writer of the Mahan school his watchword was aggressiveness.[45]

Since an invading enemy of the United States might readily turn the harbor fortifications, McClellan believed that a strong mobile army was also essential to American defense. Even as far as holding the fortifications was concerned, high quality troops were de-

sirable. As McClellan saw it, the success of the Russians in pro-
longing the defense of Sevastopol had owed more to the character
of the Russian troops than to the inherent strength of the fortifications:

But, in our admiration of the talent and energy of the engineer, it must
not be forgotten that the inert masses which he raised would have been
useless without the skilful artillery and heroic infantry who defended
them. Much stronger places than Sebastopol have often fallen under
far less obstinate and well-combined attacks than that to which it was
subjected. There can be no danger in expressing the conviction that the
siege of Sebastopol called forth the most magnificent defence of fortifications that has ever yet occurred.[46]

Therefore the United States should heed the lesson:

That mere individual courage cannot suffice to overcome the forces
that would be brought against us were we involved in a European war,
but that it must be rendered manageable by discipline, and directed by
that consummate and mechanical military skill which can only be acquired
by a course of education instituted for the special purpose, and by long
course of habit.

An invading army of 15,000 or 20,000 men could easily be crushed
by the unremitting attacks of superior numbers; but when it comes to
the case of more than 100,000 disciplined veterans, the very multitude
brought to bear against them works its own destruction; because, if
without discipline and instruction, they cannot be handled, and are in
their own way.[47]

Here was another clear statement of the professionalist thesis.
McClellan did not offer detailed prescriptions for providing the
United States with an army of "consummate and mechanical military skill." He was writing an official report of his European tour,
and to offer a military policy for the United States was not his task.
The few suggestions he did put forth, however, emphasized the
expansible army formula; like Halleck, McClellan urged a mat-
ing of the ideas of Calhoun and Mahan. He suggested that the
regular army be made as large as the defense of the frontier required, which implied an increase. Beyond that, he held that the
number of officers and NCO's should be exceptionally large, in order
to provide for expansion with the greatest possible ease and speed.
The army should be one of skilled specialists, an army of potential
leaders, and special care should be devoted to the training of its
most professional arms, the artillery and the engineers. Since the

engineer troops were pitifully small in number in the American army, the artillery must be prepared to perform functions which in other armies would fall to the engineers, notably the preparation of its own battery positions. The equipment of the army should be of the best available types; McClellan recommended the adoption of various items he had seen in Europe, such as Austrian bridging equipment which could prevent losses such as had occurred in Mexico, from inability to bridge streams and ravines.[48]

McClellan believed that along with a well trained and well equipped regular army, there should be a penetration of the militia and volunteer systems by regular army influences, so that the material for wartime expansion could readily come from those systems. The militia and the volunteers should receive a coherent organization, presumably one which would facilitate their absorption into the command system of the regulars. They should have regular army officers as their instructors. The regular army should use all possible means to diffuse its military knowledge among them. The systems would still have shortcomings; but the intelligent course was to minimize them by offering as professional as possible a training and by putting the militia and volunteers under increasing professional control.[49]

McClellan's colleagues in the American military commission to the Crimea, Richard Delafield and Alfred Mordecai, emphasized technical information on European developments in their own specialties, military engineering and ordnance, respectively. When Delafield briefly ventured into broader questions of American military policy, his conclusions were substantially those of Halleck and McClellan. A specialist in engineering, he urged the high value of completing and strengthening the American coastal fortifications and of fortifying strategic points generally. He emphasized that the key Russian fortress at Sevastopol, the famous Malakoff Redoubt whose name had become a byword for defensive strength, first threw back the allies when it was a weak and unfinished work, and that its earthworks and armament never approached the strength of the best American permanent fortresses. If so much could be accomplished by an incomplete and faulty fortress, Delafield asked, how much more could be done with properly constructed works?

But though he was an engineer, Delafield argued too that the Malakoff had become a byword through the caution and lethargy of the allies. If the allies had pressed the attack against it when it was not only unfinished but largely unsupported, the Malakoff would have fallen readily. The crucial factor in the Crimean campaign had again been the zeal and force in the attack. A vigorous offensive should have won for the British and French the quick collapse of Sevastopol; the lack of such an offensive condemned the allies to a costly and discouraging siege and to limited rewards at the end. The offensive as the highroad to military success was the doctrine of the engineering specialist Delafield as of the cavalryman McClellan, the scholar Halleck, and the teacher Mahan.[50]

Delafield was Mahan's senior and for many years his colleague in the shaping of West Point, serving as superintendent of the Military Academy in 1838–1845 and 1856–1861. Eventually Mahan's students began to join him as West Point colleagues; notable among them was George W. Cullum of the class of 1835. Cullum's literary production was small, except for his monumental *Register of the Graduates of the United States Military Academy*. But he was a well known and influential figure in the professional officer corps, and in 1864 he did write a noteworthy book review for the *United States Service Magazine*. Reviewing Halleck's translation of Jomini's *Life of Napoleon*, he illustrated the persistence of professionalist doctrines among Mahan's students and Jomini's preeminence as the European preceptor of American military thought well into the Civil War.[51]

Cullum used the occasion of the book review to write a brief survey of American military history. In it he emphasized again the contrast between the failures of untrained soldiers in the Wars of the Revolution and of 1812 and the successes of the regular army in the War with Mexico. Writing with the Civil War uppermost in his and his readers' minds, he had to acknowledge that the United States must rely on citizen soldiers rather than on regulars in major wars, and that citizen soldiers in time could become good fighting men. But against the background of the Civil War, Cullum saw cause more than ever to urge the highest standards of professionalism in the American officer corps. The deficiencies of citizen soldiers made the attainment of the best possible officer corps imperative.

And to Cullum, the best possible officer corps was the best educated officer corps. It was a corps of professionals, in the fullest sense of the word:

In our days we no longer believe in what Chatham called "heavenborn generals." It is agreed that modern warfare is the offspring of science and civilization,—that it has its rules and its principles, which it is necessary to thoroughly master before being worthy to command, and that it is wiser to profit by such lessons of history, as taught in the work before us than to purchase experience by the blood of battle-fields. The brief span of a single life avails little in working out the great problems of science; but education supplies the piled-up aggregates of human knowledge.[52]

We wish to impress upon our rulers the necessity of thorough education, both theoretical and practical, to attain that excellence in arms which the disciplined mind of our people has already secured in nearly all the arts of peace. England neglected her military schools, and failed to employ her best talent to lead her dauntless soldiery in the Crimea. Hence Alma was won by blood and not tactical skill; Balaklava was a blunder and butchery; Inkermann, a surprise only redeemed by valor; and the Redan, a fatal and unpardonable repulse. How humiliating it must have been to proud Albion to witness the contrast in the military knowledge, strategical combinations, tactical evolutions, and the perfect adaptability to circumstances of her educated ally! Though the French had conducted but a single great siege—that of Antwerp—in forty years, the lessons learned in her military schools taught her vast army how to skilfully dispose itself before Sebastopol.[53]

With an uncritical enthusiasm that would have astonished the French themselves, Cullum urged the United States to look again to the French for its military model. He urged a return to the writings of Jomini, "the most learned strategist among ancient or modern authors," "long . . . regarded in Europe as the highest authority among military writers," of whom "Napoleon himself, in his autobiographical memoirs dictated at St. Helena, says that . . . of all his critics, [he] best understood his system of war." [54] The United States needed an officer corps of the highest professional standards, and the best foundation for such a corps, said Cullum, was the study of Jomini's *Précis,* and also of the military history embodied in his *Life of Napoleon:*

Jomini does not in the present work formally discuss strategy, but, what is better, in narrating the operations of each campaign he deduces the true principles of the military art, and illustrates them by the various plans of Napoleon and his opponents. . . . *In other words, he teaches strategy by applying its principles as a scientific test to the facts of history which he narrates.*[55]

Thus Cullum returned to the first theme of Dennis Mahan, professional study and primarily the study of military history as the foundation of success in war. Mahan's students had in their own writings consistently emphasized the themes which Mahan had stressed. They had urged the value of the study of military history and handbooks of military doctrine, although in Halleck, Mahan's complementary emphasis on pragmatic flexibility had fallen into the background. They had continued to regard the offensive as the true mode of victorious war, though in Halleck and McClellan there was a greater emphasis than in Mahan on the defensive uses of fortifications, especially seacoast fortifications. But all had remained substantially consistent with Mahan's precepts, and Mahan's students had carried on and elaborated Mahan's professionalist ideas, urging the need of the United States for a strong regular army and for a thoroughly professional officer corps.

One influence of the West Point of Mahan and Thayer, then, was to instill in the American officer corps a quest for high standards of professional excellence. The Civil War was to demonstrate that West Point had succeeded in producing an officer corps imbued with respect for military study, and ready to display the adaptability to strategic and tactical circumstance that Mahan had praised. They were skilled in the technical procedures of fortification and gunnery, but guided nevertheless by a dedication to the offensive and the attack.

Another influence, however, was to leave West Point graduates unprepared psychologically as well as doctrinally for the command of the vast citizen armies that fought the Civil War. While West Point in the era of Mahan grew strongly committed to the Washington-Hamilton tradition, the nation at large still clung to the Jefferson-Jackson tradition in things military. The West Pointers thought in terms of armies of skilled regulars. Their education gave them little confidence in an unskilled citizen soldiery. But the Civil War compelled them to make armies of just such a soldiery. The result was that some of them demanded from their Civil War armies complicated maneuvers of which green troops were incapable, while others developed an excessive caution rooted in a lack of trust in their men. In either case, the conduct of the war was hampered and the blunders and the delays on both the Confederate and Union sides were multiplied.

The West Point of Thayer and Mahan was divorced from the main intellectual currents of Jacksonian America. Its isolation enabled it to give the regular army high standards of excellence, but the price of isolation was high. Standing apart from American life, American military leaders failed to address themselves to the discovery of military programs in accord with that life. Justly proud of their professional growth and of the record of their regulars in Mexico, they felt confidence in the prowess of their professionalized regular army. But they avoided extensive thought about the fact that any major war would have to be fought not so much with regulars as with militia and volunteers. Jacksonian America was not going to provide a larger regular army or even an expansible army on the Hamilton-Calhoun plan advocated also by Halleck and McClellan. When the professional officers led Americans to war, they would have to lead armed citizens, whatever their deficiencies, or lack the numbers to fight a serious war. But the professionals gave scarcely any thought to preparing for this fact by evolving a military doctrine designed to draw the highest usefulness from an armed citizenry.

The professional officers of the Jacksonian era were isolated from realistic thinking about how to fight an American war. They expected society to adapt itself to their mode of warmaking; they made little effort to adapt their ideas on warfare to American society. Thus they were little prepared for the full dimensions of the Civil War, not only for its becoming a war of mass armies of citizen soldiers, but more for its becoming a total war of nation against nation, a war of violence foreseen by Clausewitz, but not foreseen by Jomini.

VI WILLIAM T. SHERMAN AND ULYSSES S. GRANT *The Rise of Total War*

> We are not only fighting hostile armies, but a hostile people, and must make old and young, rich and poor, feel the hard hand of war, as well as the organized armies. WILLIAM T. SHERMAN

> But above all, he [Grant] understood that he was engaged in a people's war, and that the people as well as the armies of the South must be conquered, before the war could end. ADAM BADEAU

SHERMAN and Grant were originals. They were graduates of West Point, but they never fit into a West Point mold.

From one point of view, Grant never attained Dennis Mahan's standards for the fully professional officer. He was not a student of the art and science of war, of its history and governing principles, nor even of its technical trappings. When he sought to drill troops at the beginning of the Civil War, he had continued the study of war so little, that he found it necessary at first to acquire a book of tactics and to work by the book. He discovered that the tactics were essentially the drill he had learned at West Point, which was organized common sense, and which he could readily master. Not a student of war, he possessed a genius for those inspired *ad hoc* solutions to military problems whose value Mahan had recognized, but believed should be grounded in the discipline of knowledge. Grant did not know enough about the skill of regulars to be oppressed by the deficiencies of the volunteers he commanded; he was willing to use green volunteers for the daring winter campaign to Forts Henry and Donelson and to rely on them in the terrible battle of Shiloh.

Sherman was closer to the Mahan concept of the professional officer than was Grant, for he had a respect and appetite for formal knowledge. He was not out of place as a college president just before the war, and he kept abreast of current military ideas, especially after he returned to the army and a military career. His extension of the army school system is significant. But Sherman was that rare individual who could absorb the formal knowledge of his profession without being imprisoned by it, using it when it served him but going beyond it when it did not answer his needs. His mind well stocked with the conventional military knowledge of his day but still turning freely to new ideas, Sherman was to recognize that the Civil War was a new kind of war not foreseen by the West Point textbooks, and that it demanded new methods to win.

Grant almost by intuition, and Sherman by acute perception recognized that the textbook precepts on the undoing of enemy armies, rooted in eighteenth-century warfare, did not fit their problem in the Civil War. They were fighting an angry people, not just armies. Therefore they devised their own mode of war, carrying the fight to the enemy people as well as to his armies, and in the process breaking from the conservative military tradition of West Point to join in the revolutionizing development of total war. Sherman contributed more to that development than Grant, because of the circumstances in which he found himself during the war and because knowing more than Grant about conventional war he was more aware when he was doing something new. He rationalized every important move he made while Grant's actions had much the character of a force of nature.

The wars of the French Revolution and Napoleon had furnished the first great impetus toward total war by placing the military revolution of the nation in arms beside the political revolution. Even the wars of the French Revolution and Napoleon, however, continued to be fought on the assumption that the primary objective of warfare is the surrender or destruction of the enemy's armed forces. Even Clausewitz, famous as he has become for his doctrine that warfare is unfettered violence into which the introduction of limitations is absurd, emphasized that the ultimate objective of war is the subjugation of the enemy army. The American Civil War introduced the principle that with the war of monarch against monarch giving way to the war of people against people, the ob-

jective is the destruction of the whole fabric of the enemy's society. Carry war to the enemy people, the Civil War seemed to
teach, destroy the cohesion of the enemy society, and the enemy
army will collapse of its own weight.

The new mode of war, the war against peoples rather than merely
against armies, was implicit in Sherman's marches through Georgia
and the Carolinas, and for that matter in Philip Sheridan's devastation of the Shenandoah Valley. Such campaigns, designed to destroy
the warmaking resources of the enemy, to leave his people desti-
tute, and to ruin his morale, had occurred often enough through
history until the close of the Thirty Years War, but thereafter they
were rare in the period of dynastic wars with limited objectives.
Now the Americans not only restored such campaigns, but led by
Sherman they gave them a rationale. They incorporated into their
military thought the principle that the enemy society rather than
simply the enemy army constitutes the logical objective of war.
This principle received explicit enunciation in certain American
writings on war which the Civil War inspired.

William T. Sherman's contribution to the rise of total war lay
not only in his Georgia and Carolina campaigns but also in his
rationalization of them. And he developed a cogent rationalization
of his new mode of war partly because he was a thorough student
of the old warfare. His revolutionizing impact on war was greater
because of his deep roots in the conservative military tradition. Up
to a point he was a disciple of Mahan on the model of Halleck or
McClellan, but his conservative roots made him more appreciative
of the newness of the ideas the Civil War had thrust on him, more
articulate in their expression, and thus better able to introduce
them into military doctrine. Furthermore, thoroughly grounded as
he was in the conservative American military tradition, he could
recognize what remained of value in that tradition even in an age
of changing methods of war. As commanding general of the army
from 1869 to 1883 he could contribute to the retention of what was
valuable in that tradition.

Dennis Mahan's first theme had been the necessity of thorough
military study and education to an effective officer corps. Sherman
as commanding general of the army perhaps accomplished more

than any other holder of that office to advance the professional
education of the American officer corps, for he was the principal
founder of the army's postgraduate education system. Finding the
engineering school at Willett's Point, New York and the artillery
school at Fort Monroe already established when he assumed command of the army, he nurtured the latter through its uncertain
formative years and founded the cavalry and infantry school at Fort
Leavenworth. He stressed that while these schools were to enhance
the skill of American officers in technical specialties, he intended that
they should aim also "to qualify officers for any duty they may be
called upon to perform, or for any position however high in rank or
command they may aspire to in service." [1]

Sherman's service as commanding general occurred in a period
when foreign war seemed remote; but on one of the few occasions
in that period when he adverted even to a remote possibility of
foreign war, Sherman stressed the need for military education:

Steam and electricity [he wrote] have brought all parts of the earth into
such close relations that we are forced into rivalry with foreign nations
in the matter of military education and training. . . . Whilst other nations claim superiority in military affairs, by reason of large establishments and greater experience, it so happens that modern guns and
breech-loading rifles have, in late years, almost revolutionized the equipment and tactics of armies, and we are fortunately encumbered with
but few old prejudices to be unlearned, and are free to adopt what is
excellent among the discoveries and improvements of every land.[2]

Such a union of the theme of education with a reminder of
change and improvement was characteristic of the man. But he
remained faithful to Mahan's emphasis on military education. Always thoroughly realistic, he doubted that the professionalists' expansible army plan for building wartime forces around the regulars
would come to exist; but he believed the regular army might serve
nevertheless as an instrument of military education throughout the
land. Indeed, that was the purpose of the peacetime army as he
saw it: "Our Army is small and intended to be a school of instruction." [3] If national military planning must build upon the popular
acceptance of the militia-volunteer system, the regular army's performance of its educational function became more imperative:

The whole theory and practice of the Government of the United States has been, and continues to be, that the Regular Army must be small, as small as possible, and that for great occasions we as a people must rely on the volunteer masses of soldiery. No class of men better recognize this fact than the Regular Army, and as the science of war is progressive, we must keep pace with it, so as to impart to the volunteer militia, on the shortest notice, all that is known of the art and practice of war up to the moment of execution. In this sense the whole regular army is a school.[4]

Sherman's respect for military education led him to compose his *Memoirs* of the Civil War in such a way that they might guide future commanders. Few Civil War memoirs were so composed. The postwar torrent of recollections of service contributed little to the advancement of American military thought, for most of the memoirs were too much concerned with self-justification or with recovering the excitement of days of glory to serve such a purpose. On the Confederate side, furthermore, the memoir writers were reluctant to probe deeper into the causes of defeat than to cite the material and manpower superiority of the North or sometimes to quarrel with their former comrades. On the Union side, a by-product of final victory was a tendency of Union memoirists to be uncritical of anything in the Union war effort save the mistakes of their personal rivals. The Federal armies had subdued the Confederacy and had generated an awesome strength in the process, and their success had certified to many of their leaders and soldiers the sanctity of the methods that had won success, except of course that many professional soldiers held that the United States should have had a bigger army in 1861. Civil War memoirs tend to be descriptive narratives, not critical analyses seeking to capitalize the war experience for guidance in future wars. But Sherman's *Memoirs* are one of the few outstanding exceptions to this rule.

Sherman sought throughout his *Memoirs* to underline the strategic, tactical, and logistical lessons of the war. Conspicuously among the memoirists, he wrote a concluding chapter in which he tried to sum up the military precepts suggested by his experience. No other Civil War memoir comes so close to being a military textbook.

As a military student as well as a practitioner of the military art, and as a man who before writing his memoirs toured Europe and talked with the generals of the Franco-Prussian War, Sherman was well aware that European soldiers thought the American Civil War lacking in generally applicable military lessons. The volunteer armies of the Union and the Confederacy still looked like armed rabbles to the European professionals. The entrenchments thrown up by those armies seemed, to the Europeans, evidence of their lack of the discipline necessary to stand fire. The loose American tactics seemed simply an inadequate substitution of badly drilled men for the close-knit mass formations which would crush the enemy under a sheer weight of fire power and bayonets.[5]

Sherman disagreed. He shared the nationalism of his era, and he regarded his American volunteers as the equals of any soldiers in the world if not their superiors. He would not admit that any military innovations in the Civil War resulted from an inferiority of the troops. But he had better reasons than that for believing that the American Civil War in its methods of fighting had established a pattern for the great wars of the future.

He conceded that certain peculiarities of the American campaigns stemmed from American geography. American battlefields were more often wooded than those of Europe, and screened withdrawals were possible in America more often than in Europe. With the explanation of the tactics developed in the American war the matter was different. Americans fought in strong skirmish lines rather than in great masses, taking advantage of the shape of ground and of every cover, not because of the inferiority of the troops but because of the difficulties which would henceforth be faced by any attacker moving against an enemy who used rifled weapons. Henceforth the old massed lines of attack would be fit only for mass suicide on any continent and among any troops. Rifled muskets and artillery would compel all armies to dig into the earth, and those who left their entrenchments to attack would have to grope their way from cover to cover.[6]

One of the lessons of the Civil War, then, was that in the future an army standing on the defensive would have advantages over its attacker, who would have to leave his trenches and expose himself to destructive rifle and artillery fire while the defending force remained relatively secure. Sherman believed that in his campaign from Chattanooga to Atlanta the special strength of the defensive plus the difficult terrain counterbalanced his numerical advantage over the Confederates.[7]

But despite the growing power of the defensive, Sherman held to Mahan's confidence in the offensive as the only truly decisive form of war. Faced by new defensive weapons, the offensive must rely more on maneuver, which Mahan had already stressed.[8] Furthermore, with new weapons opening up the battlefield, Sherman believed a premium would be placed on the quality of the men composing an army. Although he admired the exploits of the Civil War volunteers, he encouraged the professionalists by contending that the soldiers would have to be highly trained and disciplined to fight on the battlefields of the future.[9]

With breech-loading rifles compelling a dispersal of companies and battalions, thought Sherman, "a higher order of intelligence and courage on the part of the individual soldier will be an element of strength." [10] But the soldier must possess trained and disciplined intelligence and courage; the man who fought at a distance from his comrades, without the assurance of their presence close by his side, would need the spur of good discipline to keep him on the firing line. "Therefore, the more we improve the fire-arm the more will be the necessity for good organization, good discipline and intelligence on the part of the individual soldier and officer." [11]

An officer corps ranking high in professional education, an aggressive spirit, and thoroughly trained and disciplined troops—on these criteria of military success Sherman agreed with Mahan and the West Point doctrine he inherited. But he took a new direction in the type of war he would wage with them. He would wage a revolutionary kind of war.

In the first place, he would wage war with mass armies. His views here were somewhat ambivalent, given the emphasis on discipline and training just cited. But by and large he believed that great wars now demanded massive forces and that to fail to employ them was to risk disaster. He said to Grant in 1864: "We ought to ask our country for the largest possible armies that can be raised, as so important a thing as the self-existence of a great nation should not be left to the fickle chances of war." [12]

He believed that massive armies were implicit in the type of war the Civil War became: a war of nation against nation, throwing issues that concerned whole populations into the balance.

He continued to assert, as Jomini and Mahan and even Clausewitz had done before him, that the primary aim of war is to destroy the enemy army. He always regarded his march from Atlanta to the sea as having had merely a fraction of the importance of the march from Savannah through the Carolinas, since the second march contributed directly to the overthrow of the principal remaining military force of the enemy, R. E. Lee's Army of Northern Virginia. But even while reiterating his belief in the primacy of armed forces as the objective of war, he shifted towards a new doctrine by pointing out that the will and ability of the enemy army to fight may be undermined by striking at its resources within the enemy homeland and among the enemy population.[13]

Sherman believed that the Civil War was a war of peoples rather than of governments, in a sense in which foreign wars were not. He did not fully foresee that all wars might become conflicts of peoples as well as of governments. But he recognized nevertheless that if in a popular war the will of the enemy people to resist can be destroyed, then the fighting will of the enemy army will probably collapse as well. In this idea he held the germ of the total wars of the twentieth century, and of the bomb at Hiroshima.

Of his destructive marches Sherman wrote:

I attach much importance to these deep incisions into the enemy's country, because this war differs from European wars in this particular: we are not only fighting hostile armies, but a hostile people, and must make old and young, rich and poor, feel the hard hand of war, as well as the organized armies. I know that this recent movement of mine through Georgia has had a wonderful effect in this respect. Thousands who have been deceived by their lying newspapers to believe that we were being whipped all the time now realize the truth, and have no appetite for a repetition of the same experience. To be sure, Jeff. Davis has his people under pretty good discipline, but I think faith in him is much shaken in Georgia, and before we have done with her South Carolina will not be quite so tempestuous.[14]

Or again:

My aim, then, was to whip the rebels, to humble their pride, to follow them to their inmost recesses, and make them fear and dread us. "Fear is the beginning of wisdom." [15]

Thus in Sherman's hands war became a more terrible thing than it had been in the earlier history of the modern Western world, and his precepts carried the seeds of even more horrors than he imagined. He knew that his views on warmaking were ruthless, and he did not shrink from ruthlessness. When his army set out from Atlanta for Savannah, he ordered it to "forage liberally on the country," knowing what the consequences in destruction would be.[16] He looked forward with grim satisfaction to the greater destruction and terror his troops would bring to South Carolina. He had set forth his rationale for the war against people even before his march to the sea, when he ordered the evacuation of the civil population of Atlanta so that the city might be transformed wholly into a military base. That evacuation would aid his cause, he believed, in other ways beyond sparing him the feeding of thousands of useless mouths:

I knew that the people of the South would read in this measure two important conclusions: one, that we were in earnest; and the other, if they were sincere in their common and popular clamor "to die in the last ditch," that the opportunity would soon come.[17]

Those who made war invited its terrible consequences, as Sherman saw it; if they wished to escape the consequences, they must not make war. War is by nature ruthless. Sherman would have agreed with Clausewitz that the violence of war is logically without limit. If the stakes mount higher, then the ruthlessness of war tends to mount with them. And a war of peoples such as the American Civil War, with mastery of one people by the other as its prize, will push war to its ultimate fury.

But the most fearful war is simply one which develops most fully what is implicit in all war. The cruelty of war is not something adventitious: "You cannot qualify war in harsher terms than I will. War is cruelty, and you cannot refine it." [18] "If the people raise a howl against my barbarity and cruelty, I will answer that war is war, and not popularity-seeking. If they want peace, they and their relatives must stop the war." [19] "You might as well appeal against the thunder-storm as against these terrible hardships of war." [20]

So Sherman drove the people of Atlanta from their homes, and burned the crops of Georgia and the Carolinas, and treated leniently the greater depredations of his men, assuring the people of the South that there was only one escape: "to stop the war, which can only be done by admitting that it began in error and is perpetuated in pride." Until that was done, "I will ever conduct war with a view to perfect and early success."

The Government of the United States [he said] has in North Alabama [for example] any and all rights which they choose to enforce in war— to take their lives, their homes, their every thing, because they cannot deny that war does exist here, and war is simply power unrestrained by constitution or compact. If they want eternal warfare, well and good; we will accept the issue and dispossess them, and put our friends in possession. I know thousands and millions of good people, who, at simple notice, would come to North Alabama and accept the elegant houses and plantations there.

If the people of Huntsville think differently, let them persist in war three years longer, and then they will not be consulted. Three years ago, by a little reflection and prudence they could have had a hundred years of peace prosperity, but they preferred war. Very well; last year they could have saved their slaves, but now, it is too late—all the powers of earth cannot restore to them their slaves any more than their grandfathers. Next year their lands will be taken, for in war we can take them, and rightfully, too, and another year they may beg in vain for their lives. A people who will persevere in war beyond a certain limit ought to know the consequences. Many, many people, with less pertinacity than the South, have been wiped out of national existence.[21]

To those who submit to the rightful law and authority, all gentleness and forbearance; but to the petulant and persistent secessionist, why, death is mercy, and the quicker he or she is disposed of the better. Satan and the rebellious saints of heaven were allowed a continuance of existence in hell merely to swell their just punishment. To such as would rebel against a Government so mild and just as ours was in peace, a punishment equal would not be unjust.[22]

There was another side to Sherman's nature, the side which assured the people of the South that "when peace does come, you may call on me for any thing. Then will I share with you the last cracker. . . ."[23] In practice, too, Sherman waged war ruthlessly on civilian property, but he did not war against civilian lives. Nevertheless, in his actions in Georgia and the Carolinas and in his words still more, he had contributed as much to the revolutionizing of war as did the mass armies of the First French Republic. In deed and in word he had shown the face of the war of nations:

"power unrestrained by constitution or compact." He had offered to the future the assurance that to those who refuse to submit to "rightful law and authority," "death is mercy." He had even suggested that a pertinacious people might be wiped out of national existence.

And he had read aright the grim nature of modern war, for his ruthlessness expressed a rising mood of the Northern people in the late years of the Civil War, the mood given voice by the Radicals and making itself felt in the increasing difficulty with which the moderate Abraham Lincoln resisted the political power of the Radicals in Congress, in the governors' mansions, and in the legislatures. "Did I command the army which will take [Charleston]," wrote one Northern general, "I should be sorely tempted to go through the ancient ceremonial & literally plow up its foundations & sow them with salt." [24] In a professional military service magazine, a writer praised Sherman's sternness and called for more generals like him, complaining that the other generals were excessively delicate and conservative in their treatment of the South. The other generals failed to recognize, the military writer said, that they were not fighting an old-fashioned war:

It will be different [he wrote] when it is realized that to break up the rebel armies is not going to bring peace, that the people must be influenced. . . . They must feel the effects of war. . . . They must feel its inexorable necessities, before they can realize the pleasures and amenities of peace. We want determined and unrelenting men, who can exercise their powers, with all the relentless rigors of justice. . . . Humanity was designed for peace, not for war. If we show mercy towards a legitimate enemy, it is magnanimity; if we execute a traitor, it is philanthropy. Humanity is a vulgar virtue. . . .[25]

The writer went on to quote approvingly some of Sherman's more extreme statements on the necessity for cruelty, and then he concluded: "The war will end when the moral strength of the North exceeds that of the South." [26] What he meant was that the war would end when the North carried it ruthlessly to every supporter of the Confederate government, armed or unarmed. The proposal was to wage total war.

Grant did not win the commendation of so bloodthirsty a writer. Grant did not wage a campaign like Sherman's through Georgia, and he was not addicted to making statements about the cruelty of war which could serve as rationalizations for total war. He fought as though the enemy's armies were his objective, and in his *Memoirs* he expressed a conventional view of war, emphasizing almost to excess the doctrine of the primacy of armies as military objectives. Yet he had a part in developing the war against a people as well as against armies. As commanding general of the army, he sponsored, after all, both Sherman's marches through Georgia and the Carolinas and Sheridan's destruction in the Valley of Virginia. As early as his victory at Chattanooga, Grant suggested a march across the Confederacy to Mobile which would have been similar to Sherman's marches. The march from Atlanta to the sea was Grant's conception at least as early as it was Sherman's, albeit Grant anticipated a march which would have the Confederate Army of Tennessee retreating before it and grinding itself to destruction while Sherman carried war to the civilian South.[27]

Furthermore, according to his *Memoirs*, as early as the Shiloh campaign Grant began to move cautiously away from the conventional West Point ideas about how an army should conduct itself in the enemy's country, and toward harsher policies. As he wrote during the 1880s:

Up to the battle of Shiloh I, as well as thousands of other citizens, believed that the rebellion against the Government would collapse suddenly and soon, if a decisive victory could be gained over any of its armies. Donelson and Henry were such victories. An army of more than 21,000 men was captured or destroyed. Bowling Green, Columbus, and Hickman, Kentucky, fell in consequence, and Clarksville and Nashville, Tennessee, the last two with an immense amount of stores, fell into our hands. The Tennessee and Cumberland rivers, from their mouths to the head of navigation, were secured. But when Confederate armies were collected which not only attempted to hold a line farther south, from Memphis to Chattanooga, Knoxville and on to the Atlantic, but assumed the offensive and made such a gallant effort to regain what had been lost, then, indeed, I gave up all idea of saving the Union except by complete conquest. Up to that time it had been the policy of our army, certainly of that portion of it commanded by me, to protect the property of the citizens whose territory was invaded, without regard to their sentiments, whether Union or Secession. After this, however, I regarded it as humane to both sides to protect the persons of those found at their homes, but to consume everything that could be used to support or supply armies.[28]

This policy was a modest enough departure from conventional policies, but it was a departure nevertheless from such prescriptions as those of Henry W. Halleck in his *Elements of Military Art and Science.* Where Halleck had approved seeking supplies from the enemy's country rather than a system of supply by depots and magazines only in extreme emergencies and was dubious of the policy even then, Grant's new ideas opened the way to his eventual boldness in cutting himself from his supply lines and for a time relying completely on the enemy's country during the Vicksburg campaign.[29]

More important still was the interpretation which Grant's semi-official biographer was later able to place upon Grant's new policy. Brigadier General Adam Badeau was a member of Grant's wartime staff and wrote his biography with the general's cooperation, so that statements in Badeau's biography were taken as reflecting the thought of Grant himself. It was important to American thought about the new warfare against peoples that Badeau explicitly set forth a doctrine of war which made populations as well as armies legitimate military objectives and that Badeau portrayed Grant as the author of such a method of war.

Badeau reminded his readers that the initial policy of the Union armies on Confederate soil was to treat rebel property and persons with scrupulous regard, even to the extent of restoring slaves to rebel masters. Leniency, the Union first hoped, would induce the secessionists to return to their old allegiance. But this policy failed. As Halleck put it in a letter to Sherman on the eve of the march from Atlanta to the sea: "We have tried three years of conciliation and kindness without any reciprocation; on the contrary, those thus treated have acted as spies and guerrillas in our rear and within our lines." The Confederates, Badeau pointed out, fought believing that the very foundations of their way of life were at stake, that a Union victory would wreck everything that they valued. Thinking thus, they could not be conciliated by peripheral kindnesses. They saw themselves as fighting for what was most valuable in their lives, and simply to spare their property would not win them back. "The rebels," said Badeau, "had staked all, and could lose no more than all." The Confederacy could not be cajoled into surrender; the Confederacy had to be beaten, people as well as armies.[30]

Therefore, Badeau argued, the Union embarked on a new policy, the new warfare of Grant, Sherman, and Sheridan: "Since the population, as well as the armies, of the South was united in rebellion, the population, as well as the armies, must undergo whatever was necessary for its subjection." [31] Here Badeau touched the crux of the new warfare even more firmly than Sherman had done. Populations, he stated categorically, had taken their place as an objective of war of equal importance with armies. When war thus becomes a conflict of peoples, then enemy peoples as well as enemy armies must be crushed. Badeau continued:

A change thus came over the spirit of the North, and Grant embodied and represented this change. He saw that it was necessary to deprive the South of its resources as well as of its armies, for both were part of its military power. It was he who introduced and enforced the rule that all property useful to the enemy, adding to their strength, or assisting them to carry on the war, should be destroyed.[32]

Or as Badeau could point out Grant himself said to Sheridan of the Confederate farmers in the Shenandoah Valley: "So long as the war lasts they must be prevented from raising another crop." [33]

Badeau published his biography of Grant in 1881, at the start of a new period of interest in the Civil War, when the war had faded enough into the past to take on a coloring of romance and when its generals were ready to produce their memoirs. With the memory of Grant's unfortunate presidency also fading, the popularity of the Union general in chief was rising to new heights, and Badeau sought to explain Grant's fame, to advance it, and to ensure that it would swell to give Grant a place among the great commanders of history. Writing at a crucial moment in the fashioning of Grant's image in American military annals, Badeau contended that Grant's primary claim to renown was his recognition that "American war" demanded new methods and his introduction of those methods.

By "American war," Badeau referred in fact to a war of peoples; Grant's new methods for "American war" would by implication become the methods for any war of peoples. Badeau eloquently described the new war and his conception of Grant's contribution to it in his concluding summary. He held that Grant's innovations in warfare were many, including such tactical developments as the emphasis on open order fighting and field fortifications and the use of cavalry as mounted infantry rather than in old-fashioned charges. But among Grant's innovations, he said, one stood preeminent:

> But above all, he understood that he was engaged in a people's war, and that the people as well as the armies of the South must be conquered, before the war could end. Slaves, supplies, crops, stock, as well as arms and ammunition—everything that was necessary in order to carry on the war, was a weapon in the hands of the enemy; and of every weapon the enemy must be deprived.
>
> This was a view of the situation which Grant's predecessors in the chief command had failed to grasp. Most of the national generals in every theatre, prior to him, had attempted to carry on their operations as if they were fighting on foreign fields. They sought to out-manœuvre armies, to capture posts, to win by strategy pure and simple. But this method was not sufficient in a civil war. The passions were too intense, the stake too great, the alternatives were too tremendous. It was not victory that either side was playing for, but for existence. If the rebels won, they destroyed a nation; if the government succeeded, it annihilated a rebellion. It was not enough at this emergency to fight as men fight when their object is merely to outwit or even outnumber the enemy. This enemy did not yield because he was outwitted or outnumbered. It was indispensable to annihilate armies and resources; to place every rebel force where it had no alternative but destruction or submission, and every store or supply of arms or munitions or food or clothes where it could be reached by no rebel army.
>
> Grant's greatness consisted in his perception of this condition of affairs, and his adaptation of all his means to meeting it.[34]

When the idea of Grant as the prophet of a new kind of warfare was established, a later writer in a professional service journal put the idea more succinctly. Grant's greatness as a commander, he said, was that he was the first Federal general to see "that it was the mind of the South we had to conquer, not alone fortifications and territory." [35]

Introduced by Sherman and Sheridan, rationalized in Sherman's *Memoirs* and in Badeau's biography of Grant, the new mode of warfare against peoples next established itself in a leading late nineteenth-century American textbook on war, John Bigelow's *The Principles of Strategy*. Captain John Bigelow of the 10th Cavalry was too young to have served in the Civil War himself. A West Point graduate of 1877, he was partly a product of Commanding General Sherman's influence upon the United States Army. He was an outstanding example of the young officers alert to the development of their profession who passed through Sherman's schools of application, filled the pages of the growing professional periodicals which were also encouraged by Sherman, and generally appeared in surprising numbers out of the otherwise lethargic frontier-post army. Bigelow enjoyed also the stimulus of a literary heritage, for his father, the elder John Bigelow, had been not only Lincoln's minister to France but also co-editor with William Cullen Bryant of the New York *Evening Post* and a prolific essayist, minor poet, and scholar in the New England genteel tradition. The captain's brother Poultney Bigelow was a journalist, scholar, and university lecturer.[36]

Spurred by this background and inheritance, Captain John Bigelow overcame the stultifying effects of army life in the remote West to produce numerous contributions to military journals. He authored careful studies of *Mars-la-Tour and Gravelotte* and *Chancellorsville*, and, in Fort Assiniboine, Montana, where he commanded a company of the 10th Cavalry's "buffalo soldiers," an ambitious effort toward the first complete textbook on strategy specifically calculated to meet the needs of the American service.

The Principles of Strategy was a formal textbook. Much of it did not pretend to originality, being a discussion of the organization of armies and of the basic elements of strategy as culled from the classic works of the field. The foundations of Bigelow's study were those laid by Jomini, although Bigelow carried the geometric approach to strategy much further than Jomini had done. He argued that the key to success in war is in fact the ability to discern through the complexities of a military situation the geometric relationships which shape it and which, once recognized, indicate the solution of military problems.[37]

The classic textbooks were written by Europeans and cited European examples from which they formulated the rules of strategy. Bigelow, however, proposed through the study of campaigns waged in America by American soldiers to present a text that would be more instructive than most for American officers. The American examples, plus Bigelow's cautious insertion of his own views and emphases, combined to make the book, like Halleck's, more original than the author's modesty permitted him to claim.

Bigelow began, in the manner of formal textbooks, with definitions—of war, an army, tactics, strategy, decisive points and key points, the offensive and the defensive. Since his primary concern was strategy, he emphasized definitions of the three classic types of strategy: strategy proper, or regular strategy, which seeks to deprive the enemy of his supplies; tactical strategy, which seeks to overmatch him on the battlefield; and political strategy, which seeks to embarrass or if possible to overthrow his government.[38]

In discussing all three types of strategy, Bigelow retained the now traditional American emphasis on the offensive as the preferable mode of war.[39] Like Dennis Mahan but more emphatically because of the lessons of the Civil War, Bigelow urged an offensive of maneuver rather than an offensive of headlong assaults. He recognized that no amount of training adequately prepared a man to face with steady nerves the hail of bullets from a position held with modern rifles. He reminded his readers of the fate of Lee's direct attacks on the Federal line at Gettysburg. He urged that the enemy be thrown off balance and met on terms not of his choosing, by maneuver which compelled him to look to his supplies. Indeed, he ultimately urged an offensive which would reach beyond the enemy army to the enemy nation which sustained it, for he incorporated into his textbook the lessons of Sherman's campaigns, and he saw in those campaigns evidence that attacks on the enemy nation would at last bring the enemy army to wither on the vine.[40]

Like Sherman himself, Bigelow was not consistent in his emphasis on warfare against the enemy people. "As a rule," he wrote, "the primary object of military operations should be to overpower, and, if possible, to capture or destroy, the hostile army." [41] But with the examples of Sherman's campaigns and of the Federal naval blockade of the Southern coast before him, Bigelow also went on to give special attention to political strategy, "embarrassing the enemy's government and carrying the war home to the people." [42]

In wars of popular passions, Bigelow pointed out, even attacks on the enemy's government offered no assurance of forcing a decision. If a war were unpopular among the enemy's people, the people probably would not carry it on after political strategy had overthrown their government. But if a war were popular with the enemy's people, then the people might well carry it on even after their regular government had fallen. Certainly the mere loss of their political capital was not likely to destroy the resistance of a people in a popular war: "The occupation of Richmond by the Federal army . . . would have had no more effect upon the spirit of resistance in the South than the occupation of Philadelphia by the British had upon the colonies." [43]

Bigelow suggested that carrying the war to the enemy's people was much more promising of decisive events than was carrying the war to the enemy's government. This aim as well as simply the destruction of the Confederate armies' sources of supply had carried Sherman through Georgia and the Carolinas. This aim as well as the interruption of Confederate communication with the outside world had inspired the Federal blockade of the Confederate coasts; by compelling the non-combatant South to depend on the South's own meager products, the blockade inflicted "a greater shock to the inert and indolent South of that time than even that of arms." [44]

Under the blockade, said Bigelow, not only did the South come to lack major war supplies, but Southern life lost many of the amenities which, however small, keep the spirit from despair. Coffee drinkers had to make do with substitutes brewed from sweet potatoes or melon seed, tea drinkers tried sassafras root or corn fodder, sugar gave way to sorghum molasses, readers without coal oil attempted to use a lamp contrived from a saucer of lard with a dry sycamore ball floating in its midst. Bigelow drew the implications of the sort of war the blockade represented:

War is brought home to a hostile people [he wrote] by depriving them of their civil and political rights and privileges, or of the comforts and conveniences, and perhaps the necessaries, of life; by injuring their business, or by detracting in any other way from their individual welfare.

With or without design, and despite every possible provision to the contrary, war sooner or later becomes a burden and a trial to the great body of the people concerned in it; and the mere prolongation of war in any form will finally break the spirit, if it does not exhaust the re-sources, of a belligerent.[45]

It was the function of political strategy to lend design to the burdening and trial of an enemy people through war. Thus might armies be destroyed and wars won by dissolving the armies' founda-tions. Bigelow underlined his point by quoting from Grant's com-ments on the effects of Sherman's march to the sea:

Even during this march of Sherman's [Grant had written], the [Con-federate] newspapers in his front were proclaiming daily that his army was nothing better than a mob of men who were frightened out of their wits, and hastening, panic-stricken, to try to get under cover of our navy for protection against the Southern people. As the army was seen march-ing triumphantly, however, the minds of the people became disabused, and they saw the true state of affairs. In turn they became disheartened, and would have been glad to submit without compromise.[46]

Bigelow was essentially a humane soldier, and the full face of twentieth-century warfare surely would have shocked him. Yet once he had endorsed a warfare against people as well as armies, the sheer frightfulness of twentieth-century total war was already implicit in what he wrote. He warned that warfare against people must be thoroughgoing warfare if it were to achieve the desired results:

The infliction of suffering on a people who can stand all that can be inflicted only makes the military problem more difficult by embittering them, and so the infliction of inadequate suffering is a cruel mistake. The popular support given to our government in the War of 1812 was largely the effect of a system of devastation, culminating in the desecra-tion of the capital, to which the British resorted with the object of ren-dering the war unpopular, and of making it hateful to the people by bringing its horrors home to their hearths and firesides.[47]

Half measures of horror, in short, will only stimulate a people to resistance. The soldier who undertakes the new mode of warfare must make war so utterly frightful as to beat all hope into the ground.

Thus Captain John Bigelow of the 10th Cavalry looked toward the coming total war. But his humanity persisted, and he quickly drew back from the grim prospect, reflecting that logic does not always rule, and that warfare might yet fail to reach the horrible fulfillment that logic indicated. Though a course of frightfulness may be the surest road to victory, he wrote, nevertheless such a course

may be prohibited to a commander by the law of nations, or of his own country, or by his own scruples. This is a matter in which the commander must be governed to a large extent by his judgment of the temper and disposition of the enemy's people and his own, and of mankind in general.[48]

Furthermore, Bigelow recognized that frightfulness is not the only possible mode of political strategy aimed at the enemy nation as a whole. He recognized some of the possibilities of what the twentieth century would call psychological warfare; he advocated campaigns against the enemy's war effort that appealed to the sentiments of the enemy's people against their war-making government. An army advancing into the enemy's territory, he said, ought to exert itself to detach the allegiance of the population from their old government, perhaps even through the formation of new governments.

It need hardly be stated that the form of government held out to a people with a view to detaching it from its allegiance must be such as to be preferred to its own, and even a government imposed upon a hostile people for the purpose merely of controlling it during the course of operations should be made as acceptable to it as possible. . . . All great conquerors have been masters of the politics of strategy. The wonderful successes of Napoleon are attributable in no small measure to his figuring as the apostle of republicanism, or of representative government. The campaigns of Alexander and Hannibal afford perhaps the most signal instances in the history of the strategist reckoning with diplomacy. Both commanders counted for success upon a vast augmentation of their armies in the enemy's country. The realization of this idea by Alexander and its non-realization by Hannibal may be regarded as the main secrets both of the marvelous success of the former and of the melancholy, though illustrious, failure of the latter.[49]

Diplomacy and discretion, then, might lead and permit the commander seeking to overcome a hostile people to choose forbearance. So Bigelow plainly hoped. But it must be remembered that Adam Badeau believed that such an option might no longer exist: "The rebels had staked all, and could lose no more than all." "Since the population, as well as the armies, of the South was united in rebellion, the population, as well as the armies, must undergo whatever was necessary for its subjection." And in such a case, even Bigelow pointed the way to the war of frightfulness.

In 1870, with the fame of his triumphs in the American West and the Shenandoah Valley still fresh and bright, Lieutenant General Philip Sheridan of the United States Army was respectfully welcomed by the German armies when he chose to ride with them to observe their invasion of France. Surrounded again by great columns of marching men and horses and the thunder of the guns, pugnacious Phil Sheridan enjoyed himself immensely. He hobnobbed with Bismarck and Moltke. He admired and thrilled at the military efficiency of the Germans and the drive of their leaders, although with characteristic brashness he doubted that they could match his own old soldiers. Observing the confinement of Marshal Bazaine's French army in the fortress of Metz, he remarked that all he would have needed to break out was one division of the old VI Corps. In a self-confident mood he felt free to criticize the German arrangements, and a story which has the ring of truth tells us he chided the Germans on the excessive mildness and humanity with which they waged war. If they wished to break the spirit of the French, he thought, they ought to be burning more French farms and villages, as he and his Americans would have done.[50]

> Regular troops, engaged for the war, are the only safe reliance of a
> government, and are in every point of view, the best and most
> economical. EMORY UPTON

> At the commencement of hostilities, there should be nothing either
> to new model or to create. The only difference, consequently, be-
> tween the peace and the war formation of the army, ought to be
> in the increased magnitude of the latter; and the only change in
> passing from the former to the latter, should consist in giving to it
> the augmentation which will then be necessary. JOHN C. CALHOUN,
> *as quoted by Emory Upton*

TO carry war to an enemy people in the true manner of Sherman
and his disciples demanded armies of great size and power. Small
units such as independent cavalry divisions might accomplish destructive raids, but if as Badeau said the people of an enemy nation as well as its armies must be conquered so that war might end,
then huge mass armies with power to spare must swarm across the
enemy's country. They must be so strong that they could fend off
the enemy's fighting men with one hand while they visited havoc
on his homeland with the other, as Sherman was able to leave
behind the Army of the Cumberland and the Army of the Ohio to
deal with the Confederate Army of Tennessee, while his own Army
of the Tennessee and Army of Georgia marched to Savannah,
Columbia, and Goldsboro. Sherman's doctrines of the war against
populations were doctrines befitting a young giant of a nation, with
such power to spare.

Thus the revolutionary concept of the war against peoples went
hand in hand with the older revolutionary concept of the nation in
arms, for mass armies were requisite to waging the war against
peoples. But though the doctrines of the new warfare against peoples sprang from the experience of the Civil War, and commanded

the prestigious support of Sherman and at least indirectly of Grant, those doctrines remained unassimilated into the mainstream of American military thought. For the doctrines of the new warfare implied the use of mass armies, while the professionalist tradition among the American officer corps was so strong that after the Civil War the officer corps returned to a system centering on the relatively small but highly skillful professional army. This system had little room for Sherman's theories of total war. Ironically enough, and illustrative of the hesitancy and confusion of Sherman's own thinking about the implications of his march through Georgia and the Carolinas, the single figure most influential in sealing the commitment of the officer corps to the conservative, professionalist view of war was a protégé of Sherman, Colonel and Brevet Major General Emory Upton.

Emory Upton cannot but seem an attractive and even romantic figure, and his personal history as well as the brilliance of his mind contributed to his renown and influence in the professional officer corps.[1] He was among those West Point graduates of 1861 who plunged so swiftly into battle—he was in action at First Bull Run —and won meteoric fame. The army knew of him even before he left the academy, for on the eve of secession he battled Cadet Wade Hampton Gibbes of South Carolina in a fist fight for principle that is still famous in academy annals. He was a man of principle throughout his career; from the first he was a dedicated abolitionist, a highly uncommon phenomenon in the professional army. But he also had the charm of a handsome, active, energetic young man, the winning personality seen in his sensitive, unaffected letters to his sister Maria, and the character of a man utterly loyal to trusts and friendships which illuminates the affectionate biographical tribute of his friend and West Point classmate Peter Smith Michie.

Upton rose rapidly from the second lieutenancy in the 4th Artillery with which he began the Civil War. Almost everyone who served with him found him the embodiment of all a young officer ought to be, a soldier almost without flaw. He matched headlong bravery in combat with a quick and astute intelligence and an astonishing possession of that Mahanian attribute, the *coup d'œil de guerre*. He commanded a battery on the Peninsula, and by the

Fredericksburg campaign he had received the colonelcy of the 121st New York Infantry. He could not be found in the camps of his regiment the first few days after he assumed command, and his subordinates thought he was away hobnobbing with old West Point friends. But characteristically he was spending those days visiting the regimental hospital, reviewing every detail of its arrangements to secure the maximum protection of the health of his men. It was said that he watched over his men like a father, but he was also one of the sternest disciplinarians in the army, and soon it was remarked that the 121st New York could be identified in battle by the superb precision with which it maneuvered.

By the autumn campaign of 1863 Upton was in command of a brigade of the VI Corps. At Rappahannock Station in November he captured the attention of the whole Army of the Potomac with a bold assault on a Confederate beachhead that netted 1,600 prisoners, eight colors, 2,000 stand of arms, and the enemy pontoon bridges, as well as a brevet colonelcy in the regular army for Upton himself. The feat also gave Upton a crucial assignment the following spring, when Major General Horatio G. Wright of the VI Corps needed an officer to lead the attack on the west face of the Confederates' "Mule Shoe" salient at Spotsylvania. Wright assigned Upton a task force of twelve regiments to make the major assault. Upton meticulously planned his attack on two lines of Confederate entrenchments, taking each regimental commander with him for a personal reconnaissance and a clear explanation of what was expected of the regiment, and carefully supervising the placing of artillery support and the arrangement of the assault troops into four lines of three regiments each. Upton's task was almost hopeless: a frontal attack on a fortified position defended in strength and with rifles. But Upton's planning and tactics almost carried the day. He instructed the assault troops not to pause to fire, but to plunge directly into the Confederate works. The first line then would fan out to the right and left, broadening the penetration. The second line would move forward into the Confederates' second line. The third and fourth lines would advance just inside the Confederate defenses, there to await their call as reserves. The plan unfolded almost to the letter, both Confederate lines broke, over a thousand prisoners and several colors fell into Upton's hands, but lack of support at last compelled him to withdraw.[2]

The attack on the Mule Shoe won Upton Grant's promotion to brevet brigadier general on the spot, but it also occasioned a disgust on Upton's part with such vain sacrifices. As the bloody 1864 campaign dragged on the disgust grew, reflecting Upton's feeling for the welfare of the troops and inspiring a determination that the professional attainments of American officers must be higher in future wars.

I am disgusted [he wrote his sister on June 4] with the generalship displayed. Our men have, in many instances, been foolishly and wantonly sacrificed. Assault after assault has been ordered upon the enemy's entrenchments, when they knew nothing about the strength or position of the enemy. Thousands of lives might have been spared by the exercise a little skill; but, as it is, the courage of the poor man is expected to obviate all difficulties.[3]

Or again the next day:

I am very sorry to say I have seen but little generalship during the campaign. Some of our corps commanders are not fit to be corporals. Lazy and indolent, they will not even ride along their lines; yet, without hesitating, they will order us to attack the enemy, no matter what their position or numbers. Twenty thousand of our killed and wounded should to-day be in our ranks.[4]

Upton suffered a wound in the attack on the Mule Shoe, and under Sheridan in the Shenandoah he was wounded again. He was now compelled to leave active service for several months and, as it turned out, to leave the Eastern theater for good. He was commanding a division when he fell at the Opequon, and when he returned to duty for the last few weeks of the war he again received a division, this time a cavalry force under Major General James Wilson in Alabama. Thus Upton completed the war with first-hand experience in all three arms of the service. Under Wilson he was the first to break into the Confederate entrenchments at Selma, leading dismounted cavalry forward against superior numbers of infantry and strong artillery. For that exploit he won his brevet as a major general of regulars, at the age of twenty-six.

Immediately after the war Upton put his mind to work on projects which might eliminate from future American wars much of the futile bloodshed he had so vehemently deplored after Spotsylvania and Cold Harbor. He formulated the first original American system of infantry tactics, continuing the traditional linear mode of assault but providing for greater flexibility in maneuver and opening the formations as the new fire power of rifled muskets and artillery dictated they must be opened. The army adopted Upton's tactics in 1867, and with this event he assured his position as the most promising young officer in the service.[5]

For a brief two years Upton was married. The two years were marred by frequent separation from his wife by military duty and by an illness which sapped her strength and their happiness and abruptly left him alone once more. More than ever Upton poured all his energy into the army and his efforts to improve it. For a time Secretary of State William H. Seward had contemplated securing a leave of absence for Upton so that he might travel to China and fashion a modern army for that empire, sealing Chinese friendship with the United States. The project never materialized, but it served to interest Upton in Asian military affairs. He studied the armies of Asia, and he drew up a plan for a Chinese military academy. While he was commandant of cadets and instructor in tactics at West Point he and Sherman discussed the merits of sending an American commission to observe the Asian armies, especially the British and Russian forces which in India and Central Asia pacified vast areas with small numbers in the face of problems similar to those on the Indian frontier of the United States. Upton himself was appointed to a three-man commission for a military tour not only of Asia but of Europe as well.[6]

Upton's vision of the military destiny of the United States reached beyond its Indian wars, and accordingly he proved more interested at last in the armies of civilized Europe than in the scattered forces of Asia. Visiting Europe in 1876, he experienced the customary favorable impressions of the German army. He deplored much of German militarism: the schoolboys wearing uniforms and engaging in military drill, and the Reichstag's abdication of all authority over the military for seven years by means of long-term appropriations.[7] But Upton believed the United States had much to learn from German efficiency in preparation for war and from the German system of military education for officers and men. Most important, Upton was impressed immensely by the German cadre system, where the nucleus of all wartime military formations existed in peace, the ranks filled by reserves at the touch of war. He resolved to make his report on his foreign observations a body of recommendations as well as a record of what he had seen. From Berlin, for example, he wrote:

I shall devote most of my attention to the subject of officers, and to showing our reckless extravagance in making war. When Germany fought France she put her army on a war-footing in eight days, and in eight days more she had four hundred thousand men on French territory. It took us from April, 1861, to March, 1862, to form an army of the same size at an expense of nearly eight hundred millions of dollars. We can not maintain a great army in peace, but we can provide a scheme for officering a large force in time of war, and such a scheme is deserving of study.[8]

And from Fort Monroe in 1877, while he was planning his report, he said:

West Point is, in my judgment, far superior to any academy abroad for preparatory training of officers. But, once in service, we have nothing to compare with the war academies of Europe, except the Artillery School [Sherman's school of application for infantry and cavalry had not yet appeared]. You know how ignorant our generals were, during the war, of all the principles of generalship. Here, I think, we can correct that defect and form a corps of officers who in any future contest may form the chief reliance of the government.

My report has yet to be written. I doubt not it will disappoint many people, as I intend to expose the vices of our system, instead of merely describing the organizations abroad. We can not Germanize, neither is it desirable, but we can apply the principles of common sense.[9]

Upton's report became more than the War Department had bargained for. It achieved publication as *The Armies of Asia and Europe,* but its title was somewhat misleading, since the passages of it most important to Upton were those in which he offered his recommendations for the army of the United States. "We can not Germanize, neither is it desirable," he said, but his book nevertheless marks the change from the preeminence of French influence to a preeminence of German influence on the military thought of American officers. The German cadre system now emerged in modified form as Upton's prescription for the war preparations of the United States. Thoroughly a professionalist, Upton proposed that the regular army become the center of American military planning, the regulars to be reorganized into skeleton formations with full complements of professional officers, the war army to be formed by filling the ranks with volunteers. Meanwhile the professional officers themselves would become prepared for their wartime duties through a military school system similar to the German. The American war army as an expansion of the regular army would by no means be one of the largest armies of the world, but in professional standards it might hope to equal or excel Europe's best, and this seemed to Upton the goal of first importance.[10]

Upton was not satisfied, however, with the case for an expansible regular army as he argued it in *The Armies of Asia and Europe*. He believed that cogent presentation of his arguments demanded a book devoted to American military problems alone, and therefore he could not rest until he had prepared such a book. From *The Armies of Asia and Europe* he hastened into the writing of his magnum opus, one of the principal landmarks of American professionalist military thought, *The Military Policy of the United States*.[11]

West Point officers had had to fight the Civil War mainly with armies of citizen soldiers, but they had not wanted it that way. Most of them would have preferred to have possessed even a moderately large force of regulars on which to rely from the beginning. When the war began the commanding general of the army, Lieutenant General Winfield Scott, not a West Pointer but a thoroughly professional officer, hoped to subdue the secessionists principally with even the minuscule regular army of 1861, some 17,000 strong. A trump card in the hands of the Union, as Scott saw it, was that however small it was, the regular army remained loyal except for Southern officers. The South possessed no comparable force. Therefore Scott believed that Northern militia and volunteers should be called to serve as supporting troops and auxiliaries, but that the decisive thrusts against secession should be those of the regulars. He resisted the resignation of regular officers who after Fort Sumter wished to take commissions with the volunteers. Instead he attempted to keep the regular officers with their regiments, there to provide a model army for the edification of the volunteers and, more important, to provide a spearhead for the marches southward.[12]

The plan did not work, because the South, lacking a regular army, called volunteers in such masses that they would overmatch the regular army by numbers alone. Accordingly the North had to rely on its own great masses of citizen volunteers who were enthusiastic but completely green (and kept green longer than necessary because of Scott's reluctance to have regular officers join them). The professional officers were not happy with this necessity. They long grumbled about the inadequacy of the citizen volunteers.[13] They eventually acknowledged that the volunteers became excellent fighting men after a year or more of service had made them veterans, but they hoped that in a future war they would have a substantial regular force immediately, so that they would not again suffer the waste and danger of the armed citizenry's training under fire.

Naturally, the professional officers deplored citizen officers even more than they did citizen soldiers. Such capable commanders as John A. Logan and Francis P. Blair in the North, and Nathan Bedford Forrest and John B. Gordon in the South came from the citizenry, but there seems to have been truth in the citizen officers' complaint that the West Pointers would deny them autonomous commands if possible no matter what their merits. Though the circumstances were complex, Logan's failure to receive the Army of the Tennessee in July, 1864, seems to have resulted principally from Sherman's preference for a West Pointer, even one with a relatively undistinguished combat record. For every Logan or Blair the professionals could point to a spectacularly unsuccessful citizen officer such as Ben Butler or John C. Frémont, but the most conspicuous and disastrous of all the failures of Federal officers were those of West Pointers such as George McClellan, John Pope, Ambrose Burnside, and Joseph Hooker. The point is that the professionals seem to have judged men by their military academy training or lack of it at least as much as by their merit.[14]

Not surprisingly, before the Civil War was over some professional officers took advantage of the temporary high popular regard for things military to propose a postwar military policy sweepingly redesigned along Hamiltonian lines. Since the Civil War also gave evidence of probable need for mass armies, those officers might propose substituting for the state militia a federal national guard equipped and uniformed at national expense, trained under the supervision of regulars, periodically encamped, and subject constantly to the call of the President and the governors. An editorial writer in the *United States Service Magazine* proposed to ensure the readiness of such a force by what amounted to a system of national conscription. His plan relied on the theoretical membership of all citizens in the state militia, but gave the states federal direction in their maintenance of a national guard numbering ten percent of the arms-bearing population, and in their imposition of a minimum of military training even upon those citizens not called into the national guard.[15]

The same writer proposed beyond the federalized national guard, an increased standing army "of sufficient strength not merely to form the nucleus but to serve as the backbone of the forces on a war footing." And while he hesitated to propose the system for the United States, he praised highly the Prussian military organization, notably its expansible army features. He pointed out that the Prussian reserves and militia consisted of men who had served their three years in the standing army, and that as reserves they continued to be brigaded with their old regular units, so there was constant association with the regulars and no need to form elementary organizations at the outbreak of war.[16]

By the end of the Civil War, many West Point officers categorically rejected the notion of an armed citizenry as a reliance in war. They consistently regretted that they had not possessed, at the beginning of the war, a sizeable body of regulars that could have swiftly conquered the South without recourse to volunteers. If only they had commanded a moderately large force of regulars, they believed they could have put down the Confederacy virtually with the regulars alone. Sherman spoke for many of his fellow professionals when, in his *Memoirs,* he complained of the obtuseness of politicians who for ten years could foresee the possibility of civil war but who made no military preparations for it. (Of course the political conflicts which made civil war foreseeable made such preparations impossible.) [17]

Emory Upton's *The Military Policy of the United States* was to spell out the feelings of many professionals that the regular army must be the center of American military planning and to support those feelings with an elaborate argument from the whole history of United States military policy. He did an impressive job. No similar study of American military history had ever been attempted, and to this day there is no history of American military organization and policy which fully equals Upton in the period he covered.

Upton not only expressed the respect his fellow professionals felt for regular soldiers and their distrust of armed citizens, but he went further, for in its conclusions his book was a counsel of despair. His principal solution to American military problems was an elaboration of the expansible army idea which had been outlined by Hamilton, more explicitly formulated by Calhoun, and expounded by Upton himself in *The Armies of Asia and Europe*. Under Upton's full plan relatively large regular forces would serve as cadres to be filled out in wartime not by volunteers but by conscripts, who serving under regular officers and regular discipline would be as close an approximation to regulars as possible. Even with the conscripts, however, Upton's plan ruled out a genuine mass army, for he was careful to urge that the regular army not be excessively diluted by wartime recruits. But Congress had always proved hostile to a regular army large enough to expand to substantial proportions without great dilution, and a permanent commitment to conscription was even further from congressional inclinations. Upton proposed a military system, in short, which even he scarcely expected to work in the American context. He admired the German as the best current military system, and though he denied any intention of Germanizing the United States, his proposals came sufficiently close to that to be politically impracticable. His announced purpose was to prescribe a proper military system for his country, but in all his conclusions was a despairing conviction that his country was never likely to adopt a proper system.

Upton ended in deep pessimism, and he did so in part because he failed to acknowledge that military policy must reflect the general policy of a nation and, more than that, reflect the general spirit of the nation. While one of the persistent themes in his treatment of American military history was the recurrent failure of American civilian leaders to devote the country in peace to preparation for war, he never attempted to discover the motives and the possible merits of their views. For all that Upton's *Military Policy* reveals, the cause of the unpreparedness of the United States for its wars seems to have been the sheer perversity of its statesmen. Because Upton never really attempted to understand the civilian view of military policy, he failed utterly to formulate a military policy in harmony with the American national genius. Apparently he did not reflect that the best means of establishing an effective American military policy might be to study American society at large and to fashion military institutions within its framework. Instead, he began with fixed views of military policy and then despaired because he could not shape the nation in accord with their demands.

The Military Policy of the United States is an excellent book of military history, but it is military history written in a vacuum, untouched by nonmilitary considerations. Upton has been called "the army's Mahan," referring to the philosopher of sea power, Alfred Thayer Mahan; [18] but the sobriquet is misleading, for whatever his limitations, Alfred Thayer Mahan consistently saw national policy as a whole, not naval affairs alone. Upton, in contrast, subordinated all other national considerations to the military ones. In his military interpretation of history, military preparedness seemed to be universally the primary concern of statesmen. To be sure, Upton was correct when he asserted that the United States had always fought its wars wastefully. But no one respectful of the genius of American society would have sought remedy in the prescription implied by Upton:

The military system under which, in two campaigns of seven weeks each, Prussia humbled Austria, in 1866, and subverted the French Empire in 1870, was the joint product of soldiers and statesmen, who began their laborers [*sic*] (in 1806) immediately after the disastrous battle of Jena. The military system under which we subdued the Rebellion was established by Congress in less than four weeks.[19]

A contempt for civilian leadership in military affairs continually appears in Upton's pages and suggests the Henry Wilsons, Douglas Haigs, Henri Pétains, and Ferdinand Foches of the First World War sneering at the "frocks." The tap root of the wastefulness and folly with which the United States had fought, said Upton, was control over military policy by civilians; the remedy was to place military policy in the hands of military professionals. It is difficult in reading Upton not to believe that he would have liked to confine the duties of civilian leaders in military affairs to countersigning acts of the principal military commanders to assure their constitutionality. Upton did not consider whether some military inconveniences at the hands of civilians might not be worth enduring in the light of national purposes other than military.

In the Revolutionary War, for example, said Upton: "Military legislation was thus largely made to depend upon the combined wisdom of a body of citizens [the Continental Congress] who, in their individual experience, were totally ignorant of military affairs." [20] Practically the whole military policy of the American Revolution was utterly faulty because it was the creation of civilians untrained in warfare. Here lay a principal reason for the many heartbreaking military failures of the Revolution; those failures by no means followed simply from the inherent weakness of the colonies:

Admitting the poverty of the colonies, their want of credit, their inability to provide proper clothing, food, arms, ammunition, and other supplies for the Army; also the possibilities of a confederation which might deprive Congress of the power to enforce its requisitions—all of these considerations, instead of being accepted as reasons for adopting a feeble military policy, called for wise legislation looking to a vigorous prosecution of the war with the least expense in men and money.[21]

The follies of the Revolution were not remedied but were repeated in subsequent American wars, most especially in the Civil War. Upton believed that President Lincoln exercised too much control over the army. Lincoln was an admirable and well intentioned man, but he was a civilian and did not understand military affairs:

For want of military experience, he [Lincoln] could neither appreciate nor forecast the effect of any one of these measures [which he had planned]. . . . Although constitutional Commander in Chief, he did and could not solve the military problems of the war. The pen which could trace the Emancipation Proclamation instinctively avoided strategical discussions. To his mind the narrow peninsula between the York and James rivers afforded as many chances for brilliant maneuvers as the broad plains of Manassas.[22]

As Upton saw it, a military system devised and governed by a civilian President and a civilian Congress, not the shortcomings of such Union generals as McClellan (Upton was notably tolerant of McClellan), was the cause of the excessive duration and wastefulness of the Civil War.

The surviving officers and soldiers of our armies, many of whom participated in the battle of Bull Run, will not for a moment deny that through the inexperience of themselves and their commanders the war for the Union was prolonged.

But when their mistakes are summed up and their deficiencies considered, it will still be found that the underlying causes were inherent in a military system which was a creature of law.[23]

Or again:

In discussing the events of 1862, most of our historians, according to their political connections, have contented themselves with laying the blame upon the President, the Secretary of War, or the commander of the Army of the Potomac.

The candid reader, however, if not already convinced, will discover upon further investigation that the President and his subordinates were but the instruments or victims of a bad system; that the disasters of the campaign entailing the bloodshed of the three ensuing years had their origin in the needless division of our armies, and what is still more instructive, that the cause of this division is to be found in that defect of our laws which, contrary to the spirit of our institutions, tempted the President to assume the character and responsibilities of a military commander.[24]

The underlying cause of the defects of the American military system, then, was civilian control of strictly military matters, and Upton asserted that the remedy lay in foreign examples:

In foreign armies, it is the duty of the General Staff to draw up the bills relating to military organization, which, after approval by the War Minister, are presented to the representatives of the people. The latter may refuse to incur the expenses of reforms, but do not question the wisdom of the details.[25]

What, specifically, were the defects which resulted from civilians' "questioning the wisdom" of the plans of American military leaders and even preparing their own plans? First was the inveterate unwillingness of Congress to prepare in peace for waging war. The history of American military policy was a history of "the shortsighted economy which ever prompts Congress to defer preparations for war, until hostilities are actually begun." The seeming economy of limiting military expenditures in peacetime was to Upton the falsest of economies, for in the end it was sure to cost the nation thousands of lives as well as vast treasures.[26]

The principal result of shortsighted economy was the failure of the United States ever to enter a war possessing an adequate standing army. He expressed forthrightly the conviction which he shared with large numbers of his fellow professional officers, "That regular troops, engaged for the war, are the only safe reliance of a government, and are in every point of view, the best and most economical." [27]

The United States regular army, Upton could boast, always had performed every service asked of it with more than credit:

Wherever the Regular Army has met the enemy, the conduct of the officers and men has merited and received the applause of their countrymen. It has rendered the country vastly more important service than by merely sustaining the national honor in battle. It has preserved, and still preserves, to us the military art; has formed the standard of discipline for the vast number of volunteers of our late wars, and, while averting disaster and bloodshed, has furnished us with military commanders to lead armies of citizen soldiers, whose exploits are now famous in the history of the world.[28]

Upton acknowledged that citizen soldiers as well as regulars had fought bravely, but in every war it had taken too long to make soldiers of citizens, and both national danger and excessive losses had prevailed in the meantime. The regulars were always too few. Upton cited examples similar to Halleck's. If even a semblance of a strong regular army had existed in 1812, he said, the United States undoubtedly could have conquered Canada. In the Indian wars the persistent numerical weakness of the regulars enabled mere handfuls of savages to defy the government of the United States; during the Seminole War,

for want of a well-defined peace organization, a nation of 17,000,000 of people contended for seven years with 1,200 warriors and finally closed the struggle without accomplishing the forcible emigration of the Indians, which was the original and sole cause of the war.[29]

If the United States had been infinitely more successful in the Mexican War than in the War of 1812, Upton, like his fellow professionals, was sure the explanation lay not in perfection of military policy, for that was not achieved, but "in the quality of the Regular Army with which we began the two wars." In the War of 1812 an enemy numbering fewer than 5,000 men had baffled all American efforts at invasion; in the other an American army of fewer than 6,000 combatants entered the enemy's capital in triumph. The difference was that in the 1840s the American regulars, though few, were thoroughly professional.[30]

Offering the idea Sherman was to express in his *Memoirs,* Upton argued that if in 1861 the federal government had been able to throw even 10,000 regulars onto the field of Bull Run, the rebellion almost certainly would have expired immediately. But so little did Congress appreciate the value of a trained soldiery that it had not utilized such a regular army as it possessed to instruct the civilians who now donned uniform (which was a criticism of Winfield Scott's policy as much as of that of Congress).[31]

Congressional neglect of the regular army, Upton recognized, resulted from parsimony and from the traditional fear of a standing army as a breeder of despotism. But Upton contended that the old fear could persist only from an utter misreading of American history. Such dangers of despotism as had appeared in the United States sprang not from the strength of the regular army but from its weakness. Because the American standing army was weak American wars frequently carried the country to desperation and the edge of defeat, and at such hours democracy was in danger from within as well as from without. It was then the nation tended toward dictatorship. Repeatedly the weakness of the Revolutionary army had made Washington almost a dictator:

> The campaign of 1776 demonstrated in a remarkable manner the dangers to which liberty was exposed by an unwise and feeble military policy. In his letter of September 24, Washington referred to the feeling that a standing army was a menace to liberty, yet for the lack of an adequate force of this character he found himself repeatedly compelled to exercise unwarrantable powers. . . .
>
> The almost total dissolution of the Army [toward the end of the year], the rapid advance of the British through New Jersey, and the apprehended fall of Philadelphia, the capital of the United Colonies, inspired Congress with such alarm that, on the 27th of December, it not only voted the increase recommended for the Army, but vested Washington with dictatorial powers.[32]

Fortunately for American liberty, in this crisis Washington and his army acted with the restraint that came to be characteristic of American professional soldiers. At the close of the Revolution:

The army could point with pride to its subordination to civil authority and to its devotion to liberty. More than this, it could justly claim that the dictatorial powers conferred upon its commander—arbitrary arrests, summary executions without trial, forced impressment of provisions, and other dangerous precedents of the Revolution—were the legitimate fruits of the defective military legislation of our inexperienced statesmen.[33]

In the Civil War it was again the weakness rather than the strength of the regular army which endangered liberty. Apart from its fostering of rebellion, that weakness compelled President Lincoln to ignore the Constitution and the laws while taking forceful action on his own initiative, lest the Constitution and the laws be destroyed completely. At least this was Upton's interpretation of events:

No usurpation could have been more complete [than Lincoln's in 1861], but what else could he have done? An emergency had arisen, the militia was disorganized, Congress had neglected the national defense, the military preparation of the insurgents threatened the speedy overthrow of the Government, and the situation brooked no delay. In every similar crisis however produced, history teaches that the fate of a nation may depend on the patriotic or selfish action of a single individual.[34]

Upton found in the regular army a spotless record of loyalty to constitutional government all through American history: "Great as was the devotion of the private soldier, the patriotic record of the officer was even more brilliant." Not a standing army, but the want of it, endangered democracy.[35]

This Upton believed, since the army could be a bulwark of democracy in peace as well as in war. In the history of Shays's Rebellion he found the lesson that the regular army must be strong to cope with insurrection at home as well as with war abroad. He thought that lesson was important in the new industrial age; at the time he wrote, the railroad strike of 1877 had impressed the officer corps anew with the mission of the army to suppress civil disorder. The professional journals now printed frequent articles on how the army might save democracy by crushing labor agitation. In this situation, said Upton, "The present exposed condition of all our great arsenals finds its condemnation in the history of this [Shays's] brief rebellion." [36]

Another folly of the American system of civilian control over military matters was that Congress, to the extent it gave thought to military preparation at all, frequently had taken the militia seriously. To rely on militia for defense was in Upton's view worse than to make no preparations whatever. The burden of American military history, he said, pursuing the theme relentlessly throughout his book, was that on the battlefield militia were a downright liability and worse than useless. Their presence misled commanders into depending on them, and with appalling consistency they betrayed such dependence and threw battle plans into chaos.

No words of condemnation seemed too harsh for the militia, and Upton's rule for dealing with militia was the simple injunction, do not call them out. "No matter how absolute the necessity for calling out undisciplined troops, history teaches that useless extravagance, often accompanied by inaction or disaster, will surely ensue." [37]

The lesson of the Revolution in regard to militia was "That when a nation attempts to combat disciplined troops with raw levies, it must maintain an army of at least twice the size of that of the enemy, and even then have no guarantee of success." In 1776, when the United States maintained a force averaging 40,000–50,000 men, the British with an army never exceeding 34,000 were able to inflict almost totally ruinous defeat on the Americans. "The disparity between the resources employed and the results obtained is another proof of the wastefulness of a policy based on the employment of raw troops." [38]

More than a waste of money was involved, of course; there was a tremendous waste of lives. Depending on an armed but untrained citizenry for defense led to criminal sacrifice of the citizens, and it cost more lives by encouraging enemies to war on the United States. During the War of 1812, the weakness of the militia tempted the Indians of the Southwest into hostilities; the militia system "encouraged the Indians to strive with a superior power, till in the battle of the Horse Shoe, they were nearly annihilated." [39]

In the War of 1812, the imbecile dependence of the United States upon mere armed citizens had ensured the destruction of American communities by calling down British amphibious attacks which might never have occurred if the communities had maintained a peaceful aspect:

With criminal disregard for the rules of civilized warfare, the futile defense of these [seacoast] towns [by armed citizens] only increased the distress and suffering of their patriotic inhabitants. Those who joined the militia in offering resistance, saw their houses and property ruthlessly destroyed, while such as remained peaceably at home, were rewarded by the amplest protection.

This policy speedily demoralized many of the towns exposed to attack. The people, instead of being able to rely for defense on the strong arm of their Government, looked upon its militia as the forerunners of destruction, and to save their property, made haste to throw themselves on the mercy of their enemies.[40]

The conclusion was clear to Upton: to depend on an armed citizenry in war was sheer infatuation, a very invitation to disaster, confounding the best laid plans of one's own generals and provoking needless violence from the enemy. It was a resort worse than no military activity at all. Once again, "regular troops, engaged for the war, are the only safe reliance of a government."

Bad as was any military system founded on an armed citizenry, the American militia system was an incredible compounding of evils. The system deliberately ensured that officers as well as men would be untrained, for in 1807 Congress had provided that when any militia unit tendered its services to the United States, it would retain its own officers. The result was to aggravate a deficiency of the law of 1792: "It is not necessary to discuss the military qualifications of the swarm of generals appointed by the different States, nor to dwell upon the utter lack of instruction and discipline of the rank and file of the militia. . . ."[41]

Still another iniquity was the short service feature of the militia system. The limitation of militia service to three months was rooted deeply in precedent and sanctified, at least in part, by the Militia Act of 1792. Upton returned continually to the results. The repeatedly dissolving armies of Washington in the Revolution and the departure of troops homeward from Bull Run, "to the sound of the enemy's cannon," when their three months had expired, called forth some of the most indignant writing of an indignant book.[42]

The capstone of the follies of the militia system was the dual role of the militia as United States troops and the armies of the states.

Upton believed the Revolution had demonstrated by negative example "That the war resources of a nation can only be called forth and energetically directed by one general government to which the people owe a paramount allegiance." [43] Despite that example, the fatuous system of dual control of the United States Army by states and nation had persisted in every subsequent war. Even in the Civil War, when the obvious futility of the militia system had compelled the raising of volunteers, the new volunteer regiments had been organized by the states and their colonels had been chosen by the governors. When three professional officers, Lorenzo Thomas, Irvin McDowell, and William B. Franklin, had drawn up the call for volunteers and had urged a national army on Secretary of the Treasury Salmon P. Chase (who amidst the characteristic anarchy of civilian control handled various important army matters in 1861), Chase reportedly had replied that "he would rather have no regiments raised in Ohio than that they should not be known as Ohio regiments." Chase reflected the usual civilian feeling, and consequently the volunteer system of the Civil War "was based on the theory of confederation; the troops were to be State, and not national."

The state organization system of the Civil War volunteers "sanctioned all of the extravagance of the military system under the Confederation." It placed the original task of clothing, equipping, and supplying the troops in the hands of the states. It led to a weakening of the federal forces whenever the state governors diminished recruiting of volunteers to keep strong militia forces at home. Since it kept promotion in the hands of the states, "Officers and soldiers might fight and die for their country, but with the exception of a medal or an empty brevet, they could expect no reward save from the governors of their States." The federal government had to rely largely on the governors for apprehending deserters, though the governors "could hardly be expected . . . [to] make themselves odious, by ferreting out deserters and dragging them from their homes." [44]

In creating the Civil War volunteer army, the federal government "Instead of expanding the Regular Army, and making it the chief instrument in executing the national will, . . . violated the practice of every civilized nation by calling into existence an army of a million untrained officers and men." [45]

In summary, Emory Upton regarded the military policy of the United States as a policy of weakness and folly. It rested on uninformed civilian direction, framed as it was by Congress and executed by the President and the secretary of war (if not by other cabinet members as well). It was penny wise and pound foolish. It provided a regular army of high quality but of absurdly small numerical strength. It attempted to supplement that regular army in wartime with a citizen soldiery whom history had shown to be undependable. Through the militia system it aggravated the defects of a citizen soldiery: "View it in whatever light we may, the conversion of the militia into an army of the first line . . . was a wild and impracticable scheme." [46] When the militia's futility became apparent, it resorted to a volunteer system which retained most of the faults of the militia and, in the Civil War, brought forth a good army only at an excessive cost in time, money, and lives.

How did Upton propose to remedy these weaknesses? Obviously, his suggestions would center on the regular army and especially on the professional officer corps. He also proposed remedies suggested by his inspection of the armies of the great powers of Europe. He regretted that the United States had so long been reluctant to profit from the examples of its military betters:

Whenever Congress has shown a disposition to adopt the principle of military organization observed in continental armies, it has been dissuaded from its purpose by the demagogic admonition that foreign organizations are dangerous to liberty. This cry has frequently been uttered in the Army, and is still held in reserve by those who are selfishly interested in the perpetuation of our present effete organization.[47]

Lessons for the United States were to be found by looking to Europe:

Of late no argument has been used more effectively to prevent military legislation, than the assertion that the principles of military organization abroad are designed to support monarchies, and that, if not dangerous, they are at least incompatible with free institutions. No delusion could be greater. The student of modern history cannot fail to discover that the principles of organization, like those of strategy, are of universal application, and that no nation has ever violated them, except at its peril.[48]

If excessive civilian control was the fundamental cause of American military weaknesses, then the first remedy must be to place professional soldiers in genuine control of the army. The militia and volunteers must be subjected to federal direction, so that the federal government could insist that merit and not political influence shape them. Meanwhile, in the federal government itself, the powers of the military professionals must be increased relative to those of the President and the secretary of war.

Upton believed the duties of the secretary of war should be administrative and financial and nothing more. The command of the army should be left to the generals. Though the constitutional status of the President as commander in chief could not be changed, actual command of the army should reside in a general in chief:

> The attempt to dispense with a General in Chief after our armies had become disciplined and ready for battle [in the Civil War], the detachment of McDowell [from McClellan's army], the establishment of the Department of the Rappahannock and the Shenandoah [in 1862], the creation of the Army of Virginia, and the withdrawal of the Army of the Potomac from the Peninsula will be recognized as the dominating causes of a four years' war, the blame for which it will not place upon an individual, but upon a system which, in every war since the adoption of the Constitution, has permitted a civil officer below the President, to override military commanders and bring to naught their wisdom and counsels.
>
> In every country save our own, the inability of unprofessional men to command armies would be accepted as a self-evident proposition.[49]
>
> The disasters which ensued [in the Civil War]. . . must therefore be credited to the defective laws which allowed the President to dispense with an actual General in Chief and substitute in his stead a civil officer supported by military advisers, disqualified by their tenure of office and occupations from giving free and enlightened opinions.[50]

Upton proposed that the general in chief be supported from below by a general staff corps on the German model, its members the products of a postgraduate military education of the type available in Germany and thus the exemplars of the highest qualities of military professionalism. German staff officers, Upton pointed out,

> have had the benefit of careful instruction at war academies especially designed for their education. Learning there all the principles of strategy and grand tactics and the importance of a knowledge of military geography, studying the theory of moving and directing troops in battle, impressed with the idea that their value as staff officers depends upon the assistance they can give to their generals in planning campaigns and

fighting battles, they look with contempt upon any official occupation which may tend to degrade them to the position of clerks.[51]

The staff officers attached to American line commanders were hardly more than clerks; few of them performed duties higher than those of an aide-de-camp. A staff corps of the German type would insist on and deservedly receive more important duties:

In every military system which has triumphed in modern war the officers have been recognized as the brain of the army, and to prepare them for their trust, governments have spared no pains to give them special education and training.[52]

For one thing, an American general staff corps could take the preparation of army organization bills out of the hands of civilians. The civilian branches of government might then approve or fail to approve military bills drawn by the general staff, but the civilians should not do more; they should not attempt to take the initiative in military judgments.[53]

Secondly, a general staff corps would be valuable in that, notwithstanding the appointment of a professional general in chief, political figures were still likely to receive high rank in the American army. The general staff corps could counteract the pernicious influence of such officers; just as in Germany the general staff exercised the real command of troops nominally led by members of the royal families, so in the United States the general staff could relegate political officers to figurehead status.[54]

After remedying the basic flaw of civilian direction of the army, Upton proposed the establishment of an adequate army for the professional general in chief and the general staff corps to lead. An adequate army should be created in part by enlargement of the regular army. But he knew it would be futile to advocate a genuinely large army of regulars. He professed to believe that a return to the old ratio of 1,000 regular soldiers to each 1,000,000 of the national population, which prevailed under the law of April 24, 1816, would provide sufficient numbers. He said that he agreed with George Washington that the country "Ought to have a good army rather than a large one." [55]

For wartime increases, Upton proposed the plan of the "expansive army," which was an elaboration of ideas set forth by John C. Calhoun in his "Report on the Reduction of the Army" of December

12, 1820, influenced by Upton's observation of the German cadre-conscript army. Upton recalled that Calhoun had urged an army which, with the beginning of hostilities, would require

nothing either to new model or to create. The only difference, consequently, between the peace and the war formation of the Army, ought to be in the increased magnitude of the latter, and the only change in passing from the former to the latter should consist in giving to it the augmentation which will then be necessary.[56]

Upton emphasized that the idea was not exclusively Calhoun's, but that it had appeared on other occasions. He might have pointed to Hamilton's early suggestion of it or to Halleck's discussion of it in his *Elements of Military Art and Science*. He did point out that Winfield Scott on the eve of the Mexican War had recommended an increase in the number of privates per company throughout the army, so that "Our present skeleton Army may then, without an additional regiment . . . , be augmented by 7,690 men (more than doubled)." Secretary of War William B. Marcy had supported the recommendation. After the Mexican War began, the plan actually had been adopted, although too late to be of full usefulness. Had it been accepted earlier, Upton wrote, Scott's invading army in Mexico need not have been exposed to a force three times its numbers, nor need thousands of three months men have been rushed untrained into service.[57]

The army act of June 17, 1850, Upton noted, had written the expansible principle into peacetime military legislation. It had authorized the President to expand the numbers of any or all of the companies serving on the frontier by about 50 percent. The use made of the act, Upton declared, showed that the United States need not fear Presidential misuse of such discretionary power. Not until 1853–1854, did the President avail himself of his authority, and then he increased to the maximum standard only 123 of the 158 companies in the West. Unfortunately, subsequent legislation discarded the expansible principle.[58]

Having established an American lineage for the expansible army idea, Upton characteristically turned to European, and particularly German, armies for what he considered to be modern applications that might provide appropriate examples for the United States. He suggested that American regular army battalions henceforth be recruited by territorial districts, with each battalion constantly maintaining a depot in its district. He urged that in peacetime the battalion depots supervise military training among the young men of their districts, as was the practice in Europe. At the outbreak of war, as in Europe, the wartime recruits would report to the local battalion with which they had already trained, would fill its ranks to war strength, and thus would permit the army to go into battle with an established organization in which each man knew his assignment and with professional officers commanding the whole, the new recruits, already partially trained, rapidly learning the rest of the military craft by serving beside practised regulars.[59]

Through this system the regular army would dominate all the military forces of the United States. The wartime army would simply be an extension of the regulars, its recruits absorbed into regular formations, its officers professionals who commanded the same units in peace as in war. The essence of the plan was that, as Calhoun had prescribed, upon mobilization there would be "nothing either to new model or to create." The regular army would be a full skeleton of the wartime army.

As to how the wartime recruits were to be gathered, Upton again turned to the European examples and proposed conscription. The history of the United States with its short enlistments, bounties, and armies evaporating on the eve of crucial battle in every war, proved that the volunteer system could not provide adequate armies reliable for the duration of the war and that only conscription could do so. Without conscription, the American revolutionary army virtually had disappeared again and again. The nation escaped a need for conscription in the War of 1812, Upton believed, only because the war was brief. In the Civil War the government attempted as usual to win without conscription, but this great conflict finally gave the United States a choice between conscription or defeat.[60]

Furthermore, Upton believed that conscription was a beneficial device, a "truly democratic doctrine," based on "the broad republican principle, that every American citizen owes his country military service." [61] It could bring the people of the United States into something of the admirable close relationship with their army that existed between nation and army in Germany. It would make Americans healthily conscious of their army, just as the German people were.[62]

For all that, Upton's advocacy of conscription stands apart from the other elements of his expansible army plan. It does not dovetail with the rest of the plan. Conscription was a program unacceptable to the United States except in wartime, yet Upton was offering a plan for preparation for war, not for the conduct of war already begun. Knowing that conscription was practically out of the question in peacetime America, Upton did not propose a standing army large enough to absorb hordes of conscripts. His discussion of conscription was peripheral; his main emphasis was a larger regular army but one which was still relatively small, to be expansible to a size comparable to that of a likely European expeditionary force in America but not to that of a full European army. The focus of Upton's thought was on quality rather than quantity. He barely hoped to attain high quality in America, let alone mass as well as quality.

Turning to reforms more feasible than conscription, Upton proposed changes of detail in the existing regular army. He suggested that the traditional American infantry regiment, tactically a single battalion, should become a three-battalion regiment, better suited to maneuvering on a modern battlefield, and making possible a depot battalion for each regiment, on the German model.[63] But the main purpose of *The Military Policy of the United States* was to propose reforms intermediate between reforms of detail and so sweeping an innovation as conscription. It was to advocate thoroughly professional command of a thoroughly professional regular army, expansible by the addition of recruits who would resemble professionals as much as possible in the shortest possible time.

Upton died before *The Military Policy* was complete. His survey of American military history in support of his recommendations goes no further than 1862. But the circumstances of his death may have added to Upton's influence. Now he would be remembered as one of the most promising and heroic of American officers, whose promise had been denied fulfillment by tragedy. His impact upon the imagination would be greater to those who recalled that he wrote *The Military Policy* in spite of a mounting throbbing in his head, a mysterious ailment which denied him sleep except when he was utterly exhausted, ensured that once awakened at night he would sleep no more, and made concentration on any mental task a heroic endeavor. Upton was suffering from a brain tumor. With it came periods in which even an iron will could not force the mind to think rationally and responsibly. Recognizing that the increasing frequency of such periods would soon leave him incapable of performing his duties, in 1881, Upton wrote out his resignation from the United States Army and then shot himself.[64]

The tragic circumstances of its writing are in keeping with the pessimistic tone and conclusions of *The Military Policy of the United States*. For it is obvious that Upton doubted that the United States would follow his recommendations to turn its back on civilian direction of military policy, strengthen the regular army, and through the expansible army plan and conscription provide a wartime army comparable to the military forces of the great powers of Europe. The whole weight of American history made military reform unlikely, short of some great military disaster. "Since the Rebellion, with a fatuity pregnant with future disaster," the United States had settled down in the comfortable military delusions of the past.[65] Furthermore, even if the general outlines of Upton's expansible army plan should win popular acceptance, no likely enlargement of the standing army would render it big enough to provide a skeleton for more than a moderately large wartime force. No conceivable change of American opinion would create a standing army large enough to provide, without excessive dilution, the nucleus of a genuine mass army, comparable to the wartime armies of Europe. *The Military Policy of the United States* offered a legacy of profound pessimism.

Upton had shown parts of his manuscript to General Sherman. Colonel Henry A. DuPont had aided him in research, and after Upton's death DuPont assembled the unfinished manuscript. In this form it circulated among certain army officers, including Sherman and Major General John M. Schofield, and knowledge of the manuscript and of its ideas reached a wide circle in the army. In 1885 Peter Smith Michie's *Life and Letters of General Emory Upton* gave knowledge of the manuscript and of its basic tenets to the world at large. Finally, when Secretary of War Elihu Root tried to reform the army after the Spanish-American War, he found some of Upton's ideas pertinent, especially in regard to a general staff and postgraduate military schools, and he had *The Military Policy of the United States* published as a government document in 1904. Publication assured Upton an influence persisting long into the twentieth century. The professional officer corps's great familiarity with his work and the carefully documented support he seemed to give to ideas widely shared in the army had already established him as the major prophet of American professionalist military thought.[66]

VIII JOHN A. LOGAN *The Rebuttal for a Citizen Army*

> Our armies were composed of men . . . who knew what they were fighting for, . . . and so necessarily must have been more than equal to men who fought merely because they were brave and because they were thoroughly drilled and inured to hardships. ULYSSES S. GRANT

> When the clarion voice of war resounds through the land, the country throughout its vast extent becomes, if necessary, one bristling camp of fighting men. JOHN A. LOGAN

NOT since John C. Calhoun left the office of Secretary of War had there been an important civilian thinker on military policy. In the decades between the close of the Civil War and the opening of the brief era of imperialism, military thought in the United States continued to be the almost exclusive monopoly of the professional officer corps. During the founding of the Republic, in the debates over the Constitution at Philadelphia, throughout the states, and in *The Federalist,* political leaders of all types had interested themselves in military issues. The United States was then weak in a warlike world, and to provide for the common defense was among the most pressing concerns of statecraft. But in the long nineteenth-century summer of the *Pax Britannica* the world no longer seemed warlike, and the United States seemed safe. No likely foreign enemy existed, at least none who could cross the Atlantic in force, and in the Civil War the United States had proven its ability to mobilize tremendous military power. Under such circumstances only professional soldiers thought much about American military policy; and as the professional soldiers became more committed to defense by the regular army, few civilians troubled to argue with them or were even aware of their thinking. Civilian America was too busy with other things. Against the professionals and their dedication to professionalism, the old idea of a citizen soldiery had few defenders.

The volunteer soldiers of the Civil War were duly praised in memoirs and popular histories, but this was more a matter of standard patriotic gesture than of reasoned consideration of military policy. A few Civil War memoirists did devote real thought to the kind of soldiers they had commanded, and such an original as Ulysses Grant, never fitted to the standard professional mold, concluded that the citizen armies of the Civil War had been in many ways superior to European professional soldiers. Grant's tribute to the citizen armies that fought at Shiloh became famous:

The Confederates fought with courage at Shiloh, but the particular skill [superior to that of the Federals] claimed [for them] I could not and still cannot see; though there is nothing to criticize except the claims put forward for it since. But the Confederate claimants to superiority in dash and prowess are not so unjust to the Union troops engaged at Shiloh as many Northern writers. The troops on both sides were American, and united they need not fear any foreign foe.

The armies of Europe are machines: the men are brave and the officers capable; but the majority of the soldiers in most of the nations of Europe are taken from a class of people who are not very intelligent and who have very little interest in the contest in which they are called upon to take part. Our armies were composed of men who were able to read, men who knew what they were fighting for, and could not be induced to serve as soldiers, except in an emergency when the safety of the nation was involved, and so necessarily must have been more than equal to men who fought merely because they were brave and because they were thoroughly drilled and inured to hardships.[1]

Such statements, however, were merely incidental to Grant's *Memoirs*. They were not a full-scale answer to Emory Upton's professionalist argument, they were not even comparable to George B. McClellan's brief statement of the professionalist viewpoint in his book devoted mainly to European armies. Grant's voice on behalf of the citizen soldier, influential as it was, was no more than a whisper breaking the general silence of the champions of the citizen army.

But amidst civilian indifference and army hostility, one voice spoke loudly in a large-scale answer to the professionalists. The exception to the post-Civil War civilian indifference and silence on the appropriate nature of the American army was the Republican political boss of Illinois, United States Senator, and Republican vice-presidential candidate of 1884, John A. Logan.

Logan was Major General Logan, "Black Jack" Logan, the volunteer officer who combined political influence (at the start of the Civil War he was an important War Democrat) with military ability to rise to the command of the XV Army Corps. He led the Army of the Tennessee when it threw John B. Hood badly battered into his fortifications in the battle of Atlanta of August 22, 1864. Logan rose to that great day only to be denied permanent command of the army, with the evidence suggesting strongly that despite Sherman's denials Logan's principal handicap was his lack of a West Point education and thus of the status of a professional. Logan had his personal grievance against the professionals, a grievance magnified by Sherman's postwar criticism of him in explanation of the army command decision. The grievance doubtless helped nourish Logan's reply to the professionalist military spokesmen, and the latter could more easily dismiss Logan's reply on that account. But Logan's indignation toward the professional officer corps was more than personal.[2]

Logan's statement of the Jacksonian citizen-soldiery argument took the form of a huge book, *The Volunteer Soldier of America*, a work running to more than 700 pages and weighing two pounds, forceful through a sheer sweep and weight that suggest the raw power which was the essence of Logan's personality. The book is discursive, ill organized, and even by the standards of Victorian political literature often badly written. It awards as much space to irrelevancies as to support for its arguments. Its contentions are overdrawn in the impulsive fashion that was a principal defect of Logan's battlefield generalship. It uses painstakingly compiled statistics to support dubious conclusions. It is so extreme an expression of the Jeffersonian-Jacksonian tradition that notwithstanding caveats on some pages it nearly implies on others that any professional military education is superfluous. Its argument against military professionalism weakens itself through identification with Logan's Jacksonian defense of the spoils system against any professional bureaucracy civilian or military. But with all its faults it forcibly drives home its main point, that the West Pointers' devotion to professionalism and their contempt for military amateurs had left the United States unready for foreign war and with no idea of how to get ready.

Logan's argument was most labored and verbose and least convincing when he sought to discredit the whole existing concept of West Point (and of Annapolis as well). It was here that his Jacksonian suspicion of the expert led him close to a flat denial of the value of military education. He argued that history proved greatness in war is not a product of education but of a genius inherent in certain individuals, susceptible to some cultivation by training, but bound to manifest itself whenever opportunity arises.[3] He devoted many of his pages to reviews of the careers of Americans who won high success in war despite their lack of the benefits bestowed by West Point: George Washington, Philip Schuyler, Nicholas Herkimer, John Starke, Oliver Hazard Perry, Thomas Macdonough, William Henry Harrison, Andrew Jackson, Zachary Taylor, Alfred H. Terry, Dan Sickles, and a host of others. What he said about Nathanael Greene can represent what he said about all the rest and show the gist of his argument:

The case of General Nathaniel Greene is one of the most striking and at the same time one of the most instructive in the annals of military history. Without any enlarged English education, except such as he acquired through his own tutorship after being grown; with no military tendencies about his family and social surroundings to give his mind a bent in that direction; with no friend or teacher to inflame his young imagination with tales of war and "hair-breadth 'scapes by flood and field;" without apparent aspiration for other than the arts of peace—under the magic touchstone of opportunity his military genius blazed out with the suddenness of the full-faced sun as it quickly emerges from behind a fugitive cloud. . . .

Hence, it must appear to the most ardent advocate of preliminary military education as a prerequisite of military greatness, that Greene's case suggests embarrassing perplexities to the sweeping theories of the scholastics. Within the narrow scope of his education there had not been embraced even the outlines of mathematical instruction, though through the spur of ambition he acquired some knowledge of Latin and of mathematics in the moments of rest from his work, and by the friendly light of the blazing forge. But he was as unlearned in engineering as in the modern languages, and he knew no more of the elements of military science than he did of the ordinary routine of military drill and tactics. With simple patriotism he entered the service of his country, and in less than eighteen months thereafter he had proved himself an accomplished military leader. Considered in all of its bearings, his case must be held to afford remarkable negative proof against the common belief that high military talent and successful leadership can only be the product of a set course of instruction by a military academy.[4]

Logan concluded, in short, that the sort of military education purveyed by West Point was of doubtful necessity. He went on to argue that history showed West Point to have been a wasteful failure at best and a danger to American democracy at worst. In support of these contentions he adduced three principal arguments.

First, he contended that the political system of appointments to the Military Academy filled the academy and the officer corps of the army with men whose principal dedication was not to the nation and the service but to party and section. His evidence lay in the defections of Southern-born West Pointers to the Confederacy, or, as he put it, to treason. Under the political system of appointments, he said, the cadets of West Point and the officers of the army would always reflect the predominant political and sectional views of an era, not broad national views. With Southern Democrats dominating the national government before the Civil War, Southern Democrats had also dominated the officer corps. Before 1860, the Southern states had sent one cadet to West Point for every 5,757 of their population, the Northern states only one cadet for every 8,330 of their population. Composed disproportionately of Southern Democrats, the officer corps proved disloyal to the higher claims of the nation when, in 1861, the nation needed them most.[5] Indeed, the education at West Point under Southern influence seemed less valuable to the nation than no professional military education at all, since the enlisted men of the army and navy, not exposed to West Point, remained loyal to the United States in 1861 even as their officers defected.[6]

Second, Logan argued that even if West Point did succeed in producing men loyal to country rather than to party or section, it produced soldiers only when fortuitous circumstance intervened. The political system of appointment did not draw men whose inclinations were necessarily military ones; again political connections rather than military aptitudes were what counted. Within the academy, scholarly attainments and even punctiliousness of conduct, rather than military promise, kept a cadet in good standing and determined his final rank in the cadet regiment. Logan demonstrated through a survey of the careers of all first-honors graduates of the academy from 1802 to 1860 that many had not even become soldiers and only two or three had won high distinction in war.[7] West Point, he argued, had produced many outstanding engineers, lawyers, bank presidents, and the like, but that could be said of any university; the purpose of a military school was to produce soldiers.[8]

West Point graduates who did prove to be outstanding soldiers, Logan pointed out, rarely won high honors at the academy. Two defects seemed implicit in the record: those appointed to the academy were not appointed because they were potential soldiers, and the academy program itself was suitable for producing educated men perhaps but not geared to the specific task of producing leaders for war. On both counts, the West Point system was wasteful.[9]

Third, Logan argued that West Point was not only wasteful but was also a danger to democratic institutions, in that the existing military system based on West Point graduates confined "knowledge of the military art" to a small part of the people. Thus there existed a small group who "would possess the power, even should they never entertain the inclination, to control, or, to put it more broadly, to conquer the rest of the community." Furthermore, the graduates of West Point tended to become an aristocracy, for in Logan's Jacksonian view aristocracy followed from life tenure in office. Democracy depended, he argued, upon absolute political and civil equality. Life tenure in office, apart from judicial office, amounted to the granting of special privilege and was the reverse of democracy. Nourished by special privilege, the officer corps tended to develop the attitudes of an aristocracy; and here lay another explanation of the eagerness with which West Point graduates had abandoned the democratic cause of the North for the antidemocratic, caste-oriented cause of the South in 1861.[10]

Each of Logan's three arguments against West Point has manifest flaws. No system of appointment to the academy would have been likely to prevent the defection of Southern-born officers in 1861. No system of appointment was likely to ensure that most of the graduates, especially the honors graduates, made careers of the army when the era was one in which the army offered little stimulation or opportunity for advancement. Life tenure in office for experts, civil or military, provides problems for a democracy but does not nullify equality before the law or equality of opportunity. As for the merits of military genius over military education, even

Logan conceded on his more sober pages that education had its values—we shall see it included in his recommendations. The possibilities open to untrained talent were becoming slighter with advancing military technology even as Logan wrote.

Yet each of the three arguments also had a certain merit, in Logan's day at least, and the third reached the heart of the problem created by the evolution of the Washington-Hamilton school of military professionalism into the Calhoun-Upton school. The existing West Point system did confine "knowledge of the military art" to a small circle, and that circle's low opinion of the uninitiated did prevent the diffusion of even rudimentary military knowledge.

As the repository of our military knowledge and resources, the Government habitually looks to its army and navy class [Logan wrote] in all matters pertaining to those branches of administration, and, briefly stated, the result of our system has been to constitute both the army and navy the closest corporations in the country. The entrance to a recognized career in either one or the other service lies only through the picket lines of West Point or Annapolis. All knowledge not obtained there is spurious, and all soldiers and sailors not made there are considered mere pretenders . . . . the corporations named have become supreme in the management of the military policy of the country: they have controlled the whole organization of military affairs, and they have regulated all the appointments of the army and naval services. They have arrogated to the graduates of the national academies the appellation of *regular* officers in opposition to volunteer officers, who by contrast have become *irregular,* and, as a consequence, pretenders in the profession of arms. Hence, from the earliest operation of our present system the regular officer has climbed over the head of the volunteer officer, without regard to real ability or qualification, in all promotions for which the two classes were competitors.[11]

With important military posts almost monopolized by the West Pointers, and with little adequate military training available outside the regular army, the nation possessed a military system too narrow to protect its interests. In wartime greater numbers than the regulars mustered would have to be mobilized, but the regular army gave only lip-service recognition to that fact:

Strangely enough the military interest of the governing classes of our country has always centered in the small body of men—a mere national police force—called the "regular" army of the United States. Since the effective establishment of the Academy at West Point this institution has been constituted the special repository of the entire military establishment. Instead of its functions being limited to imparting an education in the science and art of war to such pupils as may be sent there for the purpose of receiving it, the institution, arrogating to itself the sole military knowledge of a people military by natural impulse and by the general habits and surroundings of their life, has for years taken possession of the military interests of the Government and has conducted those interests as the sole property of the select circle which by the decrees of West Point has been constituted the only true exponent of the art of war upon the American continent.[12]

In short, the citizen soldiers who would have to win any American war remained neglected by the military leaders of the country. Logan did not give a detailed solution for the military problems of the United States. He did not claim to possess a full solution, and he held that even if he had one he ought to defer to a full public discussion. But he did set forth the general lines along which he thought changes should be made, and the first necessity he saw was for the regular officer corps to acknowledge the superb fighting qualities of the American volunteer and to prepare to use the citizen soldier. Much of Logan's book consisted of a panegyric to the citizen soldier, and much of what he said on the subject was as extravagant as his extreme claims for natural genius in officers. But withal there was less extravagance than truth in his tributes. He conceded that citizen soldiers had proven unreliable until they had gained a year or more of seasoning in the field; but he was correct in arguing that once they were trained and seasoned the soldierly performance of the American armed citizens had been excellent. An armed citizenry could become a good army; that they first needed training and experience was more reason not to neglect them in peacetime but to fit them in peace as well as in war into American military planning.[13]

But it was into an *American* military system that the armed citizenry would have to be fitted. Here was a point that Logan emphasized and Upton had minimized:

In the fabrication of a military system for the United States which shall be wholly adapted to the necessities of our peculiar form of government, but little aid can be borrowed from the nations of Europe. One great mistake of many of our public men has lain in the direction of endeavoring to follow the precedents of monarchical governments in establishing the institutions of a republic.[14]

Despite his claims for natural genius, Logan recognized that a military system for a citizen soldiery must center on military education and training. He argued that three considerations must underlie a military education program suited to American needs: the program must be divorced from politics, it must leave entrance into the army and navy officer corps open to all on the basis of merit, and it must diffuse military knowledge among the people at large. To accomplish the first two aims, he proposed that appointments to the military schools be removed from congressional hands and instead be based on a national competitive examination. With all three aims in mind, he proposed that the officer candidates selected by competitive examination go to their state universities, each of which would have a military department to teach the rudiments of military knowledge. Graduates of such departments might then take additional competitive examinations, and men of proven military inclinations and abilities could be selected to enter West Point and Annapolis, which would now teach military science beyond the rudiments. Graduates of the academies would be commissioned as before, but a larger proportion of them could be expected to remain in the military service and be successful there. And all those receiving officer training in the state universities would be prepared to take commissions in an emergency.[15]

Meanwhile, Logan proposed, the curriculum of the public schools should include physical training and the drill of the infantry soldier, so that all young men would receive a minimum introduction to the military world. Beyond that, each state ought to improve its militia system and encourage young men to participate in it. Logan did not offer a plan for raising the state militia to federally established standards. Unrealistically, in the light of his own historical survey of the militia, he held that it was enough to assure federal standards that the same voters supervised both federal and state governments. But he did recommend that each state adopt a plan similar to the original Henry Knox plan, whereby systematic training for all militiamen and extensive initial training for young members would be assured. By all means, he argued, military training must be extended to the nation at large, to the citizens who in wartime would have to be the country's principal defense.[16]

Of course the Upton plan had called for an extension of military training also, but only to such numbers as the regular army could absorb and regular officers could control. The great defect of Upton's expansible army plan, apart from the fact that it could not win public acceptance, was that its army was not expansible enough. The way to assure adequate numbers for American defense against a major enemy was to escape the belief that only regular officers were capable officers and that only an army shaped to the regular pattern could fight well. The militia had often failed, as Upton demonstrated; but with proper preparation citizen soldiers had often been both good officers and good fighters, as Logan asserted. There was this much cogency in Logan's argument for natural genius versus military education: American history had given numerous examples of proficient wartime officers who had lacked the full professional training which Upton thought so important.

Logan argued that given a genuinely American military system shaped to the characteristics of American citizen soldiers, with training for part-time soldiers and part-time officers, the United States could develop military power superior to the professional armies of Europe:

Practically considered, then, the nation has no army in time of peace, though, when the clarion voice of war resounds through the land, the country throughout its vast extent becomes, if necessary, one bristling camp of armed men. This is a most interesting circumstance, and one that has challenged the attention of men of all nations and of all creeds. It is a circumstance quite unique in character. . . . It is so new that it has no precise parallel in all history: it belongs to the genius of the American Republic; and it is possible only to a government founded upon a basis substantially identical with that upon which our free institutions so securely rest.[17]

Here was the revolutionary military tradition in full bloom, a reassertion that the new political institutions of the United States demanded new military institutions. But by the time Logan's book was in print, Logan himself was dead and his political power was no more. There were no circumstances in his death to capture the imagination as Upton's death had done, and Logan had been speaking almost alone while he was alive. No one paid much heed to the dead man's words, neither the civilians indifferent to military affairs nor the West Pointers engrossed in Upton's rationalization of their professionalist inclinations.

IX   *The Disciples of Emory Upton*

As the Congress has so utterly failed to properly provide for a "well-regulated militia" or national guard, it might naturally be expected that due provision has been made for some other military force, as represented by the regular armies of modern nations. A. D. SCHENCK

Lulled to sleep in fancied security, confident that our great wealth and numbers have made us unconquerable, our energies are devoted to trade and the arts of peace, and we have no time to devote to the consideration of possible disasters. JAMES S. PETTIT

NOT only did the United States in the post-Civil War era lack plans for the mobilization of a wartime military reserve, either of an Uptonian professional type or a Loganian citizen-soldier type; the regular army itself was faulty, unprogressive, and small. The instrument upon which Emory Upton hoped to build a better military policy was itself not a model of military efficiency, and for this reason the pessimism of Upton's writing was deep and the pessimism of his followers deeper still.

The regular army after 1876 had an authorized strength of 25,000, but it usually numbered somewhat less. It was organized into five regiments of artillery, ten of cavalry, twenty-five of infantry, a battalion of engineers, and the cadets of the Military Academy. The soldiers were scattered along the seacoasts and mainly across the vastness of the West. Rarely did the companies of a single regiment unite. As late as 1895 the commanding general of the army was still pleading in vain for the permanent concentration of at least one full regiment of cavalry at Fort Riley, Kansas, for the purpose of holding regimental maneuvers. Even on paper, the army was merely a conglomeration of regiments; no corps or divisional organization existed. Strategic and logistical planning was practically unknown, either for defensive war or for some conflict that might involve the dispatch of an expeditionary force overseas (such as the Cuban insurrection of 1868–1878 suggested might occur).[1]

Even tactical arrangements within the regiments were faulty. Emory Upton had been correct in his call for the abolition of the single-battalion infantry regiment, a clumsy mass which open-order fighting made impractical to maneuver effectively; but despite the fact that every commanding general from Sherman onward agreed with Upton, the unwieldy single-battalion regiment remained to fight the Spanish War. Organizationally the cavalry regiments were in a better pass, but the five regiments of artillery suffered from a complete lack of regimental cohesion and from haphazard assignment to duties from seacoast to field to infantry service.[2]

The army displayed a hardening of the arteries. While many of its officers, Sherman and numerous junior officers, sought to keep abreast of new developments in the art of war, too many who had served against the Confederacy seemed unable to escape infatuation with the methods of the Civil War and were blinded to the worth of improvements.

The Civil War quartermaster general, M. C. Meigs, for example, clung to his post until 1882, and he resisted organizational improvements in his department with an attitude that was characteristic of many of his colleagues. He opposed any effort to unite his Quartermaster's Department with the Subsistence Department, a step which at last had to be taken on the eve of World War I. "Two such perfect machines," Meigs wrote in defense of the old system, "should be preserved distinct in readiness for the call of war. You will remember how both expanded in a moment at the touch of war in 1861." Such an expansion "in a moment" was precisely what those with accurate memories did not recall. But Meigs went on to argue that the Quartermaster's Department as it stood

has grown up in the course of many years, is adapted to the genius and habits of our people, it admits of expansion at the outbreak of war, while able to teach new officers their difficult duties, and an arm which has served so well should not now be experimentally broken or thrown aside.[3]

Even an officer so unwedded to the traditional as Phil Sheridan found little that might improve the American army when he observed the Franco-Prussian War. "I find that but little can be learned here to benefit our service," he wrote back to Sherman. "We are far ahead in skill and campaign organization."[4]

Infatuation with the techniques of the Civil War was especially dangerous because as late as the 1890s field officers and even subalterns were men who had entered the service during the war or immediately afterward. The officer corps of the American army in the late nineteenth century was an aging officer corps. A writer in a professional journal pointed out in 1891 that the youngest captain in the American artillery was older than the oldest artillery captain in the British army, a force never noted for its rapidity of promotion. There was not a single American artillery captain under forty years of age. The average age of the oldest ten artillery captains was fifty-six; the average age of all artillery captains was a fraction over fifty years. Among forty-four first lieutenants of artillery, the average age was forty-five. Lacking adequate mandatory retirement regulations for officers who failed to achieve promotions, the army simply was too small to keep open avenues of advancement which would ensure it young and vigorous subalterns, much less relatively young field and general officers.[5]

Although such was the army of a third-rate power, in the late nineteenth-century age of seemingly secure isolation few civilian Americans cared. The United States neither faced foreign threats nor had foreign policy aims to require the maintenance of a powerful army. In size, apart from its other deficiencies, the small army of the 1870s and 1880s was appropriate to the needs of the country. There was boastfulness and blindness but also a large measure of perception in an observation made by Secretary of War Redfield Proctor in 1890:

The military resources of the nation have been so recently demonstrated [presumably in the Civil War, a generation earlier] and its network of railways is so adapted to a rapid concentration of troops on any threatened point, that no hostile force is likely to seek an encounter with us on our own soil. A small army sent upon our shores could not hope for success; it is not probable that any large one will incur the risk. We have, therefore, little to fear from invasion, and are free from the necessity of maintaining large standing armies or of fortifying against land attacks.[6]

But Proctor's truths were difficult for professional officers who had not succumbed to lethargy to accept. Devoting their lives to preparation for war, they could not believe that war was so unlikely to come. They wrote articles in their professional journals about war as a constant of human experience, and believing war to be the ordained lot of men, many of them had to share Emory Upton's pessimism when they contemplated the military policy of the United States.

One result of the parlous condition of the United States Army was a considerable departure from the emphasis on offensive strategy and tactics which had characterized American professional military thought since the early years of Dennis Mahan. Professional officers, seeing no prospect of possessing the bodies of trained troops needed to seize the military initiative, became preoccupied with plans for passive defense. The one major expression of civilian concern for possible foreign wars was a movement for strengthening the seacoast fortifications. This movement appealed to civilians because it seemed to offer defense without the costs and dangers of a large standing army; but professional officers joined in support of the movement too, for there seemed to be no other respectable weapon that they were likely to get. Now the American interest in coastal fortifications, already evident among Mahan's students, grew into an obsession.

The rifled guns of the Civil War had battered into rubble masonry forts like Sumter and had compelled a modernization of the seacoast fortress system. As early as 1869, Sherman urged the systematic replacement of prewar fortifications with defenses better able to resist modern artillery. He recommended that the masonry forts along the coasts give way to "barbette batteries of earth, with deep parapet, and a liberal number of bombproof and magazine traverses." He asked that their prewar and wartime guns be replaced by the most modern and heaviest pieces available, with "disappearing carriages" so that they might be depressed below the parapets for reloading. He urged emplacement of numerous heavy mortars, preparations for the mining of harbors, and construction of harbor entanglements to hold a hostile fleet under the guns of the forts.[7]

Sherman urged this program in 1869 and through the 1870s, but so great was civilian indifference to military matters—or civilian perception of the absence of real danger—that even his considerable influence could not persuade Congress to adopt the program. The secretaries of war seconded Sherman's plan, and after Sherman retired his successor Sheridan took up the same cry. But the seventies gave way to the eighties, artillery advances of almost revolutionary scope made the old fortresses more vulnerable, and still nothing was done. By the late 1870s and early 1880s Congress was not appropriating enough funds even to keep the old fortresses in repair. Whipped by coastal winds and by the tides, the great red hulks of masonry fell sadly into decay.[8]

By the middle 1880s the decay was so advanced that even a preoccupied nation could no longer ignore the worthlessness of its coastal defenses. The Chester A. Arthur administration, furthermore, had an uncommon interest in things military, and its influence had won from Congress the first modern steel ships of the United States Navy, the famous cruisers *Chicago, Boston,* and *Atlanta.* The rebirth of the navy then called attention to the defenseless condition of the harbors in which the navy would have to be based. Accordingly, in 1885 Congress at last heeded the perennial calls of war secretaries and commanding generals for stronger coastal defenses, establishing under Grover Cleveland's secretary of war, William C. Endicott, a board of officers charged with undertaking a thorough study of seacoast defense needs and preparing a plan to restore adequate fortifications.[9]

The Endicott Board recommended the erection of new fortresses to protect the twenty-seven (later twenty-eight) principal harbors of the country. Surprisingly, it recommended the fortifying of the Canadian border as well as of the seacoasts. It proposed forts composed of earthworks, and of masonry protected by steel armor plate. Finding the guns of the old fortresses as obsolete as the masonry walls, it called for the fabrication of 677 modern high-powered guns and 824 mortars. It noted the precarious state of the American gunmaking industry, and it seconded the recommendations of the earlier Gun Foundry Board (1883) on how to achieve improvements. Since no American manufacturers were capable of producing modern steel artillery, the Endicott Board followed the Gun Foundry Board in recommending that private steel companies be commissioned to equip themselves to provide steel forgings for heavy ordnance, while the Watervliet Arsenal in New York and the Naval Gun Factory at Washington would be expanded to enable the army and navy to complete most of the heavy guns for themselves. Meanwhile the Endicott Board, like General Sherman before it, urged that the guns of the coastal defenses be supplemented by mines in the adjacent waters.[10]

In the years that followed, the report of the Endicott Board was slow to do anything but fill the pages of the professional military journals with discussions of harbor fortresses and their guns, and to give American professional military thought an unwonted pre-occupation with passive defense. Though the report reached Congress early in 1886, that body did nothing about it until September 22, 1888. It then provided for the establishment within the army of a Board of Ordnance and Fortification, composed of officers of engineers, artillery, and ordnance under the chairmanship of the commanding general, John M. Schofield. The board was to pass upon detailed proposals for carrying out the Endicott recommendations, the first expenditures for which were authorized at the same time. In the following months the Schofield Board approved plans of the Corps of Engineers for commencing the new defensive works in a few of the most important harbors, for the purchase in Europe of samples of modern ordnance, and for proposals calling for bidders to supply steel forgings for eight-inch, ten-inch, and twelve-inch steel guns and twelve-inch breech-loading rifled mortars.[11]

Despite the activities of the Schofield Board, by the early 1890s the visitor to the American coastline would have found few substantial evidences of the discussion and activities which had taken place since 1885. Private contractors were supplying twelve-inch mortars more rapidly than the army could use them, and the Secretary of War had to report that fortification of positions even for the completed mortars was just beginning in New York, Boston, and San Francisco.[12] On the other hand, despite the tardiness of the Endicott and Schofield plans in materializing, seacoast fortification was now more than ever the topic of such military discussions as the United States voiced.[13]

The attitudes, civilian and military, of those who urged the pushing of the Endicott and Schofield plans are illustrated by an article in the *North American Review*, quoting a Senate address by George F. Hoar of Massachusetts:

Judge Hoar said two years ago, in the Senate Chamber: "Our condition is well known to foreign nations. The absolutely defenseless condition of all our coast is well known abroad. The late Minister of Foreign

Affairs in France said to one of our statesmen, not long since, 'How about your defenses? In the intelligence department of our War Office,' said he, 'we have a drawing of every military work of consequence on the whole American coast line, with comments on their strength. There is not a first-class fortification among them all. Do you know how long it takes to build a first-class modern gun?' said the French Minister. The American replied that he did not. Lacour said: 'It takes a whole year. Your cities would be shelled and sacked and laid under tribute while you are creating a navy; and how could you rebuild your fortifications with one-thousand pound shells falling about the ears of your working-men? Be sure'—now mark this—'Be sure that the defenseless condition of your country is thoroughly well known and commented upon by every power in Europe that will gladly see you humbled, for, as I said, your prosperity is a dangerous menace to all the nations of the Old World except France.' "

Will the nations that would gladly see us humbled be uninfluenced by the sight of our unprotected coast, dotted with wealthy seaports? Can we expect that they will hesitate about taking part themselves in the humbling process, when a favorable opportunity is presented? [14]

Thus it was a curious, Elizabethan-sea-dog war that the proponents of the Endicott plan envisioned against the United States. Foreign nations were expected to strike against American prosperity not only to curtail the growth of a dangerous rival but to plunder that wealth for their own treasuries. The *North American Review* writer painted a terrifying picture of the effects of hostile naval bombardment on the population of New York City, suggesting that "The only alternative to such a bombardment would be the payment of a ransom, which, in the case of New York, would probably be not less that one hundred thousand dollars." [15] The Endicott report itself had spoken similarly of ransom, saying, ". . . the contributions which could be levied by a hostile fleet upon our seaports should be reckoned at hundreds of millions." Even reports of the commanding general of the army mentioned the idea.[16]

The realities of the late nineteenth century were often hospitable to economic interpretations of international affairs, but visions of an attack on the United States by a major power with its principal purpose the extortion of ransoms from American seaports were visions of a highly unlikely war. Nineteenth-century humanitarianism and militant nationalism joined forces to ensure that wars among civilized powers were no longer fought for such petty purposes, and with such limited aims and methods. Yet much of the advocacy of the Endicott plan rested on the assumption that the country must guard against yielding tribute to some modern corsair. The Endicott fortresses could not protect the country against foreign invasion, for as a critical naval officer remarked, "Even if the fortifications were sufficient to protect our ports, the defense is incomplete. There are many points along our coast not included in the army scheme." [17] Encouraged by civilians seeking cheap national defense and prodded by realization that it was not prepared for a mobile war with a major power, by the 1890s the army allowed the Endicott program to become almost a substitute for any other form of military policy.[18] But the fatal weakness remained: relying on the forts in the principal harbors, how did the army propose to deal with an invasion directed at some other point along the 2,870-mile American coastline?

Official army policy emphasized the Endicott plan because in the late 1880s and early 1890s it seemed impossible to accomplish anything else. But with the Endicott plan a fatally flawed substitute for a military policy at best, and with the plan itself existing more on paper than in fact, professional army officers unofficially turned to seek a better military policy. Any realistic policy would have to provide for defense against foreign invasion rather than mainly against raids on the seacoast cities, and there was no way to defend against foreign invasion without a mobile navy and a mobile army. In the 1880s and 1890s a growing interest in foreign commerce and in the activities of Stephen B. Luce and Alfred Thayer Mahan began to provide the former. There was still no great popular support for the latter, but army officers turned to the problem, and their thoughts about a strong mobile army led many of them to the ideas of Emory Upton.

One of the most promising younger officers of the army, Captain William H. Carter of the 6th Cavalry, regretted in 1889 that Upton's *Military Policy* "lies pigeon-holed in the War Department, and it is probably forgotten entirely by those who had the power to render any of his thoughts and plans effective." [19] But Upton's *Military Policy* would not remain forgotten if younger officers such as Carter could help it, for in the last years of the century those officers repeatedly filled professional military journals, *United Service*, the *Journal of the Military Service Institution*, and the *Army and*

Navy Journal, with Uptonian arguments for a reformed army.[20]

A suitable example of many such articles was First Lieutenant Arthur L. Wagner's "The Military Necessities of the United States, and the Best Provisions for Meeting Them." Wagner's subject was supplied by the United States Military Service Institution for its prize essay competition of 1883–1884, and his essay received the first award from a board of three eminent professionals, Generals Sherman, William B. Franklin, and Zealous B. Tower. Wagner was to become a leading reformer of the army's postgraduate school system.

His arguments were familiarly Uptonian. Wagner conceded that militia must be used as reserves, but he stressed his hope that federal supervision might improve their efficiency. Despite the existence of the militia, he believed that the United States would need as professional as possible a force of 100,000 men at the outbreak of any serious war. Therefore he argued that the regular cavalry and field artillery should be strengthened to provide all the soldiers of those arms necessary in a force of 100,000. He believed that it required two years to fashion good cavalry and good artillery from civilians, so that all the cavalry and artillery needed at the start of war should be ready at the first shot. The infantry for the 100,000-man first-line army should be the product of the expansion of the peacetime army, to be accomplished by filling up a skeleton third battalion in each regiment and by raising the other two battalions to war strength. Wagner believed that a proper expansible organization could enable the existing infantry force of about 9,000, for example, to grow quickly and without undue dilution to 22,000.[21]

Wagner thought most likely to occur conflicts with Great Britain over Canadian issues, with Spain over Cuba, or with Mexico over American property interests there. He believed that with a good navy and adequate coastal fortifications the United States would find a ready army of 100,000 men ample for any of those wars, strong enough to permit its use as an expeditionary force in Canada, Cuba, or Mexico, to carry the war away from American soil. But without such a force, a British war especially might bring initial defeats and even the capture of American cities. Wagner's bow to the militia was little more than a gesture of politeness. He proposed a professional force large enough to fight with its own re-

serves any conflict that seemed likely, without calling on the militia
for front line service.[22]

The militia was enjoying something of a renaissance in the late
nineteenth century, with labor disturbances impelling the states
to improve their armed forces to permit them to suppress strikers,
but with much of the improvement bringing about a restoration
of some military efficiency. Even the best of the new "national
guards" were still far from finished soldiers, and the Uptonian professionals sought means to consign them to such a limited role as
Wagner suggested. Wagner's attitude toward them and the attitude
of the Uptonian professionals was well summarized by another of
the Uptonian article writers, Captain A. D. Schenck of the regular
artillery, who echoed Upton in saying:

> Even the very short period of our country's history has clearly demon-
> strated that the constitutional "militia" has proved but a broken reed
> upon which to lean for our security, and it has now fallen upon such ill
> repute that our citizen soldiery consider it a stigma to be termed
> "militia," and, consequently, organize outside of the terms of constitu-
> tional law and parade as national guards. . . .
> As the Congress has so utterly failed to properly provide for a "well-
> regulated militia" or national guard, it might naturally be expected that
> due provision has been made for some other military force, as repre-
> sented by the regular armies of modern nations.[23]

The 1890s stimulated the professionalist inclinations of the
Wagners and Schencks of the regular officer corps by suggesting
that the occasion to use a thoroughly trained and mobile force of
regulars might no longer be remote. The American war which
Wagner had envisioned with Spain over Cuba, sped toward reality,
complete with the need to dispatch an American expeditionary
force to Cuba. But in the new climate of rapidly intensifying na-
tionalist and imperialist sentiments a Cuban expedition seemed
only one of several possible military adventures overseas. Fighting the British over Venezuela, the Japanese over Hawaii, and
even the Germans over Samoa appeared possible at various times.
The expansionist doctrines of Dennis Mahan's naval son reflected
and stimulated the new public interest in war and diplomacy. Alfred
Mahan especially called attention to the project of an isthmian
canal and with it to the whole field of United States relations with

the Latin countries to the south. The intellectual vogue of Darwinism and the rise of Social Darwinian doctrine of a struggle for existence among nations and races suggested that in a world red in tooth and claw there could be no national manifest destiny without strong military preparation.[24]

By 1897 a writer in the *Journal of the Military Service Institution* was basing his Uptonian expansible army arguments on the possibility of Social Darwinian wars of conquest, not simply on pleas for national defense. Lieutenant J. G. Harbord of the 6th Cavalry wrote:

Surely the United States is fated to some day overshadow and dominate all other states on this hemisphere. The instinct of conquest is in the Anglo-Saxon blood and long before our population is as dense and the ownership of arable land as difficult of attainment as in the best part of Europe to-day, our people will clamor for the extension of our borders, and the Latin-American with his indolence and improvidence will give way before the energetic and resourceful Anglo-Saxon American.[25]

Harbord was typical of professional officers when he went on to argue that such a destiny could be attained only through reliance on military professionals,[26] but he was not so typical in his confidence that a bright destiny could be attained. For despite its sharing in the mood of jingoism and expansionism of the 1890s, civilian America rushed toward the Spanish War with little thought for the army. Fortunately for the success of the coming campaigns, the modern steel navy continued to grow; but on the eve of war the regular army was still tiny and scattered along the coasts and across the West with no plan for mobilization. The national guards, however much improved over the old militia, still constituted about forty separate armies with their officers more often political than military in abilities.[27] A representative military writer commented bitterly as the Spanish War approached that "The most inconsistent feature of the speeches of the political agitator is the fact that while he would forever keep down the military, he is constantly endeavoring to foment international trouble by appealing to the prejudice of the masses by every means of jingoism." The evidence of the professional journals is that the professional soldiers were by no means in the forefront of the call for an aggressive policy toward Spain.[28]

The record of the army in the Spanish War justified much of
their pessimism. The want of a system of reserves meant that the
war had to be fought practically by regulars alone. Only one volunteer regiment (the famous 1st United States Volunteer Cavalry,
the "Rough Riders") and one national guard regiment volunteered
for federal service (the 71st New York) participated in the major
campaign of the war, the struggle for Santiago de Cuba. The national guard and volunteer regiments at their camp at Chickamauga
Park, Georgia, proved unready to cope with the elementary military problems of camp hygiene and sanitation, let alone a foreign
foe. Lacking a mobilization plan and a corps and divisional organization, the regular army could be gathered together and then transported to Cuba only with heartbreaking difficulty. Once in Cuba,
its lack of reserve strength meant that it was too small even to capture Santiago without running the most severe risks; after the
casualties of a few minor engagements, Las Guásimas, El Caney,
and San Juan Hill, the commander of the expeditionary force in
Cuba had to consider a withdrawal to recoup his losses. In the end
the army stumbled to victory less because of its own prowess than
because of the even greater disorganization and demoralization of
the enemy.[29]

The enlisted soldier of the regular army fought with all the skill
and toughness with which Uptonian writers had credited him, and
the Spanish War seemed to demonstrate that man for man and
company for company, the United States regular army was as good
as any in the world. Also, the army proved capable of profiting
quickly from experience, and the dispatch of its expeditionary
forces to Puerto Rico and the Philippines came off much more
smoothly than the earlier embarkation for Cuba. Even the volunteer regiments, including again national guards volunteered for
federal service, mastered the fundamentals of camp and campaign
service sufficiently well to perform creditably in Puerto Rico and
the Philippines. To combat the Filipino Insurrection, furthermore,
the government heeded the animadversions of Emory Upton and
his disciples against state troops and organized federal volunteers
under federally appointed officers, including regular officers. The
results partly confirmed Upton's predictions and partly contradicted
them. Federal control exercised through qualified officers made the

national volunteers a better force than the state regiments in a shorter time, as Upton had assured it would. However, under good officers the citizen soldiers of the national volunteers became valuable fighting men in a shorter time and with less training and experience than Upton's emphasis on regulars had implied was possible. Thus the Spanish War and the Filipino Insurrection brought heartening as well as discouraging developments.[30]

But the discouraging developments predominated. In its only full-scale campaign against a civilized power, the United States Army had performed abominably in every respect save the individual courage and prowess of the troops. The Spanish War seems to have deepened the pessimism of Upton's followers among the professional officer corps.

In the years immediately following the war the nation responded to evidence of military inadequacies and permitted the adoption of the famous army reforms of Secretary of War Elihu Root. Although Root was by no means an Uptonian in the professionalist sense—he believed, for example, that the national guard could become a useful reserve—he was impressed by Upton's indictments of American military weaknesses. Upton's *Military Policy* helped shape the Root reforms, and Root arranged for publication of Upton's manuscript in 1904.

As part of the Root reforms the three-battalion infantry regiment was at last achieved, though without the skeleton third battalion and thus without so much expansibility as Upton had desired. The Army War College was the sort of capstone to Sherman's school system that Upton had advocated. It assured continuous professional study of American military policy, and it brought to fruition the professional ideals of Sylvanus Thayer and Dennis Mahan by fostering the study of war and of military art and science with great concentration and penetration. It assured that the United States would not again go to war with so little strategic and logistical planning as it had in all the wars of the past. It contributed directly to the birth of another of the Root innovations, the American general staff. This instrument grew partly from Upton's recommendations, but it included with Upton's Germanic central planning and directing agency characteristics derived from other sources which retained the American principle of civilian control over the military. Finally, the Dick Bill of 1903 was a compromise between the champions of the state militia and those who wanted a federal reserve. It favored the states, but it did bring increased uniformity to the various state national guards by establishing minimum federal standards that must be met to receive federal financial aid.[31]

These reforms were accompanied by an increase of the peacetime standing army from 25,000 to about 65,000 men,[32] but even then they did not allay the pessimism of the disciples of Emory Upton. For if the Spanish War brought certain reforms and an enlargement of the United States Army, it also brought increased international responsibilities and dangers that made the reforms and enlargement seem inadequate to the professionals. Improved as the regular army was in organization and large as it was by previous American standards, it was still far from comparable to the armies of the great powers of Europe and Asia.

Yet the aftermath of the Spanish War, combined with the continuing outward thrust of other nations' imperialisms, threw the United States into direct competition with those powers. The United States more and more seemed to be in competition with Germany and Japan, the most formidable military powers of their respective regions of the globe. Plunging into the race for overseas territory and prestige almost simultaneously, Germany and the United States early found themselves in friction with each other. The problems included the Samoan dispute of the late 1880s, truculent relations between Admirals Dewey and von Diedrichs at Manila Bay, the heavyhanded political intervention of the German commissioner in Samoa to secure German supremacy there in 1899, Germany's condescension to the United States in her effort to secure a naval base in the Philippines, and the bumptious efforts of Germany to extend her power into the Caribbean in Theodore Roosevelt's day. Even before his presidency, Roosevelt believed the time would come when Germany "will make us either put up or shut up on the Monroe doctrine; they counting upon their ability to trounce us if we try the former horn of the dilemma." [33]

In view of Germany's European entanglements, Japan was more likely than Germany to pose a direct threat to American interests. Japan's victory over Russia in 1904–1905 left the United States, with its Open Door policy and its outpost in the Philippines, the principal obstacle to Japan's hegemony of eastern Asia and of the western Pacific. The new posture of American-Japanese relations thus created revealed itself in the war scare of 1907, and the American government began to receive alarming reports of unofficial Japanese expression of extreme ambitions and remarks from Europeans that Europe expected an American-Japanese war which Japan would win.[34]

A war against either Germany or Japan, rising out of threats to the Monroe Doctrine, the Philippines, or Hawaii, would enable the United States to rely on its formidable navy rather than on its weak army. But the officer corps of the army were uneasy at the thought of any war with Germany or Japan when the American army was so small that, as Roosevelt put it, "neither its recent decrease [a small reduction under Roosevelt] nor any possible increase would be large enough to be so much as considered even in England, not to speak of the military nations on the Continent or of Japan." [35] So the Uptonian mood of pessimism deepened, despite the Root reforms, in the first decade of the twentieth century.

What sort of contest with a European power or Japan did professional officers expect? Captain Alfred W. Bjornstad of the 28th Infantry expressed a representative opinion in his article "The Military Necessities of the United States and the Best Provisions for Meeting Them," the Military Service Institution gold medal essay for 1907. Proposing an Uptonian expansible army, Bjornstad acknowledged that invasion of the United States by a foreign army on a scale equal to that which threatened many European powers was extremely improbable. He considered it equally unlikely that the United States would find itself carrying out an invasion of Europe or Japan single-handed. Therefore he saw no need for the United States to match the enormous armies of Europe. But he did believe that colonial rivalries might involve the United States in a war with one of the great powers. Such a war, even if not bringing upon America the full weight of the enemy's military strength, would demand the rapid mobilization of a more substantial force than the United States could muster under its existing military system.

Bjornstad argued that the Manchurian campaign of the Russo-Japanese War indicated how much strength the great powers might commit to a war beyond their principal territories and thus how much enemy strength the United States might have to face. Russia and Japan had each thrown 250,000 well trained troops of their standing armies into the field, and each had eventually mobilized enough secondary troops to form armies of about a million men. At the time of Bjornstad's writing, the Japanese regular army had grown to 300,000—"immediately available . . . for use, let us say, in the Philippines, Alaska, Hawaii, and Panama." Germany, despite its growing interest in the Western hemisphere, could not afford to send too much of its force abroad, lest it excessively weaken its European position. But Bjornstad believed that the Germans would be able to dispatch to America half their regular army, a force of 290,000 excellent troops, enough to overbear several times the available American forces. He believed France could carry out a similar effort. England, he pointed out, had dispatched 400,000 men to South Africa and had maintained 250,000 there at one time. Like Japan against Russia, the European powers would eventually reinforce regulars sent to America with high quality reserves.

In view of these calculations, Bjornstad believed that the United States needed 250,000 first-class troops ready for immediate mobilization and a good second-line force of about 700,000 men.[36]

Bjornstad proposed to acquire such a force through enlargement of the standing army and through its reorganization along Uptonian expansible lines. His fellow professional officers offered a similar prescription. But the great difficulty of the Uptonian expansible army plan in the face of the mass armies of the twentieth century was the same great difficulty inherent in it from the first, now vastly aggravated: no likely enlargement of the American standing army would render it big enough to provide a skeleton for more than a moderately large wartime force; no likely enlargement of the American army would make it big enough to escape being engulfed and dissolved by the recruits of a wartime mass army, and unable to fix its influence upon them. Yet the Uptonians had no confidence in troops not molded to the approximate shape of regulars. Now that the United States might confront European or Japanese mass armies, they clearly foresaw the submergence of the regulars among hordes of recruits, and the Uptonians grew more pessimistic than ever.

Finding the necessary recruits now posed a problem: it seemed necessary to propose conscription.[37] When professionalist writers followed Upton himself to do so, they encroached on the rival amateur military tradition, for the idea of the nation in arms had been the original property of that tradition. But the concept of the nation in arms had acquired new connotations since Germany had demonstrated the possibility of turning it to professionalist purposes, keeping the professional soldiers in control and molding the conscripted citizen in the image of the regular. With the large American population numbers of soldiers could be found somehow; the principal concern of the military professionals was still for the quality of American wartime armies.

The melancholy volumes of Homer Lea revealed the shadow of the European and Japanese mass armies lengthening over America in the first decade of the twentieth century. Touched with sickness and phantasms, these books offered prophecies of danger so circumstantially presented and so truly rooted in the dark soil underlying the twentieth-century world that it was difficult to read them without shudders of fear. Homer Lea forecast for the United States dangers of invasion and worse.

Nurtured on romantic tales of Napoleon, burning with military ambition but imprisoned in a hunchbacked body, he was involved in the comic yet ominous revolutionary societies of Chinese students in his native California. He went on to play (probably) some mysterious role as military adviser to Sun Yat-sen. In the books he wrote Homer Lea fought the battles his body prevented him from fighting in fact. He discharged his venom against the American civilization which in its pride of material power and disdain of weakness had no use for misshapen men like him. He depicted tremendous battles of the future, requiring American armies mightier by far than even disgruntled army officers envisioned, and still carrying the country, unless American society underwent a heroic reform, to decline and fall.[38]

His books formed a trilogy. In *The Valor of Ignorance* (1909) he forecast the coming American war with Japan, a war virtually inevitable in a Pacific Ocean theater which made rich but militarily weak America the chief obstacle in the path of militant, aggressive, expansionist Japan. In *The Day of the Saxon* (1912) he elaborated on that theme, setting the American-Japanese war in its larger context as part of the general struggle of the rich and satisfied Anglo-Saxon powers to preserve themselves against the combined onslaughts of jealous Germany and Japan. Though the outcome of that struggle was doubtful, Lea saw that even an Anglo-Saxon victory would leave Great Britain and the United States tired and weakened in the face of a still greater threat than Germany and Japan had presented. Lea planned to depict the threat of an awakened and industrialized Russia in a third volume that he never finished, *The Swarming of the Slav*.[39]

Homer Lea's views were not those of the American officer corps, and his prophesying was a compound of resentment and a disordered, hyperactive imagination. Such a statement must now be made partly as irony, but it must be read in part also as the simple literal truth. On the one hand, Lea included in *The Valor of Ignorance* a description of the coming conquest of the Philippines by Japan that proved to be strikingly similar to what occurred in 1941–1942. On the other hand, Lea included also in *The Valor of Ignorance* a description of the coming Japanese conquest of the Pacific coast of the continental United States, a description which greatly overrated the power of even so militant a nation as Japan to mount and sustain an amphibious attack across the breadth of the Pacific Ocean.[40]

Lea based the latter section on a painstaking study of American topography west of the Sierra Nevada, and an invading army which could have reached the area might well have behaved much as he predicted. But the study rested on unrealistic assumptions.[41] Lea excessively underrated the military capacities of the United States. His romantic militarism convinced him that a business civilization such as America must be a decadent civilization, and his involvement in the modish Social Darwinism of his time led him to regard the decadence of a business civilization as the symptom of a more profound racial decadence of the Anglo-Saxons. Grown soft and complacent, Americans would not be able to fight the tough Japanese. American softness seemed all the more serious to Lea because he conceived of warfare in brute physical terms and failed to recognize the military value of American industrial power.[42]

Yet Homer Lea must not be dismissed because his imagination

was hyperactive and his resentments almost mad. His thinking was not so far from the main currents of American professional military thought as it might seem. His fear of the decadence of the Anglo-Saxon powers was akin to the racialism of army officers who poured their fears of the new immigration into the pages of the military journals.[43] It was no more fantastic than a *Journal of the Military Service Institution* article which advocated a more attractive uniform for the United States Army which would entice into the army more biologically desirable men and draw to them more biologically desirable women, who would produce children of superior fitness growing up respectful of military values.[44] Furthermore, Lea's castigations of the business civilization as destructive of the fighting qualities of the race found frequent echoes in the military service journals. For that matter this theme of Lea's was simply a statement in more extreme form of one of the favorite doctrines of Theodore Roosevelt.[45]

More to the point, Homer Lea's prophecies of foreign invasion did not seem so fantastic to contemporary military men as they do to a generation more familiar with the difficulties of conducting amphibious operations across great distances. His account of the Japanese invasion of the Pacific coast rested on the fact that American garrisons west of the Sierra Nevada were pitifully small and would continue to be so even if the whole regular army were dispatched there. Lea had an Uptonian opinion of unseasoned troops. Therefore he reasoned that a Japanese invasion force consisting of a handful of good divisions would have no trouble landing at unguarded harbors, establishing beachheads, cutting off San Francisco from aid from the mainland, and pushing inland to the Sierras. There they would have months or years to entrench themselves, while drawing to their own uses the resources of California, Oregon, and Washington. The United States mobilization of its military capacities for an assault across the Sierras would give the Japanese more than ample time to prepare themselves.[46]

Some professional officers found this picture of the Japanese conquest of the Pacific coast as persuasive as did Lea himself. The *Journal of the Military Service Institution,* for example, printed a translation of an Austrian staff officer's strikingly similar forecast of an American-Japanese war. The Austrian officer gave more serious and realistic attention than Lea to the problems Japan would face in opening and holding naval supply lines across the Pacific, but he believed that those problems could be solved and that Japan could go on to overrun the whole Pacific slope. Apparently the American soldiers who thought his views worth printing were inclined to agree.[47]

In this context Uptonian professional officers found little cause for cheer. Even an optimistic regular officer, who believed that with adequate preparation for regulars to train them good soldiers might be made of volunteers in time to avert national disaster, and that "Yankee pluck, luck, enterprise, or whatever you may call it" would eventually win out in any future war, expected unhappy events at the beginning of war:

Our immediately available first line [he said] probably will not exceed 75,000 men; a mere advance guard of the larger force that will be needed. At best, troops will be rushed to the front illy equipped for the serious task of war and with little or no instruction in the simplest duties of a soldier. Before a determined and aggressive enemy we will indeed be fortunate if such a war as we here have in mind does not open under a cloud of defeat and disaster which will hang over the country until experience under fire has made seasoned soldiers of some, and time has permitted us to make trained soldiers of others farther to the rear and away from the turmoil of the battle-field.[48]

In 1905 the Military Service Institution chose as the topic for its annual essay competition the question, "How Far Does Democracy Affect the Organization and Discipline of our Armies, and How Can its Influence be Most Effectually Utilized?" The first prize went to a paper by Lieutenant Colonel James S. Pettit of the 8th Infantry, a paper that found America's place in the twentieth-century world, seen in an Uptonian perspective, cause for a gloom deeper than Upton's own.

Pettit's essay was explicitly Uptonian. Much of it, in fact, was a summary of Upton's *Military Policy*, reciting the lugubrious tale of ineptitude which Upton had regarded as the history of American wars. Many of Upton's most pungent criticisms received direct quotation. The ghost of Upton rather than Colonel Pettit wrote much of the essay, because Pettit believed of *Military Policy* that "A careful reading of its pages will give a complete answer to the title of our essay."[49] He might better have said that for him Upton answered the first question of the title, "How Far Does Democracy Affect the Organization and Discipline of our Armies?"; Pettit found little to say about "How Can its Influence be Most Effectually Utilized?"

Pettit did advance suggestions along the latter line, Uptonian suggestions for an enlarged and expansible regular army with a first reserve of discharged veteran regulars. But his suggestions were not hopeful ones. Pettit saw no reason to expect that Congress would be willing to authorize a regular army which even expanded for war would muster more than 150,000 men, and he had no confidence in the militia reserves Congress was likely to offer as supplements.[50]

Serious questions are arising [he said], upon the solution of which our great experiment in self-government must stand or fall. After forty years of effort to substantiate our claim that all men must be equal in the pursuit of life, liberty and happiness, we are forced to admit that we have failed, and are now drifting on a turbulent ocean with no land in sight. Labor and capital are as much apart as ever, and the greed of corporations and trusts is concentrating the wealth of the country in the hands of a few. The socialist vote grew from 60,000 in 1900 to 600,000 in 1904. . . . We are also assuming the role of peacemaker and arbiter in the affairs of other nations, which lends material to those who preach the end of wars. We offer asylum to the wanderers of every nationality in the world. Some come to escape military service at home, and would probably add their influence and votes to the opposition. A great many of our people would oppose any substantial increase in our military organization. The masses are indifferent. Labor organizations are not friendly to the militia, and political parties cater to their wishes to obtain their votes. The Democratic party promised a reduction of the Regular Army in a plank of its platform. . . . The lessons taught by the Spanish-American War have almost if not entirely been forgotten.[51]

The conclusions Pettit culled from his Uptonian review of American military history deepened the bleakness of his outlook. Under the American system of government, the power to raise and support armies and to make rules for their conduct resided in Congress, and Pettit's opinion of that body was much like Upton's. They were a body of men of whom "few have given any thought to the military history of our country," a body of mediocre talents, an institution where finally "legislation for the army comes out of the hopper greased with the slimy oil of political spoils and party expediency unredeemed by the salt of honest, manly independence and belief as to the right and justice of the cause and needs of the country."

Under the American system the President was commander in chief of the army, but tradition had so much entangled his military powers with the dispensing of patronage and the service of politics that no President could escape. And a President strong enough to resist political calls on the military was likely to follow the unhappy example of Lincoln and assume actual command of the army, botching the job through his civilian ignorance as Lincoln had done.

The evils of the President's position were compounded by the characteristics of his deputy, the secretary of war. As history showed he was also likely to issue orders to armies in the field and to depart from his proper sphere of supplying the army with the men and equipment to wage war, leaving actual warfare to the generals. Disastrous in themselves, most of these deficiencies of the American federal government were repeated again on the state level, there to interfere with militia and volunteers and to be compounded by the divided controls which states' rights imposed on the army.[52]

Beyond the machinery of democratic government, Pettit observed, was the real "dominating power," public opinion. "It is the real government—presidents, senators, governors are its servants." But the public opinion of the American democracy offered little hope to the military. Immigration had aggravated its indifference or downright hostility to the army and had sapped its patriotism. Lax in the enforcement of all laws, it failed to enforce military laws, overriding the verdicts of military courts through executive clemency when it did not affect the courts-martial themselves, sheltering even deserters from military punishment.[53]

Lulled to sleep in fancied security, confident that our great wealth and numbers have made us unconquerable, our energies are devoted to trade and the arts of peace, and we have no time to devote to the consideration of possible disasters.[54]

A government with these characteristics cannot maintain an organization or discipline comparable to that of little Japan. We must recollect that war augments the political and social evils of the time. A government that is weak and lax in time of peace will not become more virtuous in war.[55]

Even little Japan put the United States to shame in military matters. As Pettit saw it:

It is a self-evident proposition that a democracy based on the will of millions of people, expressed through devious and changing channels, cannot be as skillful or efficient in the conduct of military affairs as a monarchy headed by a wise and powerful chief.

Monarchies had that unity of command essential to military strength. They could impose strict discipline, because heredity made their officers accustomed to command and their men accustomed to obey. Relatively free from popular pressures, monarchies could pursue fixed military policies without change; they escaped the inconsistencies of democracy. The kings were usually educated as soldiers; Clausewitz and Helmut von Moltke had tutored the rulers of Prussia. Monarchs knew that their countries and their own claims must ever be ready to stand the test of war, and therefore they prepared constantly for war. Their subjects naturally accepted conscription, so desirable but unattainable in the United States. A glance at the monarchies of the world made the relative military weakness of the United States yet more obvious:

National characteristics, which become governmental ones in a democracy like ours, make it impossible to organize and discipline an effective army from the point of view of military experts.[56]

Here was the nadir of Uptonian pessimism and the logical outcome of Uptonian thinking: as a democracy, the United States could not maintain an effective army. And Pettit was not alone in his conclusions. His essay received an annual prize of the Military Service Institution, and of the ten letters which the *Journal* of the Institution published to represent readers' responses, only two took direct issue with his strictures against democracy, and those two were not from full-fledged professionals. The professional officers who responded in print found little to criticize in Pettit's essay.[57] Captain Matthew F. Steele of the 6th Cavalry, a military scholar and historian, was even more blunt than Colonel Pettit:

Colonel Pettit remarks that "a careful reading of" General Upton's "Military Policy of the United States" will give a complete answer to the title of our essay." [*Sic.*] It, however, will only give the answer to the first half of the title; it will tell "how far does democracy affect the organization and discipline of our armies" but it will not answer "how can its influence be most effectually utilized?" Nor does Colonel Pettit's splendid paper answer this question. There is no answer.[58]

The *Army and Navy Journal* added:

We are ruled by an arbitrary and irresponsible popular opinion which, through a certain sublimated optimism which is at once benevolent and baleful, treats military service as inconsequential and renders it well-nigh impossible to maintain that rigorous discipline which is indispensable to an effective army.[59]

Upton had pointed the way to such conclusions by blaming the basic folly of civilian control of the military for all the various follies of American military policy. To Upton, the American system of government precluded a genuinely sound military system. When Upton's assumption that the American form of government could spawn only military ineptitude persisted into a period when the threat of war against efficient European armies seemed much greater than in Upton's day, despair for the military future of the United States was the only possible result.

Appropriate commentary on the sterility of Uptonian doctrine had been uttered before the writing of Upton's *Military Policy*. Major General John Pope, a professional officer but not a professionalist, speaking in 1873 to the Society of the Army of the Tennessee, had reflected with sorrow that as the Civil War drifted into the remote past, the bonds which had united the army and the people in common sympathy during the war were sure to dissolve:

Shall we especially of the Regular Army be willing to contemplate without sorrow the certainty that . . . the strong affection which unites us to so many comrades who have returned to civil life will also perish, and that the unhappy and well-nigh fatal divorce which for years had separated the Regular Army from the people and which required a great civil war to reconcile, shall again be pronounced upon our descendants?

Why was such a divorce between the regular army and the people unhappy and well-nigh fatal? Because, said Pope, the only sound military policy possible for the United States was one rooted in understanding between the army and the people, in which military policy took shape from the nation at large. Any attempt by the army to imitate foreign military systems would fail; the military policy of the American army must be an American policy.

The well-being of the people equally with the well-being of the Army requires a common sympathy and a common interest between them. . . .

If bad military organization, the feeble imitation of foreign systems, and worse customs of service drawn from the same sources, have made the private soldier in peace less or other than this [that he should be], to you comrades who have returned to civil life must be committed the task of giving us an army organization in harmony with our free institutions and with the feelings and habits of our people. Ours will be the duty to conform our customs of service to such an organization. . . .

So long as the soldier remains one of the people; so long as he shares their interests, takes part in their progress, and feels a common sympathy with them in their hopes and aspirations, so long will the Army be held in honorable esteem and regard, and so long will the close ties which now bind together the soldier and the citizen be perpetuated among us. When he ceases to do this; when officers and soldiers cease to be citizens in the highest and truest sense, the Army will deserve to lose, as it will surely lose, its place in the affections of the people, and properly and naturally become an object of suspicion and dislike.[60]

The warning had been given, but Emory Upton and his disciples had not heeded it.

X JOHN M. SCHOFIELD *An American Plan of Command*

Nothing is more absolutely indispensable to a good soldier than
perfect subordination and zealous service to him whom the national
will may have made the official superior for the time being. JOHN
M. SCHOFIELD

THE Uptonian conclusions of Colonel Pettit were intolerable. With
them not even the most thoroughgoing professionalists could rest,
for to do so was to admit that the American military situation was
hopeless and an American military career futile. For the nation
and the officer corps alike, an escape had to be found.

The first ingredient in an escape from Uptonian despair would
have to be a reconciliation between the professionalists and the
American system of government. Believing civilian control of military policy the underlying cause of all American military difficulties,
Upton had urged that the military powers of the secretary of war
and by implication even of the President be constricted to the narrowest limits and that the professional commanding general of the
army, assisted by a professional military staff, become the real
source of military policy. But civilian America simply could not
accept such a plan, and if despair were to be overcome, the army
must come to terms with the constitutional position of the secretary of war and the President.

A way had been suggested by a professional officer as early as
Upton's own era, and at the very time when Pettit wrote his
lugubrious essay, the Root reforms were following it. Among the
readers of Upton's manuscript before its publication had been
Major General John M. Schofield, who was engaged in thought
about the American structure of military command. Schofield had
a special reason to be interested in the command problem, for he
had a unique opportunity to view it from both the military and the

civilian sides. He was a professional soldier, a West Point graduate of the class of 1853 and in the Civil War the commander of the Army of the Ohio in the campaign from Chattanooga to Atlanta. In the winter of 1864 he had fought the battle of Franklin to help break the force of John Bell Hood's invasion of Tennessee. During the postwar years he served as superintendent of the United States Military Academy as well as commander of the Military Division of the Pacific and the Military Division of the Atlantic. Before the century was over he rose to a lieutenant generalcy and, from 1888 to 1894, occupied the post of commanding general, the post to which Upton wished to give so much power.

But Schofield was not only a professional soldier. For a time before the war he had been a college professor, scholarly and scientific inclinations having carried him out of the army to a chair of natural philosophy at Washington University in St. Louis. Even his Civil War service had been almost as political as military, for as commander of the District of St. Louis of the Department of Missouri, and then of the Department of the Ohio, he had had to thread his way through the maze of border-state politics in Missouri and Kentucky. He had lost his way sometimes, and quarrels with Missouri civilians had compelled his removal from St. Louis. But the experience had been broadening. Most important, after the war Schofield had served as secretary of war, a compromise holder of the office in the final months of President Andrew Johnson's administration, after Edwin M. Stanton had resigned. His ability to win acceptance as war secretary in troubled 1868 testified to his capacity to link military and civilian viewpoints, to get along with politicians and with soldiers.[1]

Balding, round-bodied John Schofield drew from this background a more complex attitude than Upton's toward the problem of the command of the army. He recognized the obvious dangers in civilian control of military policy if that control would not allow itself to be tempered by professional advice; but he recognized as Upton did not the dangers to constitutional government and to sound national policy in a plan which would have reduced the President as commander in chief and the secretary of war to ciphers.

The command of the United States Army had posed a vexed question almost since the establishment of the War Department under the Constitution; Emory Upton was not alone in finding fault with the nineteenth-century system. Viewed broadly, the issue was one of civilian versus military control of military policy; viewed narrowly, the issue was that of delimiting the spheres of the secretary of war and the commanding general of the army.

Under the Constitution, the President was the commander in chief of the army and navy. Since the President usually did not find it possible to exercise his authority as commander in chief in person, however, on August 7, 1789, Congress established a Department of War and the office of secretary of war, through which the President might wield his authority. The secretary of war was the President's customary instrument of communication with the army and, more than that, the President's representative at the head of the army. When speaking for the President he embodied the constitutional power of the President; the secretary of war was in practice the day-to-day commander of the army. As the United States Supreme Court had put it:

The Secretary of War is the regularly constituted organ of the President for the administration of the Military Establishment, and rules and orders publicly promulgated through him must be received as the acts of the Executive, and as such must be binding upon all within the sphere of his legal and constitutional authority.[2]

So much was clear. But both the President and the secretary of war were civilians, and therefore it was desirable that they should exercise their command of the army through professional military men. In 1821, Congress created the office of general in chief of the army (later to be known as the office of commanding general). Much of the shaping of the office took place after 1841, when it fell to its most eminent early occupant, Winfield Scott. Unfortunately, Scott's eminence and formidable character revealed the implicit deformities of the office.

For the office of general in chief proved to be an anomaly. Winfield Scott not unreasonably interpreted the law of 1821 and subsequent appropriation acts as making him the commanding officer of the army. But if under the Constitution the secretary of war commanded the army on behalf of the President, what constitutional place was there for the general in chief? If the general in chief truly commanded the army, he violated the constitutional prerogatives of the secretary of war. If the secretary of war truly commanded the army, the general in chief became a cipher, his office honorific.[3]

For example, in 1846 General Scott discovered that Secretary of War William R. Marcy had secured from Congress authorization for two new major generals and four brigadiers in the regular establishment, without consulting the supposed professional commander of the army. When Jefferson Davis became secretary of war under President Franklin Pierce, he refused to allow Scott to travel from place to place with government compensation unless the general made the trips on written orders from the secretary of war. He further questioned Scott's action in granting a leave of absence to an army officer without consulting the secretary. The tendency of such incidents was to nullify the office of general in chief. The response of Scott's imperious temperament was to pen several of his famous letters of protest with their spectacularly inept phrases (his "fire upon my rear" letter emerged from Marcy's additions to the officer corps) and then to remove his headquarters to New York rather than associate closely with Jefferson Davis. The effect of the latter move was virtually to abdicate command of the army to the secretary of war.[4]

The post-Civil War period brought little improvement in the command problem. During the last year of the war the prestige of General Grant and the exigencies of the Union cause led the Lincoln administration to give Grant a unique freedom from War Department interference. Grant's prestige along with the politically inspired Command of the Army Act continued to uphold the prerogatives of the commanding general during Grant's brief tenure in the office after the war. But Grant's successors, Sherman and Sheridan, found themselves repeating the same role that Winfield Scott had played. Like Scott, Sherman grew so disgusted with his helplessness in relation to the secretary of war that he moved his headquarters away from Washington to distant St. Louis, where he was close to the troops on the frontier. Sheridan with characteristic impetuousness sought a showdown to vindicate his authority almost as soon as he became commanding general, but the showdown went against him, and he served in irritated frustration.[5]

The focus of the command problem through the Sherman and

Sheridan periods, and as Upton and Schofield saw it, was the relationship of the staff departments in Washington to the commanding general and the line of the army. The chiefs of the staff departments (that is, the adjutant general, inspector general, judge advocate general, quartermaster general, commissary general of subsistence, surgeon general, paymaster general, chief of ordnance, chief of engineers, chief signal officer) regarded themselves as subject not to the orders of the commanding general but directly to those of the secretary of war. Not only did the Constitution suggest this arrangement, but so did the regulations of the army, which read:

187. The command exercised by the commanding general of the Army, not having been made the subject of statutory regulation, is determined by the order of assignment. It has been habitually composed of the aggregate of the several territorial commands that have been or may be created by the President.

The military establishment is under orders of the commanding general of the Army in that which pertains to its discipline and military control. The fiscal affairs of the Army are conducted by the Secretary of War through the several staff departments.

188. All orders and instructions from the President or Secretary of War relating to military operations or affecting the military control and discipline of the Army will be promulgated through the commanding general.[6]

Since the domain of the commanding general was defined as "habitually composed of the several territorial commands," the staff departments were not included. Fiscal affairs of the army were to be conducted by the secretary of war through the staff departments. The result of these provisions was that the staff departments came to be independent of the commanding general; as Sherman put it, "we . . . have the absurdity of a General commanding the army with his chief staff officers reporting to somebody else."[7] Furthermore, if the commanding general did not command the staff departments, he did not fully control the operations of the troops of the line. The staff officers could choose supplies and means of transportation and send them to the troops regardless of the opinions of the commanding general. They could divert supplies and transportation from one area to another in similar disregard of the desires of the chief line officer. They could send their own orders to officers of the staff departments in the field without the knowledge of the commanding general or the commander of the geographical division involved, perhaps in direct contradiction of the orders of the latter officers.[8]

The result of these arrangements, as Schofield observed, was a chaotic multiple command of the army:

Thus the orders of the general commanding the army may be practically annulled at any moment by orders to his staff officers respecting the transportation or supplies, or even the personnel of his command, coming to them from their staff superiors in Washington, and without the knowledge of any military commander.[9]

The worst results of the situation could be averted by the good will and common sense of the officers involved; but the independence of the staff departments from the commanding general and the larger problem of the anomalous relationship between the commanding general and the secretary of war were potentially disruptive of the most critical operations of the army even in time of war. Under this system, the commanding general of the army was likely to find his experience and abilities largely wasted, his office merely a dignified retreat offered him as a reward for earlier outstanding service. The secretary of war was likely to discover that friction between him and the commanding general prevented his availing himself fully of the professional advice of the first soldier of the land. The system played directly into the hands of such a professionalist as Emory Upton who sought to indict the whole principle of civilian control.

If the United States Army were to become an adequate instrument of national policy, it was necessary to resolve the problems of the high command. It was imperative to end the ambivalence of the relationship between commanding general and secretary of war and to utilize fully the military talents of the senior professional soldier. But did these ends demand the acceptance of Emory Upton's prescriptions for destroying the constitutional authority of the civilian commander in chief and secretary of war and resigning American military policy to the professionals? Here was a central issue in the controversy between the Uptonian professionalists and their adversaries.

Virtually every professional soldier from Winfield Scott onward had believed that the only way to resolve the issue was for the civilian authorities to yield military policy to the military. Here was still another pernicious fruit of the divorcement which the professional army had allowed between itself and civilian America. Isolated from the civilians and contemptuous of them as soldiers, the professional officer corps was not inclined to accept the highest military direction from citizens who impressed them as military incompetents. Scott, McClellan (whose contempt for the military judgments of President Lincoln was blatantly unconcealed), Grant (until he became President himself), Sherman, and Sheridan—all these generals in chief had sought an Uptonian solution of the command problem. All had contributed to a conviction among American professional soldiers that military policy must be left to military men alone. The officer corps had lost sight of the Clausewitzian dictum that war is but an extension of politics by other means. There had grown in the American officer corps a reluctance to concede that in war military judgments cannot be exclusively military, that they must be shaped by political purposes, and that they must ultimately be decided on by the civilian political leaders of the state.

John M. Schofield, however, had been secretary of war before he was commanding general. He was not simply a professional soldier, and he dedicated the principal efforts of his later military career to resolving the command problem in a manner that would contribute to sound military policy but would also accord with the basically political nature of war and with the requirements of the United States Constitution. He devoted much of his memoirs, published in 1897, to examining the problem rather than to recalling and justifying his war activities.[10] He could not destroy the propensity of the officer corps to underestimate the political implications of military policy and to believe that military matters must be left to the military professionals; that tendency would persist well into the twentieth century. But he did much to give the American army an effective system of command.

Unlike his predecessors Schofield believed that the command problem must be resolved in favor of the secretary of war, albeit in some way that would assure the usefulness of the army's leading professional soldier. Civilian supremacy must be assured because in a democracy only the responsible representatives of the people could determine the purposes of a war, and such determination was involved in the way the war was to be fought. Differing choices of military means could alter the scope and the nature and intent of a war, and therefore the ultimate choice even of military means must reside with the civilians.

When Schofield wrote, military thought in Europe was enamored of Clausewitz's other dictum, that "to introduce into the philosophy of War itself a principle of moderation would be an absurdity. . . . War is an act of violence pushed to its utmost bounds." [11] In the United States Clausewitz was little read (there were few references to him, for example, in the military journals), and there was no American edition of *On War*. But Sherman's methods of war suggested the same absolutist principle as this quotation from Clausewitz, and Emory Upton's call for the subordination of civilian to military policy in war harmonized with this aspect of Clausewitz's thought (though not with the whole of it). Schofield was against this trend to an absolutist conception of war. He did not believe that to introduce moderation into war was absurd, either in philosophy or in practice. He believed that wars could differ in purpose and thus in the methods they employed. He believed that limited wars had their place.

Military action may have as its object, said Schofield, the destruction or capture of the enemy's armies and the complete elimination of his power. Such is the case when the purpose of waging war is to suppress a rebellion, as in the Civil War, or to secure the total conquest of a foreign country. On the other hand, the purpose may be less than total conquest, whereupon the "all-sufficient, and hence best" strategy is simply that of "defeating in battle or outmaneuvering the defending armies" without seeking their utter destruction. In the Civil War the worst strategy was that which aimed simply at the occupation of territories, since the purposes of the North could be achieved only through complete destruction of the fighting power of the Confederacy. But not all wars aim at the total conquest of the enemy, and a territorial strategy may sometimes be appropriate. [12]

In the philosophic terms of Clausewitz, Schofield rejected an absolutist view of war because such a view generated wars fought

by passion rather than by reason. Rejection of a principle of moderation gave free rein to the indiscriminate destructiveness of warlike
passion, but wisdom called for the application of reason to defining
the purpose of any war and the consequent adjustment of methods
to the reasonable purpose. In contrast to those Darwinian contemporaries who regarded war as a stimulus to the vitality of a
nation, Schofield believed that the Civil War proved the regres-
sive consequences of war, "that this country had, in accordance
with a general law, suffered permanent national injury, irreparable
in all future time, by the Civil War." This unfortunate consequence
was more pronounced because the war had been shaped by passion:

> It would seem that the official correspondence of that period ought to
> be a sufficient warning to deter any future generation from bringing
> the country into a condition where even some of the most distinguished
> citizens, statesmen, and soldiers seem to be governed more by passion
> than by reason in the conduct of public affairs.[13]

The scope and purpose of a war did not follow from the workings
of a natural law but were the appropriate objects of choice. And
the choice between limited war and total war must be in the
United States the prerogative of the civilian government, not because civilian decision ensured the predominance of reason over
passion but because the question was of national policy and in a
democracy belonged to the elected representatives of the people.
Not only did the Constitution so decree, so did sound policy, since
the expertness of professional soldiers was specialized and did not
extend to the determination of national policy and national purposes. Since different means and methods of fighting, furthermore,
tended to remake purposes in their own image, civilian control of
military policy demanded civilian control over military means and
methods.

Schofield rejected the Uptonian call for civilian subordination to
the military in all military affairs, for there could be few strictly
military questions. The American soldier, thought Schofield, ought
to adopt as his motto, "the President's policy is my policy; his orders
my rule of action." "When the people have chosen their chief to
lead them through the fierce storms of civil war," he wrote, "he
alone must guide the ship, or else all must perish." The same rule

held for foreign wars: "Nothing is more absolutely indispensable to a good soldier than perfect subordination and zealous service to him whom the national will may have made the official superior for the time being." [14]

If civilian control of military policy was essential to safeguard the larger national policy, Schofield knew that professional knowledge and skill were equally essential to the proper conduct of war. Indeed, he knew it better than Emory Upton did, for more than Upton he was aware that technology would make military science esoteric and complex.

Science [he said] has wrought no greater revolution in any of the arts of peace than it has in the art of war. Indeed, the vast national interests involved all over the world have employed the greatest efforts of genius in developing the most powerful means of attack and defense. [15]

The valor of great masses of men, and even the genius of great commanders in the field, have been compelled to yield the first place in importance to the scientific skill and wisdom in finance which are able and willing to prepare in advance the most powerful engines of war. [16]

Some means must therefore be discovered to couple technical military proficiency with civilian control of policy. During Schofield's brief tenure as secretary of war he had been able to avoid a collision with the command problem because the commanding general was busy campaigning and preparing for the presidency, and abdicated his prerogatives to the secretary. [17] Perhaps this situation put Schofield on the road to his ultimate solution. During Grant's presidency, Schofield was assigned to give specific study to the command question, but nothing came of his recommendations, and he himself did not long remain satisfied with them. But by the time he was commanding general, in 1888, he had hit upon the scheme he advocated the rest of his life. [18]

As commanding general, Schofield began by abandoning the pretensions for which Scott, Sherman, and Sheridan had fought so hard. He informed the adjutant general that no orders were to be issued by or in the name of the commanding general without the knowledge of the secretary of war. [19] This abdication transformed the constitutionally anomalous and unworkable office of commanding general; Schofield made himself in fact, though not in name, the chief of staff to the secretary of war and the President:

Upon my assignment to the "command of the army" in 1888, I determined to profit so far as possible by the unsatisfactory experience of Generals Scott, Grant, Sherman, and Sheridan. . . . In fact, long study of the subject, at the instance of Generals Grant and Sherman, earnest efforts to champion their views, and knowledge of the causes of their failure, had led me to the conclusion . . . that under the government of the United States an actual military commander of the army is not possible . . . ; and that the general-in-chief, or nominal commanding general, can be at most only a "chief of staff"—that or nothing,—whatever may be the mere title under which he may be assigned to duty by the President.[20]

Schofield was sure that here was the only constitutional solution to the command problem. He was surprised that his plan had not been advocated widely before, since it was derived from the practice of European states. "It is only in this country," Schofield remarked, "where the chief of state has generally no military training, and his war minister the same, that a chief of staff of the army is supposed to be unnecessary." [21]

The chief of staff plan was the constitutional plan, and it ought to prove satisfactory in practice. The relations between the President and his chief military adviser should be close and confidential; mutual trust is essential. Under the chief of staff system the President might appoint the officer he trusted most to the principal professional position in the army, without the old obligation to appoint the senior general to the nominal leadership.

Not by any means the least benefit would be the education thus given to officers of the army in respect to the relation in which they stand to the commander-in-chief, and in respect to the reasonable limits of military ambition in a republic where the President is and must be commander-in-chief.

Conferring with his chief of staff, the President ought to adopt the plans agreed upon in consultation as his own. Thus the President could actually exercise the chief command imposed upon him by the Constitution. The army would enjoy the advantages of trained leadership, yet civilian control of the military would be a reality.[22]

During his tenure of command, from 1888 to 1895, Schofield found the results of his experiment gratifying.

Perfect harmony was established between the War Department and the headquarters of the army, and this continued, under the administrations of Secretaries Proctor, Elkins, and Lamont, up to the time of my retirement from active service.

The President acted on matters important enough to demand his attention, and the orders issued were actually his. There was no ground on which to challenge the constitutional authority of directives sent to the army in the President's name by the commanding general.[23]

When he retired from active service, Schofield turned to campaigning for permanent acceptance of the chief of staff system, regarding it as the first step to an integrated general staff. He made his memoirs a sounding board for the plan, and with the army's mistakes and inefficiency in the Spanish War he spoke forth with renewed vigor. When Congress established a war investigating committee to seek the causes of American military shortcomings against Spain, Schofield was called upon to testify. He reiterated his belief that the commanding general must give way to a chief of staff, and he argued that the war experiences confirmed his view. So cogently did he state his case that the committee endorsed his views in its final report, stimulating interest by carrying the Schofield plan to a nation worriedly reexamining its military policy.[24]

The chief of staff plan was much discussed because of Schofield's efforts and because of European examples, when the Spanish War and the new responsibilities of the army touched off a movement for reform of the command system. Secretary Elihu Root came to the War Department determined to adjust the army to at least some of its twentieth-century responsibilities. The alert younger officers at his side stressed the necessity for a general staff system including the abolition of the office of commanding general, with the chief of the general staff to be military adviser to the secretary of war and the President. Emory Upton too had urged a general staff system, but the new suggestions followed Schofield rather than Upton in their provision for the clear acceptance of civilian control of the military. In 1901 Secretary Root's annual report to Congress called for a general staff on the plan suggested by Root's younger military advisers, and early in 1902 the War Department submitted to Congress a bill to move towards a general staff through consolidation of several of the existing independent staff departments.[25]

But the long effort to make the professional commanding general the center of military policy was still a strong influence in the professional officer corps. Root's proposals received little enthusiasm among the active senior officers and were directly opposed by the commanding general, Lieutenant General Nelson A. Miles. When the Senate Military Affairs Committee called for Miles's testimony on the proposals, the general treated them to an uncompromising castigation of staff department consolidation and the general staff system. He implied that the Root plans were un-American, warned against a dictatorship over the army by the civilian secretary of war, and uttered an emotional appeal to Civil War veterans not to discard the methods which had won such glorious victories in the past.

Root's reply to Miles's attack was to bring before the Senate committee and its Civil War veterans an old chieftain with a more distinguished record than Miles's. On April 9, 1902, Lieutenant General John M. Schofield, ponderously impressive in white muttonchop whiskers and his brass and blue, testified in favor of the general staff system. He reviewed his long study of the command question, and he urged again that the substitution of a chief of staff to the secretary of war for the commanding general would solve questions military and constitutional. Lieutenant Colonel William H. Carter, Schofield's escort from the circle of Root's advisers, rejoiced that Schofield based his testimony "on knowledge of facts and conditions, and not at all on sentiment," as Miles had done. By all accounts, Schofield's impact more than outweighed Miles's. *Harper's Weekly* said that Schofield's opinions made Miles's seem more than ever unreasonable and factious, and the press in general rallied to Root's support.[26]

In the end the Root reforms were achieved. The creation of the Army War College in 1901 completed the army's postgraduate school system and also created an agency for the study of American military problems which could serve part of the function of a general staff until such a staff was appointed. In 1903 the Dick Bill for the improvement of the National Guard won passage. The retirement of General Miles, the pressure of Root and the Roosevelt administration, and the advice of Major General Wesley Merritt and of Schofield opened the way to congressional acceptance of the general staff plan.[27]

As Emory Upton and his followers had long urged, the United States created a professional agency for strategic and logistical planning comparable to the general staff of Germany. The general staff by no means solved all high command problems immediately. Knowledge of the functions of a general staff was so slight among American officers that the new organization suffered through considerable floundering for purpose before it gained assurance and competence as the instrument of specialists in planning and organization. Furthermore, the issue of the independence of the old special staff departments remained not fully resolved. The administrative authority of the adjutant general and his role in the issuance of orders enabled him to rival the chief of the general staff in influence until Major General Leonard Wood broke the claims of the adjutant general under President William Howard Taft. Even then the worsted adjutant general conspired with congressmen fearful that the general staff corps would become a dangerous military elite to bring about a near wrecking of the staff in the National Defense Act of 1916.

But the general staff gradually overcame doubts. It demonstrated success in anticipating military tasks and readying the army to participate in them. It urged preparation to intervene in Mexico, for example, well before intervention occurred. It helped secure additional army reforms, such as the first peacetime divisional organization and maneuvers in 1912. World War I sealed the staff's permanence and ascendancy. The planning and preparation for war which the general staff had accomplished proved indispensable to United States military success. Conversely, the handicaps of the general staff brought about a near collapse of American military command. Congress heeded the lesson and authorized a wartime revitalization of the general staff which brought about improvement so manifest that the general staff was never again seriously challenged.[28]

The American general staff system was a fruition of Emory Upton's proposals and of military admiration for Germany. Upton's *Military Policy* manuscript, published under Root's auspices, helped to shape it. But the Root system combined the German and Uptonian plan of a central brain for the army with Schofield's resolution in favor of the civilian authority of the American command problem between secretary of war and commanding general. When the general staff functioned well, it demonstrated to the officer corps that effective command could be reconciled with constitutional democracy and civilian responsibility, Emory Upton notwithstanding. The Root general staff plan became a military success despite its rejection of the idea of Scott, Sherman, and Sheridan that the chief professional officer of the army must command.

The success of the Root general staff system in the first two decades of the twentieth century mitigated a source of Uptonian despair. It demonstrated the error of Upton and those of his followers who believed that the United States Army could compete with the great powers of Europe only by escaping civilian control. When the secretary of war won his long contest for authority against the commanding general of the army, the army proved the chief beneficiary. In the command question at least, the Root reforms demonstrated that there was no inevitable incompatibility between a good army and the American order of society.

XI   R. M. JOHNSTON *The Search for an*
Escape from Uptonian Despair

War as an art reaches its apogee in modern times, with the eighteenth century.

The highest trained army is the best. R. M. JOHNSTON

UPTONIAN conclusions had become intolerable by the first decade of the twentieth century, proclaiming as they did the unfitness of the United States for major war. The Schofield-Root demonstration that despite Upton's animadversions civilian control of military policy did not foreordain military ineffectuality countered only one aspect of Uptonian despair. There remained the question of how the United States could put an army matching the combination of skill and numbers that distinguished the mighty armies of Europe into the field.

Even with the new responsibilities of the United States as a great power, the people and Congress had no inclination to raise the regular army to a numerical strength adequate by Uptonian standards to new demands likely to be made on it. Even with the new American responsibilities, the people and Congress showed no inclination to make the existing regular army a genuinely expansible army. What the Uptonians desired for the United States was an army on the German model. In Wilhelm II's empire, professionals and long-term conscripts sustained a military force of almost 600,000 men in peacetime, forming cadres capable of prompt expansion to a total first-line military strength of 2,000,000 men, by the addition of thoroughly trained reservists. Second-line reservists brought the total trained military strength of the empire to 3,800,000 men.[1] Against such a force, or even a fraction of it, the Uptonians believed, the American regular army would be dissolved by sheer numbers. An American emergency army of volunteers and National Guards would be slaughtered by superior military skill. Uptonian pessimism continued to deepen.

If that pessimism were to be overcome, either of the two assumptions on which it rested had to be rejected. It had to be concluded that the United States could get along without a huge army of the European type, relying on the skill of American regulars rather than on numbers, or it had to be concluded that American citizens could become soldiers capable of meeting Europeans, without the long and professional training of European conscripts. The European armies rested upon large numbers and extensive military training; the United States had to get along without one or the other. American military policy as Uptonians saw it offered a dilemma of which either horn was likely to lead to national disaster. But the sterile despair of a Colonel Pettit could not be borne. The early twentieth century witnessed efforts to escape despair by attempting to prove that these were not horns of a dilemma but pointers to a sound military policy.

Emory Upton's strictures against citizen soldiers placed so low a value on them that the inclination of the professionalist attempting to escape pessimism was to convince himself that he might yet construct a military policy requiring a minimum number of citizen soldiers and placing its principal reliance on the regular army. To construct such a policy and to make it plausible before the mass European armies would require a *tour de force*, but so great was the professionalist reluctance to call on citizen soldiers that the *tour de force* was attempted. Professor Robert Matteson Johnston of Harvard University, the first American professional historian of the "scientific" school to devote himself primarily to military history, and a man of prestige in military circles because of his combination of scholarship with military interest, set out to demonstrate that the United States did not need a mass army. He argued that a relatively small force such as Upton's expansible army could serve American requirements.

Johnston was lecturer at Elihu Root's Army War College and professor of modern history at Harvard, and he was a prolific author of biographies of military leaders, histories of campaigns and of outstanding military epochs, and studies of the art of war. Though he wished to apply the canons of Rankian scholarship to military history, he was unable to escape a deep involvement in what he wrote, betraying it in passages illuminated by feeling: "Marlborough at Blenheim, Frederick at Leuthen, Napoleon at Austerlitz, tasted in their [sic] extreme form the joy which primitive man feels in combat but combat transformed into its most polished possibilities." [2] The emotional involvement contributed to an acute concern for the military policy of the United States. These two forces made R. M. Johnston more and less than a historical scholar; he became also a propagandist for his version of American preparedness.[3]

Johnston's proposed escape from the Uptonian dilemma began with his contention that the mass army was a clumsy and overrated instrument, even in the German version which Upton had admired. The best army, Johnston emphasized, was a small but highly skillful professional army.

Johnston's argument was from history. His *Arms and the Race* (1915) was a pioneer work in American historical writing in its examination of the changes brought to warfare by the era of the French Revolution and Napoleon and of the continuing implications of those changes. Johnston was among the first American writers to observe and report explicitly the differences between the ritualistic wars fought by standing armies for dynastic purposes in the eighteenth century and the all-consuming wars which began with the French Revolution. He wrote when European military writers were inclined to sneer at the warfare of the eighteenth century. The vogue of Clausewitz following the triumphs of his German disciples made eighteenth-century military moderation unfashionable in the light of Clausewitz's dictum that to apply to the philosophy of war a principle of moderation is absurd. But Johnston remained in the American professionalist tradition where Clausewitz had yet to become a major prophet, and he was skeptical of Clausewitz's dicta. He was not convinced that moderation in war is absurd, especially when the abandonment of moderation meant the levying of mass and necessarily unskilled armies.

Johnston's *Arms and the Race* emphasized that the mass armies of the French Revolution, for all their triumphs, had continued inferior in battle to the disciplined ranks of eighteenth-century soldiers, given anything near equal battlefield terms. For all their defects, the eighteenth-century standing armies had been superb instruments of war. Indeed, "War as an art reaches its apogee in modern times, with the eighteenth century."

The eighteenth-century army, as an instrument in the hands of its general, may be compared to the eighteenth-century orchestra. Starting on a basis of string instruments, the woods were gradually developed from the time of Montaverde to Mozart, while with Beethoven, at the close of the century, the brass comes into its own, and the three great parts of the orchestra, amply developed, give the composer ample means for employing the resources of his art. A somewhat similar evolution took place with the three great arms of the modern army: infantry, cavalry, artillery.

Frederick the Great brought the infantry to a point it has not since surpassed. It could maintain tactical cohesion under a terrific fire, on the widest front, and in complicated formations. No infantry ever equalled it in its power of forcing a decision of the combat by manœuvring against a given point and under the most violent conditions.[4]

Just when the art of war thus reached "its most polished possibilities," the French Revolution intervened to make the soldier a citizen, which was as it should be, but which destroyed the disciplinary foundation of the eighteenth-century army. At the same time the *levée en masse* flooded military camps with soldiers so numerous that they could not have been trained in the old thorough manner anyway. The armies of the French Revolution grew immensely larger than those of the old regime, but they became qualitatively inferior.

The French Republic was able to win victories despite the inferiority of its soldiers thanks to four principal assets: its superb artillery, which combined the old professionalism with the new guns and tactics of Gribeauval and du Teil; its superb leadership, which drew on the eighteenth-century heritage to create a new art of war in strategy and tactics; the social revolution, which gave the army a fine élan and enabled genius and talent to come forward from all ranks; and the sheer weight of numbers. The abilities of the French commanders, especially Bonaparte, combined with a concentration on rapid marching and an ability to live off the country to give the French army a strategic advantage offsetting its tactical inferiority to professional armies. In short, inspired strategy and rapid marching went far to assure France a victorious battle before the battle was fought.

The artillery gave further assurance. As for the infantry, strategy sought to save it from having to face its foe on level ground. Then, if battle were joined on fairly broken ground, new tactics not employing the infantry in the traditional deployment on a wide front but as skirmishers and in small columns, might drive home the victory already prepared: "A column of a half battalion was one of the easiest formations to teach a raw soldier; easiest in which to retain tactical control or cohesion; easiest in which to manœuver with rapidity from one position to another." This formation also took fullest advantage of the implications of the social revolution:

In this sort of formation, it was the head of the column that counted for everything. A dozen officers and non-commissioned officers and a dozen brave soldiers in the lead might carry along several hundred skulkers and cowards in a dash on the enemy. Now the Revolution had ordained that its armies should be made up of a large undisciplined mass, inclined therefore to skulk, and of a small proportion of men before whom it had set the greatest of human prizes. The private soldier might rise to the highest command; and he did. A sub-lieutenant of artillery became an emperor; a private dragoon became a king and so did a simple grenadier; several private soldiers became Marshals of France. These were the men who carried the tricolor at the heads of the charging columns, and gave the French armies, notwithstanding the skulkers, their irresistible quality. It was the fanaticism of the social revolution.[5]

Johnston emphasized that inspired strategy, excellent artillery, and the zeal of the social revolution were heroic expedients necessary to redeem the defects of what was, in eighteenth-century terms, a not very good army. Even these expedients required the assistance of numbers; the armies of the French Republic "generally outnumbered their opponents, and it was as well, for they sometimes required a preponderance of two to one to succeed." Therefore the French Revolution produced the levée en masse, calling every citizen to the frontier to defend it against the assembled armies of the kings. The ordinary citizen took the place of the professional soldier.[6]

The disciples of Clausewitz hailed this development as logical and therefore intelligent. If to place limitations on the theory of warfare was absurd, certainly to confine warfare to a handful of professionals was absurd. But Johnston believed the mass army was a curse, not a blessing. Militarily it could not match a professional army except through desperate expedients; from every other point of view it was a blow against civilization. Johnston suspected that this latter was true even before the First World War; as early as 1915 he was sure:

But what did conscription really signify? Take the answer in terms reaching from the French measure of 1798 to what we see in this year 1915. It meant substituting the ordinary citizen for the professional soldier; it meant sending up to the firing line not men ready and willing to face the supreme risk but men for the most part with no such disposition, ordinary citizens, professional men, lawyers, merchants, artists, even in one country to-day, priests. It is a shocking thing that modern civilization should arrive at such a system as that.[7]

As might have been expected of a shocking system, it was perpetuated by shocking ambitions and doctrines. Johnston seems to have believed that once the wars of revolutionary France ended, there was no reason why the era of the mass army should not also end. The conservative monarchs of post-Napoleonic Europe were eager to extinguish all the doctrines of the French Revolution, and a military system which relied on snatching peaceful men from their homes to create a large but qualitatively inferior army had little to recommend it. The mass army went into an eclipse. Unfortunately for mankind, the German state of Prussia discovered that reliance on a professional army left her incapable of offensive warfare, since she was one of the smaller and poorer states of Europe. Her ambition to dominate Germany required a capacity for offensive warfare and she had to find some other military system. She restored the mass army.

This act on Prussia's part was not inherent in the European scheme of things, since the Prussian legislature opposed it. The legislature recognized that Prussia was not directly menaced and that her existing army was strong enough to compel respect from any possible assailant. But Bismarck appeared on the scene, "the most forceful figure of Europe since Napoleon," and his will imposed a new mass army on Prussia and thus on Europe.

When Bismarck embarked on a ruthless policy which he candidly described as one of blood and iron, "even among high-placed officials in Berlin it was whispered that he was demented, a lunatic who ought to be locked up." But the unhappy truth was that once in power, Bismarck was able to harvest from Europe a wealth of noxious crops, which might have withered had not Bismarck appeared. His policy of violence expressed through the mass army did succeed in making Prussia the leading state of Germany, and the leading power in Europe. Therefore other states adopted mass armies, in emulation of success and in self-defense. Furthermore, the doctrines of Darwinism lay waiting in Europe to rationalize a creed of blood and iron.[8]

With Darwinism supplying the rationale and Bismarck the seeming proof of success, the mass army swept Europe toward the First World War. As in the era of the French Revolution, however, the mass army was in fact a less effective instrument than its triumphs made it seem. The Prussian army which conquered Austria in 1866 and France in 1870 was not so good as a dazzled world believed:

Very false impressions exist as to what the Prussian army accomplished in the campaigns of 1866 and 1870. Victory over opponents who were badly led, and in some respects deficient, led to the creation of a legend immensely removed from the truth. . . .

On the Prusso-German side the emphasis on numbers had produced an army numerically superior to the French, but inferior in the solidity of its infantry because the term of service was shorter. The first line of the French troops, as unit to unit, showed much greater cohesion than their opponents.[9]

Once again, the victories of the mass army depended on expedients to offset the fact that the mass army was a not very good army. The officers of the German general staff had been trained to control an immense force over great distances. Therefore they were able to achieve skillful offensive deployments when the French staff, hopelessly inferior, could do nothing of the sort. The Germans "roughly succeeded more or less well in keeping the armies in motion, getting them together on the field of battle, and feeding up the firing lines as rapidly and insistently as possible. None of these things could be done with the French army." Furthermore, the new mass army again happened to have superior artillery on its side, "used with boldness and some tactical skill, while the

French guns remained inferior at every point." Again the mass army was fortunate enough to enjoy superior leadership at the highest level, this time that of Helmut von Moltke. But the triumph of the mass army in 1870 as in the 1790s was a triumph of qualitatively inferior troops assisted by heroic expedients and supreme good luck.[10]

When German military students recognized such facts in their studies after 1870, Johnston noted, the effect was not to eliminate reliance upon the mass army but to make of it a still more shocking anomaly in a supposedly civilized world. Observing the difficulties of controlling great masses of half trained troops, the Germans decided to fanaticize the troops through intensive training in patriotism beginning in the public schools. Hypnotized by the German example, other states followed this formula.

Altogether, Johnston concluded, the history of war since the eighteenth century was a record of brutalization which had transformed war from an art to be practiced by commanders of high skill to a contest of uncontrollable masses in chaotic collision. The latest idea, that the manpower of a nation must be fanaticized through patriotic indoctrination, "was the cry of despair of the tactician at the ineffectiveness of modern infantry for getting a decision by shock." [11]

On some occasions, as in *Arms and the Race,* Johnston's view of the mass army was the resigned conclusion that now mankind was stuck with it. It barbarized war and the world itself, but it had become the reliance of the powers, and the weight of its numbers was likely to overwhelm any state which did not adopt it. Elsewhere, however, Johnston believed that drowning in a flood of superior numbers was not necessarily the fate of the army that remained professional, and even *Arms and the Race* was full of ambiguity and doubt. Johnston did not accompany the disciples of Clausewitz in their devotion to battle as the overwhelmingly preeminent object of strategy. He recognized that battle is the military pay-off; "whatever strategical advantage an army may obtain, there always comes the moment when the tactical decision must be fought for." Nevertheless, strategic advantage could prejudge the tactical decision. The mass armies of Revolutionary France and Bismarckian Prussia had overcome their tactical liabilities in part by exploiting this fact. The suggestion presented itself: might not a non-mass army offset its numerical inferiority by superior strategy? Might not its opportunity to do so be great because of its superior potential for rapid movement and sure control?

Johnston did not raise these thoughts explicitly in *Arms and the Race,* but they were implicit in his emphasis on the advantages an army can bring to the battlefield if its strategic preparation has been correct. This emphasis persisted through his works. His studies on Napoleon dwelt on the clarity with which the young General Bonaparte discerned that "an army [might] be handled so as to obtain an advantage which might prove decisive even before the tactical shock occurred."

Marengo illustrates admirably the strategic conception that overcomes tactical disability. Between the two armies that met on that field there was no comparison in point of discipline and of manœuvring power in terms of minor tactics. The French army was wretchedly inadequate to the business at hand. . . . As soon as the Austrians and French were fairly deployed face to face the result, tactically, was not in doubt for an instant. It was only because the Austrians, superior also in numbers, carelessly blundered after apparently winning an easy victory, and only because Desaix and Kellermann struck an unexpected, clever, and lucky blow, that Melas did not camp on the battlefield. But the remarkable thing was that all this mattered very little, because Bonaparte had got a decisive strategic result even before he attempted to get a tactical one.[12]

The inferiority of the French army on the battlefield had meant little, because Napoleon had used the divisional organization of his army and the rapidity of its movements to cover all the roads by which the Austrians could return to their line of communications. The strategic situation was such that a tactical setback to Napoleon was not likely to prove serious. More than that, the same methods continued to win victory for Napoleon through the rest of the Italian campaign. Repeatedly, swift movement against the jugular of the enemy's line of communications was the key to Napoleon's Italian successes.[13]

On the other hand, Johnston argued that while Napoleon won his greatest triumphs when he relied on strategy to place his enemy at a disadvantage before battle commenced, Napoleon's success diminished the more he relied on what the disciples of Clausewitz in Johnston's day regarded as the foundation of successful war, the big battalions. When Napoleon called on his strategic genius he won victories; at Marengo he won with inferior numbers. When he called on the simple mass of huge armies, his star waned. Big battalions alone were not the foundation of victory.[14]

Johnston approached the distinction which B. H. Liddell Hart was later to draw between the young General Bonaparte and the older Emperor Napoleon. General Bonaparte, according to Liddell Hart, was the heir of the highest eighteenth-century developments in warfare. He conquered by strategy, by deceptive use of the multiple tentacles that divisional organization enabled him to throw out from his army, by speed, and by rapid concentrations. The Emperor Napoleon, in contrast, relied on mass, and so he fathered the doctrines of mass warfare which Clausewitz and his disciples were to use to prepare for World War I.[15] Similarly, Johnston wrote of General Bonaparte, who "under the new conditions . . . showed a genius for war that raised him at the close of his first campaign to the select company of the great captains," and the later Napoleon, who grew intoxicated with mass:

> It is sometimes difficult to disentangle in Napoleon what is logical from what is merely craving for power.
> In 1812 he set out to defeat Russia by the sheer accumulation of numbers against her; just as de Gribeauval believed in accumulating fire and battering a hole at a given point. But the scale is wholly unsuitable, and in more than one way. He writes to Davoût: "The object of all my manœuvers is to concentrate 400,000 men at a given point." Again a pure obsession, and hopeless in practice. For at that moment he had before him two widely separated Russian armies, in a vast theater of war of scanty resources, and those armies amounted one to 100,000 men, the other to 50,000 men. A concentration of 400,000 men at either of these points, if feasible, was merely the gratification of an inordinate craving for mass and for power; as a practical measure it could only lead to the paralysing of the army from undue concentration in a poor country, while the numbers were too large to serve any adequate purpose.[16]

Here Johnston had struck fertile soil. The cumbersome mass army stood in the way of attaining that strategic advantage over the enemy which cut the risks of the tactical pay-off, the battle, to a minimum. It created difficulties of management which even the Prussian general staff, with all its preparation for the problem, had not been able to overcome. Any really probing studies of the Bismarckian wars had emphasized the looseness of army control by the high command, which, on the German side, only the hapless nature of the French command could offset. Again the suggestion was implicit: might not the smaller professional army's susceptibility to control enable it, in the proper hands, to gain strategic advantages which would more than offset its numerical inferiority to the mass army? [17]

The crucial problem of armies' control by the high commands was one which Johnston probed with thoroughness in his study *Bull Run: Its Strategy and Tactics* (1913). The results pointed to a further skepticism about mass armies. In his *Bull Run,* Johnston concerned himself with all the problems of the green troops who form a mass army newly assembled. The problems of command and control, those problems which must be solved if the attainment of decisive strategic advantage were to be possible, appeared at the heart of the issues raised by his study.

The usual plagues of straggling marchers, clumsy maneuvers, and headlong retreat cover the pages of Johnston's as of every other account of First Bull Run. Johnston with his interest in the use of pre-battle strategy to control battlefields made much of the tendency of a green army to be almost immobile. The inability of the raw Union troops to move rapidly, he pointed out, completed the impracticability of Winfield Scott's schemes for drawing together Robert Patterson's troops from the Shenandoah Valley and Irvin McDowell's in front of Washington. That immobility also did much to assure that when McDowell faced Pierre G. T. Beauregard's Confederates across Bull Run, Joseph E. Johnston's Confederates, who had the advantage of being able to move mainly by rail from the Shenandoah, would have joined Beauregard.[18]

But Johnston emphasized the problems of command at Bull Run more than those issues more frequently detailed. The Bull Run armies though citizen armies were not mass armies; yet the problems that Johnston found to have hampered their leaders were of the sort that increasing size would aggravate whenever a new army was mobilized. Some such problems could be minimized through planning before mobilization, but all were likely to cause increasing trouble as armies assumed increasing size.

One problem was that in a newly formed mass army there would be no commanders experienced in handling large bodies of troops. In the First Bull Run campaign General McDowell was inexperienced, yet even with his own lack of preparation to command a field army, the inexperience of his brigade and division commanders was such that he felt constrained to issue orders that were also instructions in how to conduct a forward movement. Even then the instructions were not sufficient. McDowell pointed out the need for advanced guards to feel his columns' way into hostile territory, but his generals proceeded to turn their whole divisions into advanced guards, continually deploying and scouting and deploying again. The slowness of the advance was the fault at least as much of the commanders as of the troops. Other evidences of the greenness of the command in the Bull Run campaign were legion.[19]

To organize a new army so its commanders could control it in battle proved another of the hardships of the Bull Run campaign, and again, enlarging an army would aggravate it. Planning beforehand could prevent such a farce as Beauregard played, when he realized only on the eve of battle that a divisional and corps organization was necessary to his army of 30,000 men sprawled over eight or ten miles of front. He then attempted to improvise such an organization in orders distributed on the morning of the battle. The improvisation did not work, and the army fought its battle awkwardly by brigades. Yet even in McDowell's army, where divisional organization took place at a more opportune moment, the divisional commanders did not establish effective control of their units by the time of the battle, and McDowell as well as Beauregard continued to give orders directly to brigades.[20]

McDowell fell into that error partly because he was badly served in the staff work of his army, and partly because he did not know how to use such staff work as he got. Beauregard had the same problem in more acute form, and Johnston returned to it repeatedly in *Bull Run* and other works. The highly trained staff officers of Germany had barely been able to manage the German army in 1870, he emphasized, and anything less than a highly trained staff would mismanage the clumsy bulk of a modern army into disaster. Napoleon had failed in the end because he never developed a staff to handle his elephantine armies, attempting to rely on personal control long after such control became impossible. Similarly, bad staff work had handicapped Washington throughout the American Revolution, nearly proving fatal on Long Island and at Brandywine when the failure of American intelligence enabled the British to unleash crushing flank attacks.[21]

During the First Bull Run campaign an inadequate staff at Federal headquarters in Washington helped ensure that the movements of McDowell and Patterson were not coordinated, and indeed that neither Patterson nor Winfield Scott was ever sure just what Patterson was supposed to be doing. Beauregard's staff work was so bad that on the morning of the battle he sent out an order for an attack by his right wing so poorly written that most of the commanders on the right wing did not recognize it as an order to attack. Partly because his staff work was bad, McDowell constantly planned his campaign against Beauregard oblivious to the fact that Joseph E. Johnston's Confederates from the Shenandoah might join Beauregard.

Because he had no functioning staff to gather knowledge of the enemy and to apprise him of all possible modes of action, McDowell planned his battle with the fixed idea that he must conduct a flanking attack on the Confederates. He ignored the possibilities presented by the Centreville ridge and his heavy artillery for forcing the enemy center or at least assailing it so vigorously as to give a flank attack the maximum chance for success. Because of bad staff work, McDowell never realized that the repulse of his left flank at Blackburn's Ford on July 18 came mainly from the diffidence of its commander; he concluded instead that the Confederate position was too strong either for a direct assault or for a move by the Union left. So inadequate was McDowell's staff work, and so little, for that matter, did McDowell understand his functions as an army commander, that he spent several hours of July 18 on a personal reconnaissance over a route he was considering for a flank march, accompanied only by a small escort. He was not accompanied even by his adjutant general or his chief engineer.[22]

The burden of Johnston's *Bull Run* is that the issue of the campaign was decided more by blundering raw commands than by blundering raw troops. The principal reason the Confederates succeeded was that the Confederates, standing on the defensive, had the easier task, and their blunders did less damage. The Confederate pursuit amounted to little because victory disorganized Beauregard's and Johnston's army as badly as defeat did the Federals; and even such pursuit as was attempted miscarried because of failures in command.[23] Had McDowell's army possessed the command and staff capacities to carry out a swifter advance, and better reconnaissance to prepare more adequate appreciations of the situation, the Union might have won the campaign.

The study of First Bull Run pointed to Johnston's conviction that the army that could win victories was the army that could be effectively led. Leadership was necessary for the army to gain a strategic advantage before it committed itself to battle; leadership was essential to drive home to victory on the battlefield. The army that could be best led was not likely to be a mass army.

With this foundation, Johnston turned to the study of a military policy for the United States. He believed the era past when the United States could muddle through without an army ready for war. While he did not share the Social Darwinian militarism of many of his contemporaries, he reflected the intellectual climate of his times in a penchant for economic explanations of historic events, and he believed that in the twentieth century economic forces would expose the United States to increasing danger of war. The world is acquisitive, materialistic, grasping, and hedonistic. In such a world moral forces opposed to war can carry little weight. The surest safety and the surest neutrality lay in armed neutrality; Germany had invaded weakly defended Belgium, said Johnston in 1915, not Switzerland with her mountains and strong militia.[24]

The United States in the twentieth century must be ready for war, Johnston believed, because the powers of Europe would cease to be the dominant powers of the globe, and America would find herself in the center of the world arena.

Clearly the bulk of Russia, now that railroads are so rapidly killing distance, overtopples that of western Europe. A grown-up Russia, half Europe and half Asia, will make the terms Europe and Asia obsolete. And in the war now being waged [the First World War] the Slavs are only just beginning to display the huge military power which the future holds in store for them. While France and Switzerland and Germany can place in the field perhaps one male in every five, Russia is as yet too poor and too uneducated to place even as many as one in twenty. France is at the end of her tether in terms of conscript armies; Germany cannot make very large gains; but Russia is only just beginning. A success in the present war may merely whet her appetite; a failure will leave her more determined than in the past to develop her resources further.[25]

But not only was Russia about to emerge from childhood to manhood and to revolutionize the world distribution of power. The Moslem world might awaken, stirring the whole vast area of southern Asia. India might come into renewed political life. Japan and China in some combination presented awesome possibilities. The Japanese had won victories over China and Russia, and they still were increasing their army and navy. Their ambition at the moment was principally toward China and its resources, but that ambition considered also the islands of the Pacific, including the Philippines and the peninsula of Alaska. For this reason if for no other the shifting balance of world politics would surely involve the United States. Johnston believed that the most likely collision of the United States in the twentieth century would be with Japan.

Germany, for all her armed strength, could not directly threaten the American continent. Before the First World War, European diplomatic alignments would not permit a major German military adventure overseas. Once the World War began, Germany was sure to be occupied for years; even if she won, she would have to consolidate her gains. The real danger to the United States came from Japan, who gave no indication of relaxing her zeal for expansion. The Philippines stood vulnerably in her path:

The taking of the Philippines from Spain may be ranked among the worst military blunders committed by any American government—it is difficult to put the matter more strongly. It is a weak, ex-centric, military position, fundamentally indefensible against any strong transpacific power, but inevitably a magnet to draw troops and ships from our shores.

Hawaii and Alaska had no assurance of immunity from Japanese attack. Some feared a Japanese invasion of California, but such a move did not seem likely if the United States gave the Pacific coast adequate military protection. Nevertheless, protection ought to be given; a militarily unoccupied California increased Japan's temptations immeasurably.[26]

Surveying these prospects and his studies of military history,

Johnston did not believe in 1915 that the United States should construct a mass army. The virtues of such an army were doubtful in any case, and even with the growing likelihood of war in the twentieth century the American position did not call for one. But the United States should adopt a reasonable military policy, and that meant a reasonable enlargement of the regular army so that the nation would possess a highly skilled force of respectable size.

Johnston believed that the Philippines could not be defended at any reasonable cost and that it would be wise to give them their independence. In the meantime a minimum garrison would have to be kept there for moral purposes. Johnston recommended that there be allocated some 23,600 men to the defense of the Philippines and the Panama Canal Zone. Alaska should receive enough troops in strategic locations to hold those locations in adversity for a number of months, until assistance could reach them from the continental United States. Hawaii's defense would have to be largely naval, but the islands demanded an adequate garrison to guard naval installations. Some 20,000 men in total, Johnston believed, should be stationed in Alaska and Hawaii. California's defense would be ensured with the establishment there of three army corps totaling 130,800 men; these troops could serve in a Japanese war as the nucleus for a mobile force in the Pacific. They could also be a reservoir from which to draw men for expeditions into Latin America, such as American policy of the day seemed likely to require. There should be a ready reserve of three army corps, another 130,800 men, available within three months of an outbreak of hostilities, to reinforce either a war effort in the Pacific or an expedition into Latin America. Within six months of the outbreak of war it should be possible to double the original force of regulars and good militia by adding another 305,200 men from a second-line reserve. To secure such a force of reserves, Johnston apparently believed that a volunteer system would suffice.[27]

The volunteers and militia used were to be well trained, and they would not be so numerous as to dissolve the regular army completely. The essence of Johnston's recommendations was the dictum, "The highest trained army is the best." [28] A comparatively small army well trained and well officered could meet America's needs without recourse to a mass army; but the training and command must be so excellent as to make the force in effect a new model army.

Repeatedly Johnston emphasized that the effective small army must be one of highly skilled soldiers, and of officers thoroughly schooled in their profession. "One of the most emphatic lessons of all military history," he said, "is that a regiment is about as good as its officers." For the training of American officers, he recommended an enlargement of West Point and the establishment of a sister military academy, probably in Colorado. He recommended an enlargement and improvement of the army's postgraduate school system and especially of the Army War College, for "the higher branches of the art of war constitute one of the most intensely difficult branches of study in the whole field of human knowledge." [29]

The training of officers should be not only theoretical. It should include regular training in the handling of brigades and divisions. Without this there could be no hope of attaining the mobility essential to successful warfare: "Let those who doubt this study the almost incredible details of Bazaine's attempts to move his columns through the city of Metz, or of McClellan's farcical efforts to get his army up the Peninsula." This point was all the more important because a relatively small army must depend upon mobility. [30]

In fact, Johnston believed that the United States Army should turn its attention to the development of mobility unrivaled by other armies; here was the most certain means of assuring that strategic advantage which could cancel out the tactical handicaps of a small force. The United States Army might apply the experience of Sheridan's Cavalry Corps of the Army of the Potomac. This had been not simply a cavalry corps but a highly mobile striking arm, capable of standing to fight infantry as well as of moving with the fastest speed possible. In the final campaign against the Army of Northern Virginia, Sheridan's mobile striking arm had become the decisive factor:

The credit of Lee's capitulation at Appomattox is clearly due first and foremost to the Federal commander-in-chief, Ulysses Grant. But the chief subordinate factor was the employment of the cavalry in the form of a massed division of mounted infantry and its brilliant leading by Philip Sheridan. The march of his corps from Petersburg to Appomattox is a great military object-lesson, and in no war from that day to this has there been so effective strategical and tactical employment of mounted men.

Here was a weapon appropriate to the small but skillful army: the marriage of the highest possible mobility to the strongest striking and staying power.[31]

The pessimism which had overtaken American professional military thought in the wake of Emory Upton had obscured the offensive emphasis of earlier American military thought. Lacking confidence in the troops with which the United States would principally fight its wars, Emory Upton's followers had neglected Dennis Mahan's doctrines of the value of the offensive and taken up a cautious preoccupation with seacoast fortifications. But R. M. Johnston, expressing confidence that the smallness of the American regular army did not condemn it to military impotence, returned to the emphasis on the offensive. Seizing the initiative was essential to Johnston's conception of war. It was only through exploiting the initiative that a small army could gain the strategic advantage which could ensure its success. The small army's virtue of superior mobility was of value principally in holding and exploiting the initiative. A relatively small army standing passively on the defensive before a mass army was likely to be overwhelmed by numbers. For the small mobile army, the offensive was the only way to victory.

Johnston recalled that Frederick the Great, Marshal Saxe, and Napoleon all had believed that troops who remain behind fortifications are always beaten, and he agreed, especially for the small mobile army. His 1907 survey of thirteen *Leading American Soldiers* returns repeatedly to the virtues of the offensive. Failure to hold the offensive was the downfall of George McClellan, while the offensive was the glory of the greatest American soldiers, Washington, Grant, Lee, and Jackson. Washington and the Confederates illustrated what could be done through the offensive, despite limited numbers. When they met only half successes or avoidable failures, the fault lay usually in their temporary reversion to the strict defensive, as with Lee at Fredericksburg. Even Washington's defense of Philadelphia in 1777, Johnston believed, should have been conducted as a tactical offensive. When Washington took the offensive at Trenton and Princeton, he scored victories despite the handicap of troops inferior in quality as well as in numbers. When Stonewall Jackson took the offensive in the Shenandoah Valley in 1862, with inferior numbers but a good army, military wonders resulted:

The Shenandoah was of vital importance to the Southern cause. . . . Its possession by the enemy would have been fatal, yet so small were the resources of President Davis that he could spare only a handful of men to defend it,—but that handful included Stonewall Jackson. If war were merely a matter of numbers, the historian might well resign his functions to the statistician, but its fascination as a study largely turns on its intellectual element, on its so frequent demonstration that one man may be worth a thousand . . . . as numbers failed him it was strategy that Jackson brought to the defense of the valley of the Shenandoah.[32]

R. M. Johnston, then, though a civilian historian, represents the American professionalist military tradition, but the professionalist tradition attempting to regain its initial hopefulness and returning to the offensive spirit of Dennis Mahan. Like Emory Upton, he believed that the only sure reliance in war is upon well trained regulars well commanded. But he believed that a moderate and practicable increase in the numbers of the American regular army, supplemented in war by moderately numerous reserves, would suffice to make the United States Army a suitable instrument for modern war. Therefore he rejected Uptonian pessimism. With regulars and good reserves numbering in wartime some 610,400 men, not a mass army on the European scale, but an army ready to exploit its superior mobility, with such a force Johnston believed the United States might face the world with confidence.

Johnston's professionalist orthodoxy was consistent, revealing itself also in his view of the objective to which his army should turn its offensive. It was appropriate to his preference for a small army that he no more endorsed the doctrine of total war waged against a whole people than he did conscription on a mass scale. He recognized that the American Revolution and the Civil War belonged to a new order of wars, in which not merely governments but whole peoples had to be subdued if the British in the one case or the Union in the other were to prevail. But he emphasized that Washington's and Lee's armies were the mainstays of their causes, and he did not suggest, on the Sherman pattern, that such armies might be destroyed indirectly through an attack on the societies from

which they sprang. He counted Sherman's march to the sea one of
the great campaigns of history, but he did not reveal an appreciation of its full revolutionary import.[33] There was much of the
military romantic in him; he believed that wars call forth the best
in men's souls, and perhaps a war against peoples was too revolting
a departure from chivalrous war for him to contemplate. He adhered to the orthodox doctrine that the objective of warfare is the
destruction of the enemy's army.

He gave curiously little attention to logistical problems, and thus
he failed also to suggest the possibility that an army might be overcome by crushing or seizing the economic resources that sustain it.
He did note the importance of supply lines in war, and his strategy
of maneuver emphasized the value of cutting lines of communications. But in discussing whether Lee's army or Richmond should
have been the primary objective of Union strategy, he considered
Richmond only from the viewpoint of its political importance, neg-
lecting the value of its war industries.[34]

Throughout Johnston's writings warfare is seen almost in a vacuum. For Johnston, the history of warfare was a history of generals
and battles, never a history of the social consequences of war. The impact of modern civilization on war, or of war on civilization, were
issues that Johnston did not probe. Only occasionally did politics
impinge on his narratives of marches and campaigns, and then he
saw political questions through military eyes, with little appreciation of their full scope. He admitted "that war is after all only a
factor of politics, and that although political considerations may
often run counter to military ones, yet it is for the general to make
the best of what must always be a necessary limitation." [35] But this
admission suggests lip-service. The total impression conveyed by
Johnston's works is that warfare is best left to the generals; that
once diplomacy has failed and war has begun, the politician should
give the soldier a free hand.

Politicians turn up in his writings on American campaigns as they
do in Emory Upton's, as nuisances who waste lives and prolong
war through their ignorant meddling in military organization and
strategy. Never did Johnston recognize in his military writings the
complexity of political problems and explain governmental actions
that from a strictly military viewpoint may have been absurd. In-

stead, he made his politicians "paltry wire-pullers who were postur-
ing as statesmen at Washington" (the Polk administration), "party
wire-pullers [who] were constantly tampering with the machinery
of the army" (again the Polk administration), or an "Administration [that] was panic-stricken and cared neither for decency, nor
discipline, nor reason" (the Lincoln administration).[36]

In particular, Johnston never displayed either sympathy with or
a real understanding of President Lincoln's problems in the early
days of the Civil War. He took the call for 75,000 volunteers as
evidence that Lincoln was a buffoon who thought that the war
could be won with that handful of men in three months; he ignored
the fact that the call was shaped by the Militia Act of 1792 and that
it was the only sort of call Lincoln could legally make until Congress assembled. When Lincoln departed from legality to begin
calling for three-years' volunteers, Johnston failed to give him credit
for it, although the action was presumably what Johnston would
have desired. In Johnston's pages, Lincoln's notions of strategy became "preposterous," the President guilty of a "long series of military blunders" and "grave faults," a man in fact who was a "fine
diplomat, clever politician, admirable patriot, but far from impec-
cable statesman." A downright anti-Lincoln bias led Johnston, as
Kenneth P. Williams has pointed out, to misquote James Ford
Rhodes in order to make it appear that Rhodes considered Lincoln
a wily demagogue. But of course, Lincoln was a mere civilian. Significantly, Johnston believed that the greatest American was not
Lincoln the civilian but Washington the soldier. He regretted that
Nathanael Greene, another soldier, could not have lived to be Washington's successor as President of the United States, rather than have
the civilian John Adams enter the Executive Mansion.[37]

Johnston's disdain for politicians was a logical product of the
fatal flaw of his work, his failure to relate war to its social context.
He could not recognize that war was changing from a knightly
joust among armies to a grim battle among peoples. He could not
recognize the inexorable rise of the mass army, whatever its shortcomings, when the military revolution begun in France in the 1790s
was approaching its apogee.

While he was an Uptonian without Emory Upton's pessimism, his
confidence in America's military future did not give him a viable

answer to America's military problems. Even as he wrote them, his affirmations of the sufficiency of a small professional army were swept aside by the experiences of Europe in the First World War and the growing American involvement in that war. For the future, Johnston's observations on the value of the highest possible mobility could inspire profitable reflection for the military men who heeded them. But for the present, R. M. Johnston's praise of the small professional army did not nullify the Uptonian dilemma. A small army was not appropriate to warfare as it developed in Europe after 1914. A small army would not solve America's military problems, and therefore reliance in one form or another on a citizen soldiery could not be escaped.

XII LEONARD WOOD *The Inevitability of*

a Citizen Army

> We must also build up a system under which officers and men for our citizen soldiery can be trained with the minimum of interference with their educational or industrial careers, under conditions which will permit the accomplishment of their training during the period of youth, and once this is accomplished will permit their return to their normal occupations with the minimum of delay. LEONARD WOOD

> Go yourselves, every man of you, and stand in the ranks and either a victory beyond all victories in its glory awaits you, or falling you shall fall greatly, and worthy of your past. DEMOSTHENES, *quoted by Leonard Wood*

IF there could be a cogent argument for a small professional army as sufficient for America's military needs, R. M. Johnston made every effort to develop that argument. And if in the end Johnston's argument failed, then at least his efforts had served to clarify the issue facing American military policy. The United States plainly was not going to build a large professional army; modern war demanded a large army; therefore the United States would have to rely on a citizen army. The only escape then remaining from Uptonian pessimism was to reject the ancient professionalist disdain for citizen soldiers and to conclude that Upton's strictures against them had been mistaken, that the national defense might rest on citizen soldiers after all.

There was no other answer. Therefore there began to appear, even in the writings of professional soldiers in the first decade of the twentieth century, a cautious reappraisal of the citizen soldiery, seeking hope for their military potential.

One prospect for hope came from the Swiss military system, which for generations had relied on a citizen soldiery and which served with the mountains to keep Switzerland so long free from invasion. American interest in the Swiss system dated from George Washington's "Sentiments on a Peace Establishment" and had reappeared at intervals ever since, including the time of the Civil War. Now that interest returned when renewed hope in a citizen soldiery became essential to escape from Uptonian despair.[1]

The same volume of the *Journal of the Military Service Institution* that carried the Uptonian lamentations of Colonel Pettit also contained a series of articles on the Swiss army.[2] The author of some of them, Captain T. Bentley Mott of the Artillery Corps, returned from a visit to Switzerland to herald the Swiss military system as "extraordinary," and his views were characteristic of a new circle of enthusiasts for the Swiss.

Out of 3,500,000 inhabitants and at an annual cost of only about $5,500,000, the Swiss Confederation formed a military force capable of mobilizing in three days 200,000 well equipped fighting men accustomed to the use of the army rifle. There was a reserve army of 300,000, 50,000 of them always armed, standing behind. This was accomplished with a permanent force of only 200 career officers, known as "instructors" of the first, second, and third classes, no more than one-fourth of whom actually commanded units.

Mott went on to remind his readers that in the United States a population which dwarfed Switzerland's could rely for defense only on a regular army of 2,200 officers and 30,000 men, supported by an organized militia of 125,000 men of dubious military quality. Application of the Swiss system to the United States, including the use of professional officers as instructors for men called up by universal military training, would substitute for the United States regular army of 32,200 a ready army of 4,500,000.

Mott did not believe the United States needed so large a ready army, and he recommended less than a thorough duplication of the Swiss system in America. But he did believe that the integration of the few American professionals with the citizen soldiery of the nation could give the United States an effective military power it had never yet possessed. When Mott wrote in 1906, the United States regular army was scattered as it had always been without regard to its possible usefulness as a training agency. In Pennsylvania, where there was a large militia, there were no regular troops to instruct. In Kansas, where the militia was small, regulars abounded.

But the regulars might as well have been in Asia for all the benefit they gave to the Kansas militia; there was little application of the regulars' skill to militia training.[3]

Mott therefore proposed a sweeping reorganization of the regular army into detachments assigned to each state for training purposes. He proposed federal legislation assuming the expenses of clothing, arming, equipping, and during training periods paying the state militia. The states would receive incentives far beyond those of the Dick Bill to merge their militias into a federal system with professional training and into an organization prescribed by the federal War Department.

> Under these laws the regular as well as the militia regiments would be recruited locally and might be called after the State. . . . The necessity for changes of station would be obviated, except for foreign service. Regiments recruited in a State would serve their whole enlistment there. Officers could be changed on a regular yearly scale, but, in order to discourage provincialism, no officer should serve in his native State. Local pride in the regular as well as in the State regiments would be developed. . . .
> Each State having a large militia would become in effect a department whose regular troops would be commanded and whose militia forces would be instructed and supervised by the "Officer Commanding the Forces (in, say, Ohio)." . . . He would have constant practice in command of a force proportioned to his grade or superior thereto.[4]

This scheme did bear some resemblance to the Upton expansible army plan, but the differences were more important than the resemblance. Unlike the Upton plan, Mott's proposals would have provided a numerically large expansion. They would have done so because Mott had developed from his Swiss observations a genuine confidence in citizen soldiers, even if they were trained for limited periods. In Mott's plan unlike Upton's, the regulars would no longer be the core of the American army, but simply its instructors. Mott pointed with approval to the Swiss plan of limiting the number of high commands which professional officers could hold, so that the greatest rewards of rising in the officer corps were open to the armed citizens.[5]

The Swiss system convinced Mott that good soldiers could be made of citizen soldiers. The way to do it, the Swiss taught, was to begin by devoting training periods to the essentials of soldiery, omitting the frills. Boys ought to receive rudimentary military instruction in the schools, and thereafter they ought to train for at least ten days each year. Such training could accomplish much if it were not misdirected, if it emphasized service in the field, not stultifying parade-ground exercises.[6]

The contrast between this [the Swiss] sort of militia training and that seen in America or England is most marked. The psychological effect on the men is certainly important. The first conceptions of the real business of a soldier, his whole reason for existence, are apt to produce a lasting impression on a young man. In our service the recruit's first enthusiasms are concentrated (and dissipated) in a grind of barrackyard drill, where no man need or is expected to use his head . . . . work in the open, among farmhouses, villages, fields and woods, seems a thing quite apart, an occasional occurrence in no way intimately bound up in a soldier's routine existence.

In Switzerland there are no parades or reviews or drills beyond the company or battalion . . . . through the push of stern necessity the Swiss has sifted out the absolute essentials to fitness for war and these essentials, field exercises and good shooting, he works at to the exclusion of everything else.[7]

Mott professed a suspicion of programs prepared by armies for the edification of foreign visitors, but his visits to the Swiss army left him with no suspicions of it. Never had he seen such intensive training, such willing soldiers as the Swiss nor such dedicated officers. Officers were selected from the ranks on the basis of military performance, as candidate-officers commanded each other in turn, underwent critical discussion after each exercise, and were promoted only by proving fitness.[8]

Mott believed the United States might also develop such an army, but he observed that there would have to be changes in the attitudes of regular officers, who now lacked the Swiss conception of their role as instructors to the nation.[9] To Mott the Swiss system meant that the military situation of the United States was not the hopeless situation which the Uptonians lamented. The Swiss example proved that the United States could have a great army; but to establish it confidence in the military abilities of the citizen soldier was the *sine qua non*.[10]

Other junior officers joined Mott in praising the Swiss system, and a few others began to work their way out of the Uptonian mood of pessimism with more affirmative reflections on the record of the American citizen soldier.[11] But the affirmations of a few junior officers, expressed in the professional journals, were not enough to signify a general change of mind within the professional officer corps nor to bring about such a change. The next steps to overcoming the Uptonian pessimism of the officer corps by substituting a new confidence in the citizen soldier came from outside the army.

The Spanish-American War and the subsequent emergence of the United States as a world power, together with the growing possibilities in the early twentieth century of a war against Japan or a war of the European alliances in which the United States might become involved, stimulated a new civilian interest in military affairs. While Theodore Roosevelt occupied the White House, a militant President further stimulated that interest. Popular periodicals began to give unwonted attention to military questions, and the long era of public indifference to the army seemed to be ending.[12]

A renewed public interest in things military meant a renewed interest by the historic opponents of professionalist pretensions. In moments of concern for the army, most ordinary citizens had not revered the regular army so much as to agree that the regulars had a monopoly on military capacity. Civilian interest in the army might now mean renewed interest in the possibilities of a citizen soldiery. So it proved to be, especially after the powers of Europe did go to war. The Plattsburg training camps movement carried thousands of businessmen and college boys into summer training camps whence they might emerge as the citizen officers of a citizens' reserve army. The assumption of the movement was the thoroughly non-Uptonian one that brief intensive military training could transform civilians into effective soldiers and effective officers.[13]

Amid the new civilian interest in military affairs considerable leadership and publicizing came paradoxically from a man who, though a civilian, claimed to be a disciple of Emory Upton. He joined the military preparedness movement quoting profusely from Upton's *Military Policy;* but there could be no clearer evidence of the growing compulsion of American professionalists to accommodate to a citizen soldiery than that this self-proclaimed Uptonian became an early advocate of the mass citizen army recruited by conscription. Upton himself had recommended conscription, but within the expansible army plan in which the regulars would mold the conscripts into the regular army image. Now the plan was for the establishment of a mass army so massive that Upton's expansible army, the heart of his proposals, had to pass into the background.

Frederic L. Huidekoper was a native of Pennsylvania residing in the District of Columbia, an attorney, a reserve officer, and by strong avocation a student of military affairs. In the late nineteenth and early twentieth centuries his name appeared frequently in the *Journal of the Military Service Institution* above scholarly articles on strategy and tactics, especially concerning the Napoleonic Wars. He began to write also for popular journals, setting forth his recommendations for an improved military policy for the United States. In 1912, he and the chief of staff of the army, Major General Leonard Wood, conceived the project of an army league to mobilize finances and publicity and to campaign for American preparedness. At Wood's suggestion that the public proposal of the league should come from outside the army, Huidekoper led in organizing it. The league was formed in Huidekoper's Washington home.[14]

When the outbreak of European war two years later gave new impetus to the preparedness movement, Huidekoper continued in the forefront of the agitation and the pressure on the Woodrow Wilson administration to ready the country for war. The Army League yielded leadership of the preparedness movement to more broadly based organizations (such as the Republican party), but Huidekoper's output of magazine articles increased, and in 1915 he published on behalf of preparedness *The Military Unpreparedness of the United States*, a volume of more than 700 pages.[15]

The imprint of Emory Upton was strong upon Huidekoper's book. In fact, much of the book was a verbatim reprint of Upton's *Military Policy*, with Upton's connective passages replaced by Huidekoper's own, but with all the most devastating indictments of American policy retained. Another lengthy segment of the book brought Upton's history of American military policy up to date, recounting as Upton might have done, the events of the last years of the Civil War, the Spanish-American War, and the Philippine Insurrection. The follies which Upton had discovered in earlier American military history were shown to have persisted and were pilloried anew.

Again there was too small a regular army, without a capacity to expand; reliance on the militia; excessive reliance on the states; short-term enlistments; and abominable organization of military resources, due to the ignorance of the civilian government.[16]

Like Upton, Huidekoper found his greatest bête noire in the militia. Because the United States had relied on that disastrous instrument, he said, in every war the country had had to mobilize at least two men to every one for its opponent. The cost of American wars in financial terms had never failed to be inordinate, and the early months of every war against a respectable adversary had been pitted with catastrophe. The history of American militia was an extended commentary on Richard Henry Lee's statement, "A government is the murderer of its citizens which sends them to the field uninformed and untaught." The final verdict on militia, Huidekoper believed, was that of Washington in his most disillusioned mood: "To place any dependence upon militia is assuredly resting upon a broken staff." [17]

Yet from the indictment of militia Huidekoper could not follow Upton to the conclusion that only the regular army, expansible in wartime but fitting wartime recruits to its own pattern, offered a reliable instrument of defense. The battles of mass armies in Europe and the likelihood that the United States might soon join them furnished the force behind Huidekoper's book. In these circumstances the American regular army could no longer bear the weight which Upton had tried to place on it. Therefore despite his Uptonian review of American military policy, Huidekoper was obliged to shift gears as quietly as possible when he recommended a new military policy.

He felt obliged to discern in the militia, for all their deficiencies, hidden merits which Upton had largely ignored. More than Upton, he paid tribute to the underlying patriotism and dedication of militiamen, and he argued that their failures were not inherent deficiencies of armed citizens but simply the product of their being misused. Their "unrivalled personal courage . . . cannot be too greatly commended," but "they have always been, and still are, the victims of a most pernicious system." [18]

The perniciousness of the system lay largely in its having been a system of state control. Upton too had laid much of the blame for

the shortcomings of militia on the states, but his vote against the
militia had sprung from deeper roots; Upton did not expect much
from any troops, federal or state, that had not experienced long
training. With Huidekoper, state control received a new emphasis
as the primary cause of militia problems. Citizen soldiers, Huidekoper affirmed, could be made good soldiers. They had performed
uniformly well in the Philippine Insurrection, when they were organized as federal volunteers, rigorously chosen under federal
physical standards, immune to state political influences, and trained
by regulars who knew their business. Federal control was the key
to success. The way to create a good citizen soldiery was to turn
their training and organization over to the federal government.
Then the job could be done.[19]

In every war in our history the State militia as such has been a dismal
failure. It would be impossible to cite a better proof that the system
is at fault than the fact that these same men, when organized into national volunteers and given proper training, have almost always become efficient troops, with a record often glorious. All the more reason
why the Federal government should at once cease to support troops
which it cannot control.[20]

Huidekoper's comments on state militia may have sounded like
those of Emory Upton, but Upton would have been less than eager
to attribute to citizen soldiers "a record often glorious" simply when
federal was substituted for state control. And although he relied so
much on Upton's *Military Policy* for his evidences of the deficiencies
of American policy in the past, Huidekoper also departed from
Upton in his recommendations for the future.

Huidekoper proposed an enlargement of the regular army to a
strength of 250,000, and he was inclined to use Uptonian terms in
praising the regulars' qualities. But he dropped the expansible army
plan. His very respect for the high qualities of regulars led him to
compare adulteration of the regular army with raw recruits to the
adulteration of foods, and to argue that both should be illegal. He
proposed that the regular army should be kept at war strength and
that its principal purpose should be to provide formations available
instantly for overseas expeditions, on the model of the British army.[21]

To provide replacements for the regular formations and to establish additional divisions, Huidekoper proposed two classes of re-

servists. The first class should be composed of veterans of the regular establishment, an Uptonian touch. Huidekoper suggested a seven-year enlistment period for the regular army, two years to be spent on active service (except for NCO's, who would remain on active duty longer), five years to be spent in the reserves. This plan could be developed, he believed, to provide a first-class reserve of 420,000 men.[22]

In addition to his Uptonian first-class reserve, Huidekoper proposed a second class of reservists modeled on the Swiss army and thus to be emphatically citizen soldiers. Like the Swiss, the second-class reservists were to train a suitable number of days annually. They were to number about 600,000. Their designation, emphasizing Huidekoper's proposal of federal control, was to be United States Volunteers. If volunteering did not bring sufficient recruits, however, Huidekoper urged that conscription be attempted. He argued that the United States Volunteers would attract more recruits than the existing state militia, since the federal force would have a worthy national purpose and would not be called on for police duty. If voluntary recruits did not fill the ranks, the American people should be reminded of the duties implied by the enjoyment of rights.[23]

Like most advocates of conscription, Huidekoper believed that benefits beyond preparedness would flow from it, with the physical conditioning and training in discipline that it would give to young men. He hoped, for example, that out of the discipline of universal military training the United States might derive a working class as well disciplined as Germany's, and indeed that in many things the United States might begin to become more like Germany:

In certain ways we Americans can derive no little profit from the example of German efficiency [Germany having conscription] and the comparative inefficiency of British land forces [Great Britain before the war not having had conscription] thus far in the present European war.[24]

Huidekoper, then, drew his historical arguments against United States military policy from Emory Upton, and he followed Upton enough to recommend a first-line army of regulars and veteran regulars called from reserve. But he departed more from Upton than he seems to have known when he dropped the expansible army idea to rely for the second line of defense on a citizen soldiery on the Swiss model, trained several weeks a year. To argue that the German army was more efficient than the British because of citizen conscripts while the British retained an army of professionals, was to take a line far different from Emory Upton's. A civilian rather than a career officer, Huidekoper was more aware than Upton of the social context of military affairs. But he considered himself a follower of Upton, and the differences between Upton's recommendations and Huidekoper's forcefully illustrate the pressure on the United States in the early twentieth century to establish a mass army and to overcome the professionalist's disdain for citizen soldiers.

Frederic Huidekoper organized the Army League in his home. His *Military Unpreparedness of the United States* came to be a textbook of the preparedness movement and of the call for a massive American citizen army, which would be raised by conscription if necessary. But textbooks are not widely read, and Huidekoper was a sober attorney who could not capture wide popular acclaim. If the preparedness movement were to achieve its massive citizen army it needed a man capable of writing short, sparkling books that would be read and capable of capturing popular attention through a forceful personality projected in speeches and in newspapers and popular journals. World events even before the outbreak of the European war had begun to shake Americans out of their traditional indifference to the army, but much more shaking was needed. From the beginning the preparedness movement included a man who had popularizing abilities to an extraordinary degree. Frederic Huidekoper with his ponderous quotations from Emory Upton was but a minor satellite of the great evangelist of a citizen army, General Leonard Wood.

Wood had been colonel of the Rough Riders in Cuba and an acting brigade commander at San Juan Hill, military governor of Santiago and then of Cuba, commander of the Moro province on Mindanao and then of the army in the Philippines, and chief of staff from 1910 to 1914. For all that, however, his appearance as propagandist for a massive citizen army represented no conversion from the professionalist tradition by the professional officer corps in general. Wood was never really one of the professionals. He was

not a West Pointer, and in any sense that would have satisfied
Emory Upton he was scarcely even a professional officer, despite
his high rank. Many in the officer corps never accepted him as one.
He was a physician, a graduate of the Harvard Medical School
who, limited in financial means and needing an assured income
promptly, became a contract surgeon with the army on the Indian
frontier. He eventually received a commission in the Medical Corps,
and through the back door received his colonelcy of the line with
the help of his friendship with Theodore Roosevelt. Politics as well
as ability were involved in his rapid promotion over numerous
seniors upward to the command of the army.[25]

Wood served a cause that had long been dear to the professionalists when as chief of staff he assured the preeminence of that post,
successor to the commanding generalship, over the bureau chiefs.
He thus won the battle that had been waged by Sherman, Sheridan,
and Schofield. But he had not won the allegiance of all the professionalists, because his rival the adjutant general strengthened his
own position by advocating a longer enlistment term and a fuller
professionalization of the army's ranks. Nor did Wood endear himself to the army's orthodox when he used the office of chief of staff
as a platform for propagandizing for preparedness. The orthodox
professionals wanted preparedness of a sort, but they did not approve of the army's principal soldier acting as an evangelist, nor
did Wood's citizen-army version of preparedness always warm their
affections.[26]

When the Democratic Woodrow Wilson administration came into
office it was among the national institutions least inclined to foster
military preparedness. With the Republican party rich in militant
leaders of the Theodore Roosevelt and Henry Cabot Lodge type,
preparedness thereafter had the flavor of a Republican political
movement. The Wilson administration was not reluctant to deprive
itself of Leonard Wood as military adviser when Wood's term as
chief of staff ended, and in 1914 the general moved from Washington to Governor's Island and the command of the First Military
District. But with fewer conflicting demands on his time, Wood now
devoted himself more strenuously to his campaign for preparedness
through the mass citizen army.

He spoke for the mass army on every possible occasion. He was not the most gifted of public speakers, but he was impressive through sheer commanding stature—physical as well as in reputation—and earnestness of conviction. A parade of magazine articles and short books carried his arguments to many who could not hear him and increased the force of his appeal to those who could.[27]

Even after the First World War began, Wood did not urge preparedness for the sake of any specific war. Until the very eve of American participation he was looking more to America's world role when the European war would have ended, than to the war itself. He based his arguments on the general position of the United States, on its status as a great power and the futility of attempting to escape responsibilities. Huidekoper had offered Social Darwinian argument to contend that the nations were engaged in a struggle for existence from which the United States could not escape. Wood took much the same line:

> An infinite wisdom has established the conditions under which we live and put in being the great law which runs through the universe: the law of the survival of the most fit. We may struggle against it, but it rules in its general application. The most fit in a military way . . . will win in war. . . .
>
> They may not be the most fit in abstract morality as relates to business relations between individuals or nations, or with regard to generosity or sense of justice. Their characteristics of selfishness, self-interest and the spirit of acquisitiveness are often accompanied by a development of the means to get what is coveted and to hold it securely.[28]
>
> Human nature in the mass [organized in a nation] is still human nature; under a little more restraint, perhaps, but still the old complex proposition of the ages, characterized and controlled only too often by expediency and self-interest.[29]
>
> Blood, race, tradition, trade and a host of other influences, capped by ambition to go on, to lead, to expand, will always produce strife.[30]
>
> War, whether it be for good or evil, is among men.[31]

His service in Cuba and the Philippines had made Wood aware of the far-flung nature of twentieth-century American interests. Together with the economic wealth and power of the United States, the overseas possessions and dependencies created, he believed, an inescapable American involvement in world politics. Sooner or later rivalries leading to war were likely to come out of that involvement. But given the nature of the world, war was less likely if the United States were militarily strong. Not only could a strong United States discourage ambitious rivals from attacking, it might contribute to the peace of the world in general. Wood was close to Theodore Roosevelt; and however much his vision was blurred by his own militarism, chauvinism, and self-assertiveness, Roosevelt as President had captured some recognition that the United States might use its new great power status to act as an honest broker among European and Asian rivalries and to enforce the peace. He had acted on that recognition in the Russo-Japanese War and in the first Morocco crisis, but to act further demanded further American strength as well as clearer vision. Wood and Roosevelt alike seem never fully to have recognized their own goals in foreign and military policy. But in both there was a hint of the sort of informed and coherent foreign policy backed by military strength with which the United States might have discouraged the opening of the First World War or at least prevented its insane prolongation.[32]

Wood found the American army of 1910–1917 inadequate for waging or discouraging war, and he could not rest while the country remained ignorant of its inadequacies:

This country has never engaged single-handed in a war with a nation of the first class prepared for war. We have absolutely no conception of what modern war means when conducted by a nation organized and ready in men and material.[33]

Justice and righteousness are not enough to insure protection, nor is an upright and blameless personal or national life a guarantee against the unscrupulous. A Pilate was found to crucify Christ; and a strong, aggressive nation, believing in its own worth and right to expand, has always been prone to crush and coerce a weaker one, regardless of the abstract justice of the weaker nation's cause.[34]

To fortify his claim of unreadiness for war, Wood turned to American military history. Naturally he made of it a lugubrious chronicle. Much of what he said was a condensation and popularization of Upton and Huidekoper (whose works in full he urged upon his readers). Once again the nation greeted every military emergency with ignorant unreadiness, once again the regular army was always too small, once again the state militias acted out their role of tragic buffoonery. As Upton had done, Wood compared the United States to China, a wealthy and tempting prize, potentially one of the greatest of powers, but for the present a vulnerable sleeping giant, an open invitation to attack. Wood lamented that the usual teaching of American history in schools and colleges ignored Emory Upton's findings, and teachers, like Fourth-of-July politicians, lulled the nation deeper into slumber by glorifying past victories won in spite of American military policy.[35]

Americans imagined, to Wood's distress, that they as Anglo-Saxons possessed superiority in military capacity. But Wood warned that such notions failed to consider that since the Civil War many other races had added their blood and their characteristics to the original Anglo-Saxon strains in the United States. And in any case, to talk of native Anglo-Saxon military superiority was folly; to expect that Americans without military training or organization could hold their own in war against men of comparable racial capacities who did possess training, such as, by implication, the Germans, was absurd.[36]

The ugly truth was that politicians' and school teachers' and patriots' appeals to the record of past American military victories were irrelevant, for the United States had never faced a situation such as would confront her in the twentieth century:

In our past wars we were not confronted by great nations with highly organized military machines; steam navigation had not appeared; our possible enemies were without standing armies of any size, and lacked entirely that complete military organization which characterizes them today. It took a long time to get troops together and prepare supplies for them, and a considerable period of time to cross the ocean. Our forefathers had more time to prepare. Then, again, they were more familiar with the use of arms; weapons were of a simple type; they could be made quickly, and instruction in their use was a relatively simple matter.

Now highly organized military establishments are the rule among our possible antagonists. Rapid steam transportation in vast amount is available. The arms of war are extremely complicated and costly; it takes a long time to make them and a long time to instruct soldiers in their use. In other words, today everything is in favor of the prepared aggressor and everything against the unready pacific nation.[37]

Wood saw the existing American military situation even more darkly than did Upton. But though he drew on Upton for historical arguments, he was not an Uptonian professionalist, and more even than Huidekoper he departed from Upton's influence to recommend solutions to America's military problems. Unlike Upton, he believed that real solutions were possible.

Wood did not share Upton's pessimism about the military future of the United States because he disagreed with Upton on the amount of training necessary to make an effective soldier. As chief of staff, Wood backed the regular army enlistment plan that Huide-koper later continued to advocate in his *Military Unpreparedness:* a seven-year enlistment, the first two years to be served with the active army, the remaining five years to be spent in the first-line reserves. The old professionals of the army objected to this plan on the ground that two years was not a sufficient period to make soldiers. Wood replied that he could train a soldier in six months.[38]

If he could train a soldier in six months, he could fashion a viable military policy for the United States. At first, while he was chief of staff, Wood advocated the military program we have already seen outlined by Huidekoper, for indeed Huidekoper got his ideas largely in consultation with General Wood. That is, Wood proposed a regular army with regular reserves to be secured through the seven-year enlistment plan, plus federal volunteers to form a second-line reserve.[39] But the First World War was not long in progress before Wood boldly advocated conscription. He believed a citizen army could become a good army, but the whole purpose of calling on the armed citizenry was to secure a mass army, and a mass army on a twentieth-century scale could be recruited only by conscription.

Wood appealed, like Huidekoper, to the principle which advocates of conscription had relied on since the first dawn of the democratic era and the beginning of the *levée en masse* in Revolutionary France: universal citizenship implies the responsibility of universal military service.

He argued that this principle was an American one. The militia system was based upon it, but the militia system had become ineffective in practice through lax management and state control. The United States had had to depart from its original principle, universal military service, to adopt the volunteer system. But the volunteer system was unfair and in a major war, unworkable. It brought out the best young men of the nation at the outset of war, while those less courageous and patriotic continued to enjoy the safety and comforts of home. After the enthusiasm of the immediate outbreak of war, the volunteer system could be sustained only through the introduction of increasingly higher and increasingly demoralizing bounty payments. The greatest American war, the Civil War, had compelled the eventual introduction of conscription despite all efforts to avoid it. Better to introduce conscription before an emergency than to do so hastily in the midst of danger.

Every good American honors the real volunteer spirit, but it is difficult to understand how any man who is familiar with our country's history can advocate the continuance of the volunteer system, with its uncertainties, unpreparedness and lack of equality of service. We have been warned repeatedly by the experience of others of the folly of depending on the volunteer system. The lack of training, the uncertainty in the way of returns, the cost, the confusion, have all served to demonstrate the danger of the procedure; the danger to us has been greatly increased by the thoroughness of modern organization and the rapidity with which armies can be transported over land or sea to deliver attacks in force.[40]

Although the United States had fallen away from a democratic system of universal military service, the Swiss system and the similar Australian one showed the appropriateness of such a system to a democratic nation. Unlike Switzerland, Wood emphasized, the United States would have to maintain a permanent regular army of considerable size. He pointed to the same tasks for a regular army that Huidekoper listed: garrisoning of the overseas possessions and Alaska, and readiness to serve immediately as an expeditionary force in any area of American interests.

Like the small permanent force of Switzerland, the regular army would provide instruction for the citizen army. To establish the citizen force, Wood recommended a universal military obligation for men between the ages of eighteen and twenty-five, or perhaps between twenty and twenty-seven. Each year about a million men in the United States became eighteen. Assuming that only half of them proved suitable for military training, each year 500,000 men would be available for the citizen army. By the time they had reached eighteen, these men should have received elementary military training in the schools, as was customary in Switzerland and Australia. They might then complete their full-time military training within three months, whereupon they would remain subject to brief annual training and be members of a ready reserve until they were twenty-five or twenty-seven. The nation would always possess a ready reserve force of about 3,500,000 men. Certain of those reserves, chosen by volunteering or by lot, should be organized into twenty-five reserve divisions, equipped and ready for immediate call to service.[41]

The reserve officer corps, Wood proposed, should be recruited and maintained from military colleges and from the officers' training corps units of nonmilitary universities and colleges. The training of the latter would be supplemented by the type of summer instruction camp for which Wood established a model at Plattsburg in 1915. A certain number of additional officers might be secured from the enlisted ranks of the army and from miscellaneous sources. Altogether, these various sources should easily supply the 50,000 reserve officers that the general staff believed were needed, and eventually supply sufficient officers for Wood's citizen army.[42]

The details of Wood's plans were important only as they rendered plausible his general theme, for Wood served primarily as the evangelist for universal military service, the abstract principle outweighing specific materialization of it. His details on how the military training of citizens should be accomplished were important mainly in adding substance to his assurance that he did not propose to disturb the normal life of America and its citizens, but that he did believe that an effective mass army could be built without great disruption. He stressed that assurance:

We must also build up a system under which officers and men for our citizen soldiery can be trained with the minimum of interference with their educational or industrial careers, under conditions which will permit the accomplishment of their training during the period of youth, and once this is accomplished will permit their return to their normal occupations with the minimum of delay.[43]

Wood was evangelizing for the principle of universal military service, not necessarily for his specific version of it. He always returned to his theme that universal military service was a democratic principle, within the American military tradition. Universal military service was the principle on which the militia had been based before it was clear that state control would hamstring the militia. It was the principle, Wood said, that Washington and Secretary of War Knox had attempted to establish through Knox's original recommendations to Congress of a three-group citizen army. It was the system that Jefferson had endorsed, especially after the War of 1812, when he wrote of the war to James Monroe:

It proves more forcibly the necessity of obliging every citizen to be a soldier. This was the case with the Greeks and Romans, and must be that of every free state. Where there is no oppression there will be no pauper hirelings. We must train and classify the whole of our male citizens, and make military instruction a regular part of collegiate education. We can never be safe until this is done.[44]

Wood argued that the nation would benefit from universal military service in other ways than preparedness for war. The regular army had suppressed yellow fever in Cuba and hookworm in Puerto Rico and had helped to control floods along the Mississippi. A citizen army, he argued, could do the same sort of thing on a larger scale. He did not say precisely how.[45] But his main argument was the necessity for the United States to prepare for future wars. Such wars were sure to come, and like Huidekoper he repeated Richard Henry Lee's maxim that "A government is the murderer of its citizens which sends them to the field uninformed and untaught."

Wood did not live only in a military world; here again he was not like Emory Upton, perhaps because he was not a professional soldier alone. He recognized that the waging of war required more than just trained military manpower:

Preparedness is based upon organization. National preparedness means far more than the mere organization of the army and navy. It means, first of all, the moral organization of the people, an organization which creates in the heart of every citizen a sense of his obligation for service to the nation in time of war or other difficulty. This is the greatest part of organization, and if once accomplished all the rest follows easily and naturally. The organization of the industrial resources of the country would place the government in possession of full knowledge concerning the capacity of each industrial plant—just what it can do, how much, and when—and at the same time would place in the possession of the various industrial organizations an exact knowledge of what was expected of them and would see to it that they are properly equipped to discharge their obligations promptly when called upon. An organization which takes into consideration transportation, communications and supply; the organization of the sanitary service, and of the various special groups of highly-trained men; an organization of the financial system of the country so that it may have the elasticity and expansibility to meet the demands of war; the organization of the economical resources of the country; the careful study of ways and means to make good shortages; organization of our chemical resources; provision as far as possible of substitutes for things which are not found within our limits, so that we may be supplied in case of loss of sea power—all these things come under organization and require much time for their consideration.[46]

Industrial production, finance, and even chemistry entered the making of modern war, Wood recognized, but even these areas could be mobilized more readily through the acceptance of universal military training. In large part it was a moral matter, to mobilize the nation in a common purpose through the moral force of the example of all young men serving their country. Like his friend Theodore Roosevelt, like so many other products of the nineteenth-century rural American background Leonard Wood believed deeply in the power of moral forces. Universal military training was to him an assurance of readiness for war, because he was confident of the prowess of American citizen armies, especially when they were animated by such a moral principle as universal military service represented. But universal military service would improve the national fiber whatever it did for physical success in war. Though not eloquent Wood had a fondness for eloquence, and he quoted on this point the call of Demosthenes to the Athenians: "Go yourselves, every man of you, and stand in the ranks and either a victory beyond all victories in its glories awaits you, or falling you shall fall greatly, and worthy of your past." [47]

More than the earnest evangelizing of Leonard Wood was required to lead the professionalist military or the skeptical nation to accept conscription. Leonard Wood was no longer chief of staff. Woodrow Wilson's Secretary of War Lindley M. Garrison turned to the general staff for recommendations to ready the army for the possible ramifications of the European war, and the professional soldiers suggested nothing beyond raising the regular army to its full authorized strength. Garrison had been influenced by Wood to some degree, however, and he responded to that feeble suggestion with dissatisfied prodding of the general staff for something better. Under the prodding such Wood men as remained were able to gain acceptance for a report on "The Proper Military Policy of the United States" which adopted the Wood-Huidekoper-Army League proposals minus conscription. That is to say, the general staff agreed to call for a regular army of 281,000 men with veteran reserves to raise it to 500,000, plus a "Continental Army" of part-time trainees roughly on the Swiss model. The Continental Army was to be a federal rather a state force, but secured through volunteering. It would number half a million, and there would be another half million volunteer reserves in a third line, ready to replace casualties.[48]

Secretary Garrison's insistence on something of the sort, the lengthening shadow of the European mass armies, and to a lesser extent the influence of the military outsider Leonard Wood prevailed upon the general staff to accept and sponsor the Continental Army plan. But to win the civilian skeptics of Congress, the representatives of the full tradition of military amateurism, proved to be another matter. The idea of a strong federal army, even a citizens' reserve army, called forth prejudices in the powerful agrarian wing of the powerful Progressive movement. It was not enough to these neo-Jeffersonians to point out that Jefferson himself favored a citizen-soldiery that was trained. More Jeffersonian than Jefferson, they looked with ingrained suspicion on militarism, federal power, and involvement in international affairs, and the Continental Army plan bore the taint of all three. The Democratic Wilson administration needed the support of the agrarian Democrats for its legislative proposals, but many of them defected, led by House majority leader Claude Kitchin of North Carolina.

Southern Democrats with the tradition of the militant South behind them did not always share the prejudices of their fellow agrarians toward anything suggesting military professionalism. But their leading military spokesman in Congress, Chairman James Hay of the House Military Affairs Committee, developed other doubts on the Continental Army plan. He questioned whether a new federal military reserve would be able to recruit as effectively as the long established National Guard units, with their deep local roots so important in a state such as his native Virginia. He doubted that recruiting a federal reserve force of 500,000 or more men was feasible, and his doubts spread through Congress and to his fellow Virginian, the President.

Hay's doubts coincided with the inclinations of the politically powerful National Guard. There were Guard leaders who were intelligently concerned about the dangers of the European war, but their reason as well as their self-interest led them to question the merit of substituting a new federal reserve for the long established and functioning National Guard. In the end, the pressures against the Continental Army plan were too great. The plan died, and Congress substituted James Hay's program in the National Defense Act of 1916.[49]

The preparedness advocates, hostile to any state influence in national defense, were bitterly disappointed by the National Defense Act of 1916, and Secretary Garrison resigned in disgust. But their disappointment was disproportionate; the new law was not really so much less than the Continental Army plan. It retained the National Guard as the principal military reserve, but it went much beyond the Dick Bill in assuring that the Guard maintained federal standards. It provided that the land forces of the United States should consist of four components: the regular army, to be increased to 175,000; the National Guard, with an authorized strength of 475,000, and with the federal government equipping and training the Guard and paying its troops during their training; a federal reserve consisting of officers drawn both from former regulars and from the graduates of the colleges' reserve officer training program and of discharged enlisted men; and a "Volunteer Army" to be raised only in time of war.[50]

Representative Hay's doubts about raising the Continental Army through voluntary recruiting were sound, but the mobilization of the National Guard because of the Mexican imbroglio soon demonstrated that even in an emergency the National Guard could not be recruited to full strength either. Hay's plan and the Continental Army plan were both inadequate; volunteering was no longer sufficient to recruit an army fit for intervention in the European war. When the National Guard could not be raised to the desired strength for the Mexican intervention, there was nothing to do but listen more attentively to Leonard Wood's continued agitation for conscription.[51]

The National Defense Act of June 3, 1916, barely had time to function. When the United States went to war in the spring of 1917, the army underwent still another reorganization to form a three-part force: the regular army, the National Guard, and the National Army. And the new National Army would be raised by conscription.[52]

Leonard Wood notwithstanding, conscription seemed to many Americans counter to principal national traditions; and professional soldiers were still skeptical of citizen soldiers. But if the United States were to muster an army appropriate to war on the European scale, there was no escape from conscription. Facts imposed the method upon Wilson, Congress, the army, and the country, and Leonard Wood had done much to prepare the way.

The tradition of the military amateur seemed at last to have won over that of the military professional, for the United States was going into its military testing as a great power with a citizen army. Through all the years of the existence of an American professional officer corps, that corps had tended to distrust the citizen soldier. The professionalist military tradition had become thoroughly the tradition of those Americans whose career it was to concern themselves with military problems. But the professionalist tradition had become divorced from the realities of American society and then sterile and discouraging even for its adherents. When the United States in 1917 at last had to play the role of a great power in a full military sense, that tradition as expressed by Emory Upton and his disciples had been incapable of affording the means.

Yet had the tradition of the military amateur really scored a victory? If so, it was a fulfillment that such an exponent of a citizen soldiery as Thomas Jefferson could neither have foreseen nor approved. The American citizen army of 1917–1918 was a far cry from a Jeffersonian or Jacksonian militia. In the years since Jefferson, Germany had demonstrated that the nation in arms could be the servant of conservative autocracy as well as of liberal republicanism. With the German use of the nation in arms now a more arresting historical example than the *levée en masse* of Jefferson's admired France, no observer in 1917–1918, could be sure of the nature of the ultimate consequences of America's adoption of the principle. The Jeffersonians and Jacksonians had thought that the citizen army was an adjunct and an assurance of democracy, but now it was plain that an armed citizenry might sow different seeds.

In the years since Jefferson, William Tecumseh Sherman and

the students of his campaigns had offered their insights into the nature of war waged by citizen armies, demonstrating that such war logically involves whole populations in a contest of rival terrorisms. By spawning the total war of Sherman, the citizen army had endangered rather than assured democracy, and of course it had endangered civilization itself. The readoption of the citizen army by the United States in 1917 harbored possible consequences unlike those foreseen in the early years of the Republic, more so since the devices of twentieth-century technology could now be put to the service of total war.

Furthermore, the new citizen army of 1917–1918 was to be turned over to the professionals as much as possible for its training and leadership. Although the professionals had neither the numbers nor the time to give what they considered adequate training, they would influence it as much as they could. The training of the citizen army had to be turned over to them, because in one way the American professionalist military tradition had not been sterile. Its very isolation from the main currents of nonmilitary American life had resulted from and contributed to its tradition of the highest professional excellence. From the days of the Maryland and Delaware Line in Washington's Continental Army onward, and especially from the founding of a true military profession in the United States after the establishment of the West Point of Dennis Mahan, the American military professionals had attempted to ensure that their small army was one of the best in quality. Inadequate financial support and inadequate organization had prevented their always succeeding, and sometimes their own conservatism had been a hindrance, especially in the post-Civil War years; but they had succeeded remarkably well.

The professional officers would control and command the new citizen army of 1917, and perhaps the new citizen army less represented the triumph of the Jeffersonian-Jacksonian tradition than the George Washington–Alexander Hamilton–Henry Knox variety of professionalism, brought up to date. In the ideas of Emory Upton and his disciples American military professionalism had diverged from its origins. Upton doubted the value of any soldiers but the most thorough professionals, or wartime recruits molded in their image, and the professional officer corps had followed Upton's type of professionalism. But Upton's professionalism was not the same

as Washington's, for Washington had not denied that citizen soldiers might become good soldiers. Washington had desired the
most thoroughly professional sort of training that was feasible
within a citizen army; he had believed that such training could
make effective fighting men of an armed citizenry even if extended
only on a part-time basis. He would have relied on regular soldiers
first, but he had believed that a citizen soldiery could become an
effective reserve.

It is significant that Leonard Wood, like George Washington,
called attention to the Swiss military system. The aim of Wood,
outsider though he was to contemporary professionals, was not to
break away from the American professionalist military tradition,
with its high standards of excellence. His aim was to rescue that
tradition from Emory Upton's transformation of it and to restore
it to its essentials as set forth by George Washington. While Upton
rejected a citizen soldiery, Wood, like Washington, was willing
to rely on citizen soldiers, though he was a professionalist in his
insistence that they receive as thoroughly professional a training as
possible. Leonard Wood's plan for a citizen army seemed to be a
departure from professionalism because in the generation before
Wood American military professionalism had fallen so much under
the spell of Emory Upton. In fact Wood's plan was not a departure
from professionalism so much as a twentieth-century reassertion of
George Washington's purpose of adapting European military
methods and skills to the special circumstances of the United States.
To that extent Wood was correct when he pleaded that his plan
accorded with the ideas of the founding fathers.

The United States went to war in 1917–1918 with a citizen army
given as professional a training as time permitted. A citizen army
went to war, however, and not even a Wood or Washington type
army, for it had not received such training for war in time of peace
as both Wood and Washington prescribed. Whether a citizen army
of the Wood or Washington type, prepared for war in time of
peace, could match good European troops, or whether Emory
Upton was right in contending it could not, had never been settled.
Whether the hastily constructed American army of 1917–1918 could
do the job was even more of a question.

XIII JOHN MC AULEY PALMER AND GEORGE C. MARSHALL *Universal Military Training*

> If American citizen armies, extemporized after the outbreak of war, could do as well as Washington's Continentals and as well as the citizen armies of Grant and Lee, what might they not do if organized and trained in time of peace? JOHN MC AULEY PALMER
>
> It is also assumed that Congress will enact (as the essential foundation of an effective national military organization), that every able-bodied young American shall be trained to defend his country. GEORGE C. MARSHALL

THE professionals were able to enjoy a triumph over Leonard Wood. The professionals commanded the army in the First World War, and they saw to it that the outsider Wood never got to lead troops in France. They did not give him a combat command commensurate with his rank and past services; they did not even allow him to take to France the 89th Division, which he trained in Kansas. His overt Republicanism contributed to his frustration, but it was less the political feelings of the Wilson administration that kept Wood at home than the resentment of professional soldiers at the man who had risen unconventionally through their ranks and then had broken convention still more to speak for the citizen army. Those two thorough professionals, General John J. Pershing of the American Expeditionary Force and General Peyton C. March, the chief of staff, disagreed about much else, but they agreed in disapproval of Leonard Wood.[1]

Yet in time Wood was able to salve his frustration with triumph over the professionals. For if they would not accept him, the powerful faction of the professionals led by Pershing were compelled by events to accept his ideas.

The United States fought the First World War with a citizen army, as Wood had said it must. The divisions designated as regular army, even the 1st Division, were laced with citizen recruits when they went into battle, so that in time the 1917 distinctions between regular army, National Guards, and National Army were dropped. The professional soldiers had to build their army from a rank and file as unsoldierly at first as any of the raw forces that had received the strictures of Emory Upton.

The result was the rout not of the citizen soldiers but of Uptonian pessimism. Forced to attempt what many of them had thought could not be done, the professional officer corps discovered that they could make a respectable army of citizens in much shorter time than they had believed. They discovered that Leonard Wood's conception of the time required to produce a combat infantryman had been closer to the truth than their own.

Pershing at first was deeply impressed by the lack of soldierly skills among his troops as compared with their British and French allies. He was also impressed and disturbed by the discouragement and defeatism of the allied armies. He was convinced, in accordance with American military doctrine since Dennis Mahan and earlier, that victory would demand taking the offensive; but the allied armies were too weary and too accustomed to trench warfare to promise a vigorous offensive, and his own troops at first were too unskilled. Therefore he established a lengthy program of additional training for American divisions arriving in France before he committed them to the front. The 1st Division, setting the pattern, remained in its training area at Gondrecourt from the arrival of its first elements on July 5, 1917, to October 21, learning basic tactical exercises and the use of various weapons from a seasoned French division. On October 21, the division began to move into a quiet sector of the front for further training, attached to a French division and with one battalion from each regiment going into the line for ten days, to be followed by the other battalions over a thirty-day period. Then the division returned to its training area to digest its experience in further tactical exercises. Not until January 18, 1918, did the 1st Division begin to take over a sector of the front.[2]

The rawness of his army and his Mahanian intentness upon

taking the offensive obliged Pershing to resort to such an elaborate training program. But in the summer and early fall of 1918 the program broke down and divisions had to go into line without the full training and seasoning Pershing had prescribed. The need for every rifleman and machinegunner to assist in repulsing the great German offensive compelled this, and then the needs of the great allied counteroffensive, the need to strike and strike again at the Germans while they were off balance, compelled further departures from schedule.

American divisions with little or no combat experience went into the Meuse-Argonne offensive, to attack a network of defensive positions twelve miles deep which the enemy must hold to prevent the breaking of the lateral railroad along his front. They suffered shocking losses which more seasoned troops would have known how to avoid, and they made beginners' mistakes that the more vigorous German army of a few months before might have turned into disasters. But they captured Montfaucon on the second day, after Marshal Henri Pétain had said that to take Montfaucon would require all autumn. By the beginning of November they were converting the Germans' retreat into a rout. Before the armistice the enemy's lateral railway and the strategic city of Sedan were under their guns. Pershing was still aware of their rawness and their consequent defects, but the memoirs he was to write reflect his pride that the citizen army he commanded had become by the 11th of November, the finest army in the world.[3]

Never again could Pershing take an Uptonian view of the qualities of a citizen army. As a thoughtful man he needed to rationalize his new respect for such an army, and for him to have borrowed his rationalization from Leonard Wood would have been an unpleasant pill indeed. Fortunately for Pershing, there had served on his staff a man as capable as Wood of developing a cogent rationale for the citizen army, but a man who also had a correct professional background. So convinced was Pershing of the merit of this officer's ideas, that when the War Department requested the A.E.F. commander to send home an officer to represent him in planning the postwar military establishment, Pershing sent the man to speak for him without specific instructions. The officer was Lieutenant Colonel John McAuley Palmer.[4]

Palmer reached the War Department, to discover that under the direction of Chief of Staff Peyton C. March, the general staff had completed a plan for the postwar army without him. March had his own ideas on the proper American military establishment, and he felt no fondness for Pershing's opinions. He had returned early from France to become chief of staff, and he had not witnessed the citizen army in its battlefield triumphs. He remained an Uptonian, and he gave the War Plans Division of the general staff no choice but to prepare an Uptonian plan for presentation to Congress. March conceded to the modern demand for numbers a proposal of universal military training, but the heart of his plan was an Uptonian expansible regular army, with a peace strength as high as 482,000 enlisted men. The corps and divisions of the regular army were to be kept usually at half strength, so that citizen recruits could be incorporated directly into them in war.[5]

Since Palmer's work seemed done before his arrival in Washington, he took up other duties as chief of the War Plans Division of the general staff. But although he and Pershing could do little while March spoke to Congress for the army, Congress did not have to accept March's Uptonian plan. Despite the rising reaction against Wilson's internationalism, most Congressmen recognized that the United States probably could not return to the military impotence of the prewar years, and Congress was willing to endorse a more ambitious military program than before the war. But Congress would not yet endorse a swollen Uptonian regular army of nearly half a million men and the disdain for citizen soldiers that such an army implied. Leonard Wood testified before the Senate Committee on Military Affairs to fuel its doubts about the March plan, and the quest for a postwar military policy stalled in the congressional military committees.[6]

Senator James W. Wadsworth, Jr., of New York, the chairman of the Senate Military Affairs Committee, wrote later that in 1919, he nearly despaired of getting a good military bill. General March and the army would not offer a bill that Congress could accept. Wadsworth wanted to give the country an effective army, but he did not believe that the goal was to be achieved by borrowing part of the organizational scheme of the defeated German army. The stubborn insistence of the professional army command on Uptonian professionalism seemed likely to kill the opportunity to install a viable military policy.

Wadsworth was to say later that he did not see a way out until he heard the testimony of John McAuley Palmer. Certain younger staff officers influenced by Pershing, Palmer, and the war experience had been urging the congressional committees to hear this officer. They noted Pershing's confidence in him and said that he was a man who had dedicated himself to the study of American military policy and would surely offer something worth hearing. Even then Wadsworth's committee did not expect more than the usual army viewpoint when in October, 1919, Palmer testified as head of one of the sections of the general staff. It was noteworthy that more officers crowded the committee room to hear Palmer than had turned up for any previous witnesses save those of the highest rank. But what really made the committee sit up and take notice was Palmer's astonishing and abrupt statement that the official army bill presented by March was "not in harmony with the genius of American institutions." [7]

Asked to explain, Palmer spent nearly two days elaborating on his objections to an Uptonian army and offering his own substitute plan. He had already joined with two other staff officers in working out such a plan when the Wadsworth committee requested the War Department's opinion on a universal training scheme before the Senate, but March had buried the memorandum Palmer prepared at that time. Now Palmer's testimony so impressed the Senate Military Affairs Committee that the members voted unanimously to request Palmer's assignment to them as military adviser. The War Department acceded, disclaiming responsibility for the advice Palmer might give.[8]

Thus after one false start, the man who would inherit Leonard Wood's mantle as the principal champion of the citizen army stepped to stage center. Palmer was to emphasize the word citizen in that phrase even more than Wood had done, for while Wood can best be defined as an intellectual descendant of George Washington, there was in Palmer's thought a notable inheritance from the Jeffersonian-Jacksonian tradition. More than Wood's, Palmer's task would be to reconcile the dual American military traditions.

One side of Palmer's career was thoroughly professional. He was

U.S.M.A. 1892. He had enjoyed a reputation as a coming man through his youthful alternation of staff and line duties before the World War. He had served as an operations officer on Pershing's staff in France from the spring of 1917, participating in the completion of the tactical organization and the general training plans of the A.E.F. He had helped on the reconnaissances and strategic studies which determined the area of operations for the force and had generally impressed his associates with his energy and solid ability. He was a small man and not a robust one, and his activities were so incessant that he broke his health, just as observers predicted for him one of the highest places in the army. But he had returned to active duty in the last month of the war to distinguish himself in the field, commanding the 58th Infantry Brigade of the 29th Division in three attacks in the Meuse-Argonne.

There was another side to Palmer, too. He was the son of Major General John M. Palmer of George Thomas's XIV Army Corps and the Army of the Cumberland, hero of Stone's River, Chickamauga, and the Atlanta campaign. General John M. Palmer was a lawyer who had become a political colonel after raising a regiment from his district. He was swept to high leadership by a combination of political standing in his state and native capacity to command. His military career was of the model of his fellow Illinoisan Black Jack Logan's, and through his father the younger Palmer stood in the line of descent from Logan as well as from the professionals. The younger John McAuley Palmer knew, because he knew his own father, that Emory Upton's strictures against amateur soldiers were exaggerated. His father had been an officer whom any professional would respect. The younger Palmer had too keen and independent a mind to permit his career among the professionals to obscure his father's memory.[9]

The elder Palmer contributed directly to the younger's military thought. Initially after graduating from West Point, the latter was inclined to accept the Uptonian ideas prevalent in the officer corps. But old General Palmer, now a member of the Senate Military Affairs Committee, warned him that it would be better to offer a second best military plan that Congress could accept than a best plan that could not pass Congress. Determined to convince his father of the wisdom of Uptonian doctrine, young Palmer nevertheless set out to draft a cogent Uptonian plan; but now his common sense collided with the principal practical defect of the expansible army idea:

When I assumed a peacetime nucleus big enough to make a real foundation for effective expansion for a great war, I found that the American people would be saddled with a big standing army in time of peace. When I assumed a peacetime nucleus small enough to give any chance of acceptance by Congress, it would result in too small a war army—unless I also assumed a rate of expansion that would be obviously absurd.[10]

Palmer returned to his father, who set him further along non-Uptonian lines:

After my last conversation with my old friend, not long before his death, I came away with another idea. If American citizen armies, extemporized after the outbreak of war, could do as well as Washington's Continentals and as well as the citizen armies of Grant and Lee, what might they not do if organized and trained in time of peace? [11]

Palmer pondered this new line of thought through the first decade of the twentieth century. In 1910, after graduating from the Staff College at Fort Leavenworth, he was assigned to the general staff and directed to prepare suggestions on army organization for the consideration of Leonard Wood and Secretary of War Henry L. Stimson. He offered a plan which would make the regular army a nonexpansible organization ready for immediate employment as an expeditionary force, while the war army would be a citizen army drawn from a reorganized national guard and from organized reserves. The plan departed from Upton more than Wood was accustomed to doing, but it impressed Stimson and he took up many of its suggestions in an annex to his annual report for 1912 in which he offered his recommendations on "The Organization of the Land Forces of the United States." [12]

Thus Palmer was a part of the stirring of new ideas in the War Department in the Stimson-Wood period. Before much could come of the stirring, the "Manchu law" of 1912 cut short Palmer's general staff assignment, Stimson gave way in the War Department to Wilson's Secretary Lindley M. Garrison, and Wood went to his already mentioned exile. But Palmer was embarked on a lifetime of campaigning for a citizen army; he had made his public break with the Uptonians, he had discovered that he could win influence to effect his ideas, and he now sought to restore and widen that influence to advance again the idea of the citizen army. In 1916, he contributed to the preparedness literature a book on the citizen army, *An Army of the People*. Recalled to the general staff just before American entrance into the World War, his study of the topic helped win him an assignment to assist in preparing a plan for universal military training, for possible submission to Congress later. When the war came, that plan provided much of the blueprint for constructing the National Army to fight the war.[13]

Now in 1919, John McAuley Palmer returned to the promotion of his citizen army ideas before Congress. As advisers to the Senate Military Affairs Committee, for ten months he and the like-minded Lieutenant Colonel John W. Gulick worked with Wadsworth's committee in framing a new army bill to create a citizen army. The Uptonians of the general staff fretted in witnessing this process, but the War Department had disclaimed responsibility for Palmer's ideas when freeing him to work with the committee, and the Uptonians profited by the example to keep the adviser to the House Military Affairs Committee tightly in rein. Nevertheless, the National Defense Act of 1920 proved to be much more Palmer's bill than a reflection of the original War Department bill; it was a measure cut to the pattern rather of Palmer and Leonard Wood than of Emory Upton.[14]

The ideas that guided Colonel Palmer as he helped write the National Defense Act of 1920 were those he had outlined in his testimony to the Senate Military Affairs Committee. He was to set them forth in greater detail in 1927, in his book *Statesmanship or War*. Those ideas shaped the National Defense Act of 1920 and continued through the 1920s and 1930s to hold the allegiance of Pershing and other officers who sought a better military policy than the Defense Act and who could no longer content themselves with Uptonian policy. Much of the National Defense Act gradually fell into disuse, but Palmer kept some discussion of the citizen army alive until general interest was restored again by the needs and events of World War II.

Palmer proceeded from a rejection of Emory Upton that was more explicit and blunt than Leonard Wood's. He rejected Upton's belief in the superiority of the German military system, and he rejected Upton's advocacy of military rather than civilian formulation of military policy. A distinguishing feature of his thought that gave him a greater kinship with the Jeffersonian tradition than Wood had possessed, was his insistence that an American military program must grow out of the American nation rather than ask the nation to adjust itself to an alien military scheme. "The form of military institutions must be determined on political grounds, with due regard to national genius and tradition," he would one day write. "The military pedant may fail by proposing adequate and economical forces under forms that are intolerable to the national genius." [15]

Palmer believed that Upton's greatest failure was in this respect. The German military system Upton had admired was suitable to the genius and tradition of Imperial Germany. It was a military system for an autocracy. "The army was officered by the aristocracy and was maintained as a school for drilling the German masses in subserviency to autocracy." It was a military system designed to wage aggressive war. The German army which Bismarck had created was kept after Bismarck's work of unifying Germany was done. After its legitimate object, national unification, was fulfilled, the swollen German army was bound to find an illegitimate object. The object was aggression.[16]

The German army turned to aggression also because Germany followed the pernicious plan, albeit admired by Upton, of delegating policy-making to the military. Once the military controlled without civilian hindrance the shaping of military policy, military policy swallowed up foreign policy. The German government so committed itself to furthering its political aims by war that it entered the area where "the extent and direction of its political aims were determined by the possibilities of military success." [17]

Such a military system, autocratic and aggressive, was appropriate to Germany (though it led ultimately to German disaster), but it was not appropriate to the democratic and peaceful purposes of the United States. Though Palmer rejected Upton's admiration for Germany military organization, he displayed a greater familiarity than Upton's with the thought of the German military philosopher Clausewitz, and he was aware of Clausewitz's dictum that war is an extension of politics by other means. Palmer's emphasis was on the words *an extension of politics.* Where Upton had treated of military policy in a vacuum, Palmer tried to keep constantly in mind that the proper function of an army was to be an instrument of political purposes, and in the United States therefore of democratic political purposes.[18]

So that American military policy might better serve democratic political purposes, and so to that end there might be more effective civilian control of the military, Palmer urged the consolidation of the War and Navy Departments into a Department of National Defense. The existing defense organization, he argued, gave no opportunity for army, navy, and the new air officers to come face to face and be made to reconcile their various objectives in the presence of civilians of superior authority charged with fitting the demands of the separate services into overall national policy. Therefore Congress and the President were buffeted to and fro by the rival demands of the services for appropriations and men, and national defense policy responded to whichever service could apply the greater pressure upon Congress and the President. No civilians were in a position to receive coherent military advice and then to adjust that advice to general national purposes. In fact, beyond a Department of National Defense, Palmer advocated a Council of National Defense in which the leaders of the Defense Department could confer with the secretaries of state, the treasury, and commerce to harmonize the national military policy with political and economic policy.[19]

Palmer believed that civilian control of the military and thus subordination of the military to general national purposes could be still more effectively accomplished by the establishment of a thoroughgoing citizen army. If the army were a citizens' institution rather than the preserve of professionals isolated from national life, the civilians in Congress and the Defense Department and the executive departments generally would be men who had served in the army. They would understand something about it, and they could not be misled by attempts of the military to make all military matters seem esoteric. Effective civilian control of the military demanded civilians with knowledge of the military.[20]

But civilian control was not the only positive advantage of a citizen army. Palmer believed that a citizen army could be effective in a strictly military sense, not for aggressive purposes but certainly for the defensive purposes of the United States. For evidence he turned, like Washington and Wood, to the Swiss army, but with a new argument at hand: the Swiss army had helped to ensure the neutrality of its country in the World War. He conceded that "Militarists find it convenient to dismiss the Swiss Army from serious consideration under the pretense that it has never been tested in war." But this view, he said, was a superficial one, since "The modern Swiss Army was created not to engage in war, but to keep war out of Switzerland." Considered in this light, the Swiss army had passed its supreme test in 1914–1918: "Its military victory was so complete that it did not have to fire a shot. Judged from the standpoint of aims achieved, no army ever had a more complete success." [21]

Palmer believed that the first purpose of the American army should similarly be to keep the country out of war, and that for such a purpose no army could serve better than an American version of the Swiss citizen army. He believed that such an army would have prevented the great American wars of the nineteenth and twentieth centuries. If every American state had possessed in 1861 a military force of trained citizens like the Swiss army, the whole maintained under federal standards, the South would not have dared to resist the federal government. For while the Southern states would have possessed trained soldiers in proportion to their population, the Northern states would have possessed a similar army in proportion to the Northern population. A struggle between South and North under such circumstances could have ended only in Northern victory, as even the South of 1861 must have recognized. [22]

Just as the Confederacy pursued its ambitions because the North was militarily weak, so Palmer believed Imperial Germany had pursued its ambitions because the liberal democracies were militarily weak. He believed that if the United States and Great Britain had commanded effective defensive armies in 1914, Germany would not have dared to go to war, and he believed the Swiss system would have offered adequate armies for that purpose. Even if war had broken out in Europe, if the United States had possessed an effective defensive army the German government could not have challenged American rights at sea nor ignored the efforts of the American government to restore peace. And even if eventually an American army had had to sail to France, an army suitable for such an enterprise might quickly have been constructed by giving further training to troops already trained for defense under the Swiss system and already organized into regiments.[23]

Therefore Palmer recommended the Swiss system for the United States. To the Senate Military Affairs Committee in 1919 and 1920 he proposed almost a duplication of the Swiss system, including conscription to secure universal military training. Not surprisingly, the committee discovered that it was necessary to prune conscription from Palmer's plan in order to obtain congressional consideration for the rest of it.[24] Thereupon Palmer argued through the rest of the 1920s and 1930s that volunteering could afford adequate numbers for his system.

He could construct a plausible argument. Switzerland, he said in order to fit the mood of the twenties, needed universal military training because from a population of less than 4,000,000 she had to mobilize 300,000 soldiers in three or four days. But the defense of the United States would be assured if 500,000 effective soldiers could be mobilized from a population of 115,000,000, and for that purpose volunteering would suffice.[25]

This argument was plausible but it was not really convincing. If the population from which the United States could draw its soldiers was immensely greater than Switzerland's, so were the tasks the American army might be called upon to perform. The First World War had demanded conscription, and so would any future emergency of similar proportions. If Palmer's arguments that citizen soldiers ought to be trained in peace were valid, all the citizen soldiers who were to be called upon in war should have had military training in peace. The climate of the 1920s and the 1930s compelled Palmer to suppress in public the universal military training part of his plan; but his plan was incomplete without universal military training, and the incompleteness was bound to be remedied whenever the occasion was ripe.

Without universal military training Palmer's plan was incomplete because it failed to meet one of the major premises of his thought. He believed a citizen army was appropriate to the United

States because it fit the national genius and political system, but he also believed it was appropriate because it offered the United States the only American means of mustering an army suited to modern war. Modern war, he believed, demanded mobilization of the whole of the potential military manpower of the nation. In 1919, before he felt obliged to gloss over this point, he emphasized it to the Wadsworth committee as one of the foundations on which everything else he said about the value of a citizen army rested:

I think this war has demonstrated, that . . . there is no measure of ultimate war strength other than the total man power of a nation; and that the military policy should be so constructed as to develop all or any necessary part of that man power in time to meet any given emergency. . . .
The very first requirement of strategy is superior numbers, and the only way to be assured of approaching that as soon as possible is to be prepared to develop the total man power if necessary. . . .

I believe that complete preparedness implies capacity to develop all or any necessary part of the man power of the nation in time to meet any given emergency, and that this can be assured only through universal military training.[26]

Basically Palmer's plan was for universal military training, but in the 1920s and 1930s he felt he could do no more than plead the cause of the citizen army against the Uptonian army. If he could win increasing acceptance for the citizen army idea, at least he would be opening the door to acceptance of universal military training when a more auspicious hour arrived.

Thus he persisted in his advocacy of the citizen army. More thoroughly than Wood, he would have had the United States adopt the organizational details of the Swiss military system. He would have reduced American regular soldiers within the continental United States to the role of the Swiss regulars. He believed that some substantial regular formations were necessary to guard the outlying possessions. But he believed that within the continental borders there should be only enough regulars to maintain training camps and technical services for an army whose officer corps as well as rank and file would be citizens first and soldiers second. Like the Swiss conscripts, Palmer's American citizen soldiers would go into military training camps for a period of each year, for sixty-five days at the age of twenty-one and for diminishing periods to eleven days at age thirty-nine. Thereafter they would not serve again in peacetime. Men with leadership ability would be selected from among the trainees for additional training. They would train and serve first as NCO's, and then the more successful NCO's would receive additional training and experience to become commissioned officers. The performance of commissioned officers would be tested each year in the annual training and maneuvers, and those who continued to display growing aptitudes would receive further promotions, until they rose to be regimental and brigade and division commanders. Such advanced training would be voluntary even if the initial training should some day become compulsory and universal.

A permanent high command would have to be maintained, but this command also could be selected from those civilian leaders who demonstrated the necessary abilities, although without discrimination against any of the small group of regular officers who qualified for high responsibility. The general staff would combine professional and nonprofessional officers.[27]

Palmer thought that mixing in all ranks of professional soldiers and civilians was among the most important assets of his program. Misunderstanding between professionals and nonprofessionals had been one of the plagues of all past American armies. Palmer would have had the professionals and nonprofessionals work together in peace so that they could learn to work together in war.[28]

His enthusiasm for citizen officers as well as citizen soldiers set Palmer apart from Leonard Wood and made him an heir of Thomas Jefferson and John A. Logan. "There will always be a place for professional soldiers such as Grant and Lee, Sherman and Stonewall Jackson and Pershing," he was to say, "but the door must not be closed to civic leaders with native military talent such as Washington and Greene, Andrew Jackson and John A. Logan."[29]

There was a distinct echo of Logan in Palmer's remarks on military officers. Palmer by no means went so far as Logan in derogation of the value of professional training, but he held that while an officer's value is the product of knowledge plus native capacity, native capacity is the far more important of the two. He compared the ineffectuality in practice of the highly knowledgeable Henry W.

Halleck with the success of the untrained Nathan Bedford Forrest, and his comparison would have delighted John A. Logan.[30] "The fact is," he said, "that military leaders, like poets, are born and not made."

Lieutenant Colonel G. Washington of the Virginia militia [he wrote] . . . cuts a much better figure even in military history than Major General Sir Edward Braddock, a war-scarred and much be-decorated veteran of His Majesty's regular army. Likewise Major General Andrew Jackson of the Tennessee militia has seen the backs of the troops that drove Napoleon's imperial eagles out of Spain. England's greatest general, Oliver Cromwell, was a typical citizen soldier. He had had no practice or interest in arms until after his fortieth year. He started with little military *knowing* but when he first drew his sword he was full of the great gift of resolute *doing*.[31]

George Washington himself would not have been likely to write a passage in that spirit. By the time he prescribed a military policy for the United States Washington had become aware of the handicaps he had suffered as a military amateur and was thoroughly committed to professional training for officers. Palmer's military recommendations seem to have been less in line with Washington's views than Palmer supposed. From his discovery in the late 1920s of Washington's 1783 "Sentiments on a Peace Establishment," Palmer consistently quoted Washington in behalf of his own proposals. He was on solid ground in seeking from Washington material with which to challenge Emory Upton. But if not an Uptonian, Washington was a professionalist, and Palmer's use of him as the champion of the citizen army required judiciousness in the selection of Washington's remarks, emphasizing those about a trained militia as "the palladium of our security" and glossing over those about militia as "a broken staff." [32]

It was the Jeffersonian strain in Palmer's thought as well as the Washingtonian that made him so direct in his rejection of Emory Upton. He did not accept Upton's attacks on state organization of military forces. What was lacking in the early wars of which Upton wrote, he said, was adequate standards of military skill. Without such standards generally accepted by civilians and by professional soldiers, federal rather than state organization would have done no good; with such standards, there was no reason why

the Swiss military system could not work within the framework of
the state national guards (though of course Palmer favored federal
supervision).[33]

The break with Upton emphatically included Palmer's rejection
of the heart of Uptonian military plans, the expansible regular army.
The whole point of the expansibility plan was to bring wartime
recruits under the influence of regulars, but Palmer preferred an
army that was always primarily a citizen army. There should indeed be peacetime formations ready to expand promptly to war
strength, he said; but they should be the citizen formations of a
citizen army. Any effort to effect the Uptonian expansible army
plan would leave the regular formations less able to defend the
Philippines, Hawaii, Alaska, and the Canal Zone, a task they could
best perform if they were always near full strength.[34]

Again sounding the Jeffersonian note, Palmer made it clear that
he rejected the Upton expansible army plan largely because expos-
ing a citizen army to the intimate influence of regulars would be
harmful, not only to the citizen army but to the nation. It would
discourage that full development of military knowledge among
citizens that was essential to civilian control. By requiring the
maintenance of a large force of regulars, it would cost too much
money. Above all, it would subvert democracy by subjecting the
citizen to the control of a group whose historic tendencies were
antithetical to democracy and by depriving democratic citizens of
the means to defend themselves on their own. "A free state cannot
continue to be democratic in peace and autocratic in war. . . . An
enduring government by the people must include an army of the
people among its institutions." [35]

Apart from military affairs the values of democracy seemed to
Palmer to be beyond debate, and he did not believe those values
needed to be vitiated by military weakness. There was no inherent
taint of military weakness in democratic political institutions. When
democracies fell before autocratic militarisms, it was because they
had allowed themselves to become too rich and too soft. But there
was no need for a democracy to become decadent. It could save
itself through the citizen army; it could save itself through the
prescription that Palmer like Leonard Wood was fond of quoting
from Demosthenes: "Cease to hire your armies. Go yourselves,

every man of you, and stand in the ranks; and either a victory beyond all victories awaits you, or, falling, you shall fall greatly and worthy of your past." [36]

Demosthenes's "every man of you," suggested universal military training. For universal military training was implicit in all that Palmer wrote even during the 1920s and 1930s when he did not wish publicly to emphasize it. With his inheritance from both of the American military traditions, Palmer stood where the two most closely approached each other and even overlapped, on the point of belief in the military obligation of all American citizens. The Jeffersonians, despite their suspicion of things military, endorsed the principle of a universal military obligation in the early militia laws. Washington approved the same principle even while he sought to select a group for special training from among the general militia. On this common ground Palmer hoped to reconcile the two American military traditions to both of which he, like his country, stood heir. He sought to apply a Washingtonian measure of military knowledge and training to a Jeffersonian citizen army. He sought to accomplish it by establishing an active military obligation for all male citizens, providing time and opportunity for the Jeffersonian citizen army to receive a Washingtonian military training.

This plan of reconciling the two American military traditions seemed to fit so well the military needs of the first four and a half decades of the twentieth century that the national indifference to military affairs in the 1920s and 1930s could not kill it. It sprang promptly into hardy life, universal military training and all, upon the coming of World War II.

Palmer's work with the Senate Military Affairs Committee in 1919 and 1920, supported by the powerful influence of Pershing's testimony before the joint Senate and House military committees, wrote much of his thought, except for conscription, into the National Defense Act of 1920. The act cut the regular army proposed by General March nearly in half, and it substituted an avowed reliance on a citizen soldiery. The regular army of 280,000 was to be organized not on the expansible plan but as an expeditionary force and a guardian of the outlying territories. The wartime army was to be built principally on the National Guard, now brought under more federal supervision, and the larger Organized Reserves, the counterpart of the National Army of 1917. The regular army would offer training to the Guard and the Reserves, but the citizens' formations were intended to be led and trained increasingly by their own citizen officers. Many of these would emerge from an expanded Reserve Officers' Training Corps program in the colleges and from Citizens' Military Training Camps on the Plattsburg model.

On the general staff itself nonprofessionals were to mingle with professional officers. Furthermore, joint general staff committees of professionals and nonprofessionals were to draw the plans for implementing the law. They prepared a scheme whereby the country would be divided into nine corps areas, with each corps area receiving one infantry division of the regular army plus an additional training staff to train in each corps area two infantry divisions of the National Guard and three infantry divisions of the Organized Reserves.[37]

"The important thing to remember," said General Pershing in summary, "is that the new law simply provides that our traditional citizen army be organized in time of peace instead of being extemporized, as in the past, after danger has actually come." [38]

Unfortunately for Palmer, Pershing, and the other advocates of the citizen army, the National Defense Act of 1920 was allowed to atrophy. As early as 1922 Congress reduced the authorized strength of the regular army from 280,000 to 125,000 and empowered the President to reorganize the army in accordance with its new authorized strength. Palmer urged that some of the regular army divisions should be demobilized. Despite the fact that Pershing was now chief of staff, preeminently the most powerful single figure in the army, and still Palmer's supporter, the Uptonians of the general staff were able to exploit the occasion to secure an expansible army plan. They persuaded the War Department to retain all existing regular divisions, albeit at greatly reduced strength, so that they might serve as skeletons for future expansion. To keep the regular formations as large as possible, they secured an abolition of the corps area training centers and the insertion of their personnel into the regular divisions. Thus the Uptonians sacrificed the program for training a citizen army to the maintenance of Uptonian skeleton units in the regular army. They did so despite

Pershing's warning that the regular army's role as an effective expeditionary force and guardian of the outlying territories would also be sacrificed. Reduced in strength, the regular army concentrated on its own problems and neglected the instruction of the National Guards and Organized Reserves, and the former sank back towards its unready condition of years past while the latter virtually disappeared.[39]

National military planning, Uptonian or Jeffersonian, reached a nadir among the euphoric world peace hopes of the 1920s and early 1930s. But John M. Palmer continued patiently to push his ideas upon anyone who would heed them, producing books and articles in his direct, commonsense, somewhat dogmatic, but highly persuasive style. He followed his *Statesmanship or War* of 1927 with *Washington, Lincoln, Wilson: Three War Statesmen* in 1930. In the latter he revealed his discovery of Washington's neglected "Sentiments on a Peace Establishment" of 1783 and enlisted the citizen army facet of Washington's thought in his own cause.[40] He was a brigadier general but was on the retired list by the time Hitler's invasion of Poland in 1939 gave new point to his arguments. He returned to public life the next spring during the German conquest of France to serve the Military Training Camps Association, an outgrowth of Leonard Wood's Plattsburg camps, by lobbying with Congress for a new preparedness program. He was able to participate in drafting what became the Burke-Wadsworth bill and the Selective Training and Service Act of 1940. His influence was not diminished by the presence of his old associate James W. Wadsworth, one of the congressional sponsors of the new law.[41]

The Selective Service Act established the principle of a universal obligation to military service in the face of the Hitler menace. But Palmer wanted acceptance of the principle of universal military service as a permanent policy, to ensure once Hitler was gone that new Hitlers would not arise or that at least they could be dealt with readily. He therefore seized the occasion to return to his long-range arguments for a citizen army, discarding his reluctance of the 1920s and 1930s to propose permanent establishment of universal military training. In 1941 he published a new book, *America in Arms.*

The occasion was appropriate. World War II was much more a war of technology than World War I had been, but it was also a war of mass armies, demanding a vast mobilization of national manpower. Furthermore, World War II more clearly created world situations that suggested the need for a constant postwar readiness to assert the military strength of the United States. It grew evident through 1940–1945 that the United States would not again be able to sink into the isolation and the concomitant military slumber that had followed World War I. Palmer offered in universal military training a plan for constant American military preparedness, and the early 1940s demonstrated that some such plan was what the United States would need. Since Palmer offered his plan in the persuasive guise of accord with Washington's wisdom and American military traditions, its aptness to the needs of the time might well have seemed complete.

Among the circle of professional officers who had emerged from World War I rejecting Uptonian doctrine and accepting the need for and the merits of the citizen army was George Catlett Marshall. Marshall like Palmer had become one of Pershing's protégés. Demonstrating brilliant promise as a staff officer in his earliest army assignments long before the World War, he had fulfilled that promise and captured Pershing's attention as G-3, operations officer, of the 1st Division and then assistant G-3 of First Army. He had arranged the secret movement of about a million men in a three-week period, over inadequate roads and railroads, from the area of St. Mihiel to the Meuse-Argonne, with the St. Mihiel offensive still in progress. That feat had won him the place of chief of operations of First Army and, at the close of the war, a position as aide-de-camp to Pershing. As his aide he helped prepare material for Pershing's advocacy of the citizen army before Congress and the country.[42]

Marshall's path had several times crossed that of John M. Palmer. Marshall had early shown high capacity as instructor in the Staff College at Fort Leavenworth in 1908–1910; there Palmer was among the promising instructor's more promising students. The two had come into some contact again when Palmer was on Pershing's staff and Marshall was G-3 of the 1st Division. Marshall was Pershing's aide and the whole Pershing circle was cooperating with Palmer

during the latter's days as adviser to the Senate Military Affairs
Committee in 1919–1920. Palmer joined Marshall among Pershing's
aides after the passage of the National Defense Act. In 1929
Marshall was among those Palmer asked to read the manuscript
of *Washington, Lincoln, Wilson,* and he reacted with enthusiasm.[43]

Marshall's staff duties in World War I did not permit him to win
the public and congressional attention that might have accompanied
line command, and line command would probably have brought
him more rapid promotion. When the war ended he was a temporary brigadier general, but he reverted to major with the coming of peace, and through most of the interwar years his advancement was disappointingly slow. During the long period of Douglas
MacArthur's tour as chief of staff he seemed to be going nowhere,
for disagreements dating from the time when Marshall was First
Army G-3 and MacArthur a division commander had been nourished into lasting resentment by MacArthur's sensitive ego. Nevertheless, Marshall had the potent backing of Pershing and of the
Pershing circle, and his personal file in the Adjutant General's Department contained as remarkable a collection of encomiums as ever
followed an American officer. When Malin Craig replaced Mac-
Arthur as chief of staff in 1935 Marshall's star began to rise. Pershing
himself interceded with Franklin D. Roosevelt to ensure the continuance of its rise, and in 1939 Marshall succeeded Craig as chief
of staff.[44]

Thus during World War II, a man whose ideas on the American
military establishment were in accord with John M. Palmer's was
to lead the army. This time planning for the postwar military
establishment would not be directed by an Uptonian Peyton C.
March, but by a friend of the citizen army. Marshall's intellectual
inheritance did not include so much of a Jeffersonian strain as did
Palmer's, despite his Virginia Military Institute background. It is
significant of Marshall's professional outlook, for example, that he
hoped during the war to be accorded the title of commanding general of the army as well as chief of staff, a hope with which Emory
Upton would have sympathized.[45] One doubts that Marshall would
have written passages like Palmer's more extreme ones on the preeminence of native capacity rather than knowledge in making a
successful general. But on the essential issue of a citizen army as

opposed to an Uptonian professional army as the proper military force for the United States, Marshall and Palmer were in accord.

The two men worked together again in 1940, when they brought representatives of the army and of citizens' preparedness groups together to write the selective service bill. Soon after the United States went to war a group to plan postwar military policy appeared in the Army Service Forces, at first concerning itself mainly with demobilization. Marshall presently broadened its scope and elevated its status, making it part of the War Department Special Staff. To ensure that it would give sound and thorough attention to a citizen army program, he recalled Palmer to active duty to serve with it and as special assistant to the chief of staff.[46]

Palmer discovered that even now there remained within the officer corps a considerable sentiment for building the postwar army around an Uptonian core of regulars. So much did such sentiment disturb him that he believed he should call for support for the citizen army from the highest level. He turned to Marshall and suggested that he prepare for Marshall a policy statement on the citizen army which could be issued over Marshall's signature as an official War Department directive. Marshall agreed, and the result was their collaboration in preparing War Department Circular 347, issued August 24, 1944. This statement became the foundation of War Department and Defense Department military recommendations for the rest of the 1940s. In it Marshall gave official repudiation to the military doctrines of John C. Calhoun and Emory Upton and endorsed an American army plan which, through John McAuley Palmer, had antecedents in the moderate professionalism of George Washington and Leonard Wood and in the citizen army tradition of Thomas Jefferson and John A. Logan.[47]

War Department Circular 347 did not include the Swiss-army details of Palmer's proposals of the 1920s and 1930s, now of dubious relevance to the American military situation. Otherwise it was thoroughly a statement of Palmer's arguments, often almost literally following Palmer's testimony to the Senate Military Affairs Committee in 1919.[48] The circular stated that there are two types of military organization through which the whole manpower of a nation may be drawn into its army. The first is the system of Germany and Japan, in which "leadership in war and the control of military preparations and policy" are concentrated "in a special class or caste of professional soldiers." In this system the common citizen is to be a private soldier or at most a noncommissioned officer in war; "only the brawn of a people is prepared for war," since the professional officers reserve all military applications of intelligence to themselves.

The second type of organization for a mass army, said Palmer and Marshall, is one in which the professional establishment is kept no larger than necessary to meet normal peacetime requirements, while the war army is created from "organized units drawn from a citizen army reserve, effectively organized for this purpose in time of peace." Palmer and Marshall made clear that they spoke of an army as thoroughly shaped by the citizenry as military necessity would permit. Not only was the professional cadre to be kept small in this type of army, but there was to be "full opportunity for competent citizen soldiers to acquire practical experience through temporary active service and to rise by successive steps to any rank for which they can definitely qualify." Facilities designed to promote the advancement in rank of citizen soldiers were to be "essential and predominating characteristics of the peace establishment." This second organizational type is the proper type for the United States.

The first type, said Palmer and Marshall, offers "no adequate provision for developing the latent military leadership and genius of the people as a whole. It therefore has no place among the institutions of a modern democratic state based upon the conception of government by the people." The second type remedies that deficiency, for "its leadership is not exclusively concentrated in a professional soldier class," but instead all citizen soldiers are encouraged to rise to the highest grades of leadership that their abilities and wishes permit. The second type has other advantages as well: with military knowledge diffused among the citizenry, it offers a public opinion well equipped for judging military issues; it provides a large war army at less cost and less strain in the support of a peacetime military force; and it is in line with the American military tradition that has always prevailed in practice and that has given the United States an effective army, ultimately, in every war.

As all our great wars have been fought in the main by citizen armies, the proposal for an organized citizen army reserve in time of peace is merely a proposal for perfecting a traditional national institution to meet modern requirements which no longer permit extemporization after the outbreak of war.

Like Palmer's books, War Department Circular 347 claimed Washington as the father of the citizen army: "This is the type of army which President Washington proposed to the first Congress as one of the essential foundations of the new American Republic." More than that, the circular held that the citizen army was the only type that Washington or any constitutionalist could advocate: "The *type* of our military institutions was determined in the beginning by the form of our government and has not changed since Washington's administration."

In 1944 it was a *mass* citizen army that the future seemed to require. The atomic bomb was an uncertain possibility, and despite the advances of more conventional military technology World War II was still demanding great numbers of troops. The coming global responsibilities of the United States seemed sure to do the same. Therefore Palmer and Marshall proposed to base their citizen army on universal military training, the plan which had underlain Palmer's ideas and those of the Pershing circle since World War I. "It is also assumed," said War Department Circular 346, "that Congress will enact (as the essential foundation of an effective national military organization), that every able-bodied young American shall be trained to defend his country." [49]

Palmer's old associate James W. Wadsworth had already introduced into Congress a bill to provide universal military training, the Gurney-Wadsworth bill of February 11, 1943. This measure would have provided for one year of military training for youths between eighteen and twenty-one, to be followed by four years in the citizens' reserve.[50] Henry L. Stimson, who with Leonard Wood and John M. Palmer had endorsed the citizen army concept when he was secretary of war in the Taft administration, was now secretary of war again and endorsed the concept once more. Furthermore, as early as 1943, President Franklin D. Roosevelt began a series of statements throwing his powerful support to the idea of universal training of youth.[51] Never had a plan for a trained citizen army enjoyed such broad civilian and military support as in the closing years of World War II; never had its Uptonian opponents in the army been so subdued as now, when chief of staff, secretary of war, and President all supported it.

In the closing years of the war, it is true, President Roosevelt became preoccupied with his vision of peace secured through worldwide international organization and through firm American friendship with the Soviet Union. American emphasis on a mass army might have run counter to this vision. Doubtless with an eye to domestic political problems also, Roosevelt with characteristic caginess suggested that the sort of universal training he desired would be only in part military, and he refused to make clear what such a suggestion meant. But with the accession of Harry S. Truman to the presidency, the trained citizen army received unprecedented Presidential support.[52]

Truman had been a citizen soldier in World War I, and he remained proud of that title and of the accomplishments of the citizen army he had witnessed in France. He became President just as Roosevelt's dreams of peace through world organization and Soviet-American friendship began to shatter under Soviet rebuffs, and American military strength seemed more important once more. Truman brought to the Presidency also a profound respect for the judgments of George C. Marshall, formed during Truman's experience as chairman of the Senate War Investigating Committee and destined to grow as his acquaintance with Marshall grew. Marshall brought his influence to bear to strengthen Truman's inclinations towards universal military training.[53]

In the message to Congress of October 23, 1945, which Truman regarded as his first State of the Union message, the President endorsed the Palmer-Marshall military program:

I recommend . . . that we depend for our security upon comparatively small professional armed forces, reinforced by a well-trained and effectively organized citizen reserve. The backbone of our military force should be the trained citizen who is first and foremost a civilian, and who becomes a soldier or a sailor only in time of danger—and only when the Congress considers it necessary. . . .

In such a system, however, the citizen reserve must be a trained reserve. We can meet the need for a trained reserve in only one way—by universal training.[54]

By the time Truman spoke, the Seventy-ninth Congress Select Committee on Postwar Military Policy had also recommended universal military training.[55] Thus in late 1945 the support for the Palmer-Marshall program seemed stronger even than it had been in the war years. A consensus on American military policy, a reconciliation of the old rivalry between citizen and professional soldiers, seemed to have been found at last.

But Palmer and Marshall were not destined to see their universal military training program become a reality. A multiplicity of bills proposing it reached Congress. The President appointed an impressive Advisory Commission on Military Training, which under the chairmanship of Karl T. Compton of the Massachusetts Institute of Technology passed ammunition to the friends of the project in a lengthy report on May 29, 1947. The American Legion and the Veterans of Foreign Wars regularly endorsed universal military training. The War Department and then the Defense Department persisted in their support, and when George C. Marshall became secretary of defense during the Korean War crisis he prevailed on Congress to endorse the principle of universal military training in 1951. But that was the high water mark. Marshall retired unable, even with his prestige, to persuade Congress to implement its endorsement.[56]

Political considerations had done much to keep universal military training stalled in Congress during the Truman years, and they did much to remove it completely from the list of Presidential recommendations when Dwight D. Eisenhower succeeded Truman as President. Despite the agreement of President, civilian War Department leaders, congressional leaders, and military spokesmen on universal military training in 1945, the program was bound to encounter political trouble. In 1945 the American electorate wanted a return to tranquility after the long years of depression, New Deal social revolution, and war; they wanted their boys home from the army, not committed indefinitely to be called into it. Many of the powerful political movements of the postwar years attest to the popular yearning to forget wars and rumors of wars and to return to a "normal," tranquil past: the Joseph R. McCarthy movement was an angry lashing out at the frustration of the desire for tranquility, the phenomenal political strength of Dwight D. Eisenhower partly a response to a figure who seemed to be able to promise tranquility. In such a climate, to propose or support universal military training and to imply that tranquility was impossible of attainment for the indefinite future was a risky business.[57]

But it was much more than political timidity on the part of Congress in the post-World War II years that killed the Palmer-Marshall universal military training plan. It was not easy for Congress to revive conscription in 1948, but in the face of the growing Soviet threat Congress did so and maintained selective service all through the 1950s, though the workings of selective service were less universal in application than the program Palmer and Marshall had had in mind. Universal military training did not die dramatically as a victim of sudden political murder, but it drifted into oblivion gradually. It did so less because of political opposition than because Congress, the Defense Department, and the army itself lost interest in it. It did so because after 1945 it came to seem irrelevant to America's military needs.

The year of President Truman's public endorsement of universal military training was also the year of the atomic bomb. Thereafter planning for the sort of major war in which mass armies would previously have clashed became planning in terms of nuclear weapons, long-range bombers, and, presently, ballistic missiles. When there was a renewed interest in nonnuclear warfare after the Korean War, it was an interest in the possibilities of limited wars which might call for considerable numbers of ground troops but not for the huge masses that universal military training would make available. In an era when warfare seemed likely to be either of limited scale or nuclear warfare of bombers and missiles, what place had universal military training? That question probably more than any other led to the disappointment of Palmer and Marshall in their retirement, and to the disappearance of universal military training from the political battleground in the years following 1951.

Epilogue

THOSE Americans who sought the way towards an American army often had been vague in their descriptions of the military necessities for which the army was intended. The principal reason for their vagueness was that through most of the history of the United States it was difficult to envision the war and the enemy that the American army would fight. Through most of the nineteenth century, the continental isolation of the United States and a foreign policy that accentuated that isolation made foreign war seem unlikely. This was one of the facts that kept Emory Upton and his followers isolated from the thought of most of their fellow Americans.

Despite American vagueness about the identity of future antagonists and about the situations which might call forth conflict, however, one thing seemed clear. If the United States fought a major war against a major power, it would be a war of continental defense, fought in North America. No one planned American forays into Europe or Asia. Jeffersonians, Washingtonians, and Uptonians all sought to construct an army to defend America against foreign invasion.

The Uptonians gradually lost ground even within the regular officer corps during the twentieth century, largely because a change in the probable functions of an American army found them less able than rival theorists to adjust. The acquisition of overseas territories through the Spanish War and the subsequent entrance of the United States into world politics made continental defense no longer the sole likely function of the United States Army in a war against a great power. The dispatch of an American expeditionary force overseas became an increasing possibility.

General Peyton C. March supported his Uptonian army plans with a conviction that the principal mission of the American army was still continental defense even after World War I. Even John

M. Palmer in his *Statesmanship or War* of the 1920s discussed the mission of the army primarily in terms of continental defense.[1] But from the beginning of the twentieth century the dispatch overseas of an American army large enough to cope with European armies was a possibility, and after 1917 it was no longer simply a possibility. Although John M. Palmer in the 1920s might write in terms of continental defense, his attacks on Uptonian theory gained conviction because he offered a better method than the Uptonians of fashioning an army capable of exerting itself against mass armies anywhere in the world.

When World War II compelled the dispatch of mass expeditionary forces overseas for the second time in a generation, the bankruptcy of Uptonian doctrine and the triumph of the mass citizen army seemed complete. There occurred the convergence of Presidential, War Department, military, and congressional support on universal military training in 1945. But just as the dual military legacy of the American Revolution seemed to be resolved into a viable consensus, the world situation abruptly made the consensus no longer viable.

Universal military training came to overshadow Uptonian professionalism as a formula for an American army when the need for readiness to face mass enemy armies overseas joined continental defense as a primary mission of the American army. At the close of World War II, readiness to face mass enemy armies overseas became again a matter of dubious necessity, and universal military training became dubious with it.

The advent of nuclear weapons, intercontinental bombers, and intercontinental missiles called into question the whole future of the mass army. Especially after the Soviet Union achieved its first atomic explosion in 1949, any future war of the great powers seemed likely to be a war of devastating nuclear attacks, in which the issue would be decided before the products of universal military training could be mobilized for action, even if they were capable of any appropriate action. Horrible as it was, the prospect of such a war had a certain attraction for Americans, since at least the tedium and pains of the foot soldier promised to be missing from it. Many Americans thought that it also promised to be a war cheaper to prepare for than a war of mass armies, since war planning based on big bombers and missiles and nuclear warheads could obviate the expense of mass armies and great fleets and thus offer war with "a bigger bang for a buck." This latter idea persisted even though war planning based on big bombers, missiles, and nuclear warheads turned out to be anything but inexpensive in fact. The prospect of thermonuclear war was the principal factor in destroying the 1945 consensus upon universal military training.[2]

Furthermore, the post-World War II period brought to the foreground of American military discussion a new type of military professional who was not committed to a strong army of either the professional or the citizen variety: the officer of the independent air force. Even while it remained a part of the army, the air force had based its doctrine upon strategic bombing campaigns that would win wars through destruction of the enemy's industry, transport, and popular will to resist, without recourse to massive land operations. After the air force won its divorce from the army in 1947, the strategic bombing emphasis grew stronger still. Atomic weapons gave it new cogency. Air force doctrine owed something to William Tecumseh Sherman's concepts of total war, which had always posed difficulties for those who would have incorporated them into the main body of American military thought. Now, carrying Sherman's ideas towards an ultimate conclusion, air force doctrine threatened to upset the fundamentals of the army's role in war. The air force was the service that enjoyed the greatest popular and congressional prestige after World War II, and its doctrine was another factor which helped destroy the 1945 consensus upon universal military training.[3]

Finally, after the Korean War of 1950–1953, universal military training ceased to fit readily into the army's own planning. Conceding that an all-out war would be a thermonuclear war waged principally with air power and missiles, the army concentrated on making itself an instrument for limited wars of the Korean type. The immediate problem of the army in the 1950s was to be ready to send formidable but not massive striking forces to any area of the world where a brush-fire war might flare up, to Korea or Lebanon or southeast Asia or the Caribbean. But the new preoccupation of the army with limited war amounted to a change in the army's concept of its purpose as thorough as the earlier shift from emphasis on continental defense to emphasis on sending massive expeditionary forces overseas.

In the new era of emphasis on limited war the army did not seem to need the huge expeditionary forces of the world wars. The army's mission was no longer to inflict the final, devastating blow upon the enemy's main forces and his heartland. The new emphasis did not require great pools of mobilizable reserves such as universal military training would provide. It required instead forces ready for immediate battle, large enough to be immediately formidable, but not so large as to make their rapid shifting around the globe impossible or to make their commitment to battle a provocation that might inflate a brush-fire war into something bigger. In proportion to their size those forces needed large numbers of highly skilled specialists in the technology of modern weapons, transport, and communications; such specialists could not be produced in the limited training periods of universal military service. Altogether, the new emphasis upon limited war required an army more akin to Emory Upton's professional force than to the Wood-Palmer-Marshall mass army. Once again, universal military training lost its relevance to America's military needs.

Therefore American military discussion again became heated debate. The search for an American army still goes on. The limited war doctrines of the 1950s and the 1960s, by calling for an army of thorough professional proficiency rather than of great size, have given the professionalist military tradition a new lease on life. They have created occasional suggestions, such as Adlai Stevenson's in the Presidential campaign of 1956, that conscription of citizen soldiers might cease entirely, and that through higher pay and other incentives a fully professional army might be restored. But those suggestions must confront doubt that an all-professional army could be sustained in sufficient size. Limited wars might not demand massive armies on the scale of the world wars, but they can demand armies that are large by any other measurement. Until now the United States has found it necessary to supplement professionals with citizen-soldier conscripts to maintain a limited war army large enough for the occasion. That necessity means that the historic problem of harmonizing the roles and interests of citizen soldiers and professionals in the same army is still alive.

But a highly professional army in the middle twentieth century raises problems for traditional professionalism. The specialized skills required by the new military technology threaten to divide the officer corps into pockets of technical specialists. They are skills, moreover, whose cultivation does not necessarily develop the broader and vaguer attributes suitable to high military command. The specialized technical skills demanded of many enlisted men, make the enlisted man different from the regular whom Emory Upton had in mind. The skills of the enlisted man are now likely to be in demand in civilian life as well as in the army, and therefore the army finds it difficult to recruit and to hold enlisted men of appropriate skills.

Nor has the United States heard the last of the Wood-Palmer-Marshall doctrines of the great citizen army. In the late 1950s and early 1960s the recurring crises over Berlin raised the possibility of a nonnuclear war in Europe. Nuclear weapons, bombers, and missiles have not offered an adequate response to Soviet threats to Berlin, since the destructiveness of those weapons would tend to paralyze the will to unleash them in the face of a Communist coup in West Berlin. But for a nonnuclear battle in the heart of Europe, ground forces of the size maintained to fight limited wars on the periphery of the Communist empire might not be adequate either.

Across two centuries the words of George Washington on foreign and military policy seem as relevant as ever:

I cannot recommend to your notice measures for the fulfillment of *our* duties to the rest of the world, without again pressing upon you the necessity of placing ourselves in a condition of compleat defence, and of exacting from *them* the fulfillment of *their* duties towards *us* . . . . if we desire to secure peace, one of the most powerful instruments of our rising prosperity, it must be known, that we are at all times ready for War.[4]

But the conflicting elements in the military legacy of the American Revolution are no more reconciled than in Washington's day. Americans still seek the proper path towards an American army.

Notes

i: *The Dual Military Legacy of the Revolution*

1. A good recent discussion of the battle of Guilford Court House is Christopher Ward, *The War of the Revolution*, II, 783–94.

2. "Professional" is used here and throughout the early part of this book to mean the opposite of "amateur," and not in the sense of "profession" as distinguished from "trade." It refers to enlisted men as well as to officers, and it is not intended to indicate that the officer corps of the eighteenth and early nineteenth centuries formed a profession, in the sense that medicine and law are today professions. Such a development will be noted later. On the other hand, while some writers make much of the fact that eighteenth-century officers were not professionals in the second sense because most of them were aristocrats first and officers second, it should be remembered that for many their way of life centered on war, and accordingly many of them developed a high skill in war which amateurs could overcome only by introducing new factors into military equations.

3. From among the many studies of eighteenth-century warfare, especially good introductions can be found in Walter L. Dorn, *Competition for Empire, 1740–1763*, pp. 80–102; Edward Mead Earle, ed., *Makers of Modern Strategy*, pp. 26–74; John U. Nef, *War and Human Progress*, pp. 147–328; Hoffman Nickerson, *The Armed Horde*, pp. 19–63; Robert S. Quimby, *The Background of Napoleonic Warfare: The Theory of Military Tactics in Eighteenth-Century France;* Theodore Ropp, *War in the Modern World*, pp. 24–42; and Alfred Vagts, *A History of Militarism*, pp. 77–96. Selections from several of the above works, together with additional material, are included in Gordon B. Turner, ed., *A History of Military Affairs in Western Society since the Eighteenth Century*, I, 1–70.

4. For example, this is a principal theme of Nickerson, *Armed Horde*, and B. H. Liddell Hart, *The Ghost of Napoleon*.

5. Liddell Hart, *Ghost of Napoleon*, pp. 118–44; Nickerson, *Armed Horde*, pp. 139–45, 202–37; Vagts, *Militarism*, pp. 190–96. Earle, *Modern Strategy*, pp. 93–99, presents a good review of Clausewitz's more extreme statements; see also J. F. C. Fuller, *The Conduct of War, 1789–1961*, pp. 59–76. It must be noted that Clausewitz's thought was more subtle and complex than those who enthroned him as the prophet of

unrestrained violence made it seem; Karl von Clausewitz, *On War,* trans. O. J. Matthjis Jollis.

6. B. H. Liddell Hart, *Strategy,* pp. 113–41; Nickerson, *Armed Horde,* pp. 64–125; Ropp, *War,* pp. 81–121; Vagts, *Militarism,* pp. 136–60.

7. Washington's generalship can be studied in Douglas Southall Freeman, *George Washington: A Biography* (6 vols., New York, 1948–1954).

8. On the nature of the Continental Army, Francis Vinton Greene, *The Revolutionary War and the Military Policy of the United States* is still useful. See also Christopher Ward, *The Delaware Continentals.* On Yorktown, see Ward, *War of the Revolution,* II, 886–96.

9. John C. Fitzpatrick, ed., *The Writings of George Washington,* VI, 110.

10. *Ibid.,* pp. 110–11.   11. *Ibid.,* p. 379.   12. *Ibid.,* p. 112. 13. *Ibid.,* p. 109.   14. *Ibid.,* p. 380.

15. Vagts, *Militarism,* pp. 96–105. A stimulating brief history of American command problems from the Revolution onward is T. Harry Williams, *Americans at War: The Development of the American Military System.* For various problems of the command of the Continental Army, see Louis C. Hatch, *The Administration of the American Revolutionary Army.*

16. Vagts, *Militarism,* pp. 96–101. But contrary to assertions of Vagts and many other writers, European *tirailleur* tactics did not derive mainly from the American Revolution but had made an earlier appearance; Quimby, *Background of Napoleonic Warfare,* pp. 84–86, 211–12.

17. Ward, *War of the Revolution.*

18. On the new style of war in America as on so many issues in American military history, much is said in brief compass in Walter Millis, *Arms and Men: A Study in American Military History,* pp. 13–46. See also Daniel J. Boorstin, *The Americans: The Colonial Experience,* pp. 345–72, and James Ripley Jacobs, *The Beginning of the U.S. Army, 1783–1812,* pp. 3–5.

II: *George Washington and Alexander Hamilton*

1. Fitzgerald, *Washington,* XXVI, 374–98.   2. *Ibid.* 3. *Ibid.,* XXVII, 360.

4. Friedrich Wilhelm Baron von Steuben, *A Letter on the Subject of an Established Militia, and Military Arrangements, Addressed to the Inhabitants of the United States.*

5. Fitzpatrick, *Washington,* XXVII, 144.

6. Henry Cabot Lodge, ed., *The Works of Alexander Hamilton,* VI, 463–83.

7. *Journals of the Continental Congress,* XXVII, 524; William Addleman Ganoe, *The History of the United States Army,* pp. 90–91; Jacobs,

Beginning of the U.S. Army, pp. 13–16; Oliver Lyman Spaulding, *The United States Army in Peace and War,* p. 116.

8. Lodge, *Hamilton,* VI, 475.

9. Fitzpatrick, *Washington,* XXVI, 396–97. John McAuley Palmer, *Washington, Lincoln, Wilson: Three War Statesmen,* pp. 3–123, and *America in Arms: The Experience of the United States with Military Organization,* pp. 5–61, emphasizes the distinctively American elements in Washington's military thought in order to establish him as the champion of the citizen army.

10. For the conditions under the Confederation which militated against a strong army or militia, see Merrill Jensen, *The New Nation: A History of the United States during the Confederation.*

11. C. Joseph Bernardo and Eugene H. Bacon, *American Military Policy: Its Development since 1775,* pp. 78–81; Arthur A. Ekirch, Jr., *The Civilian and the Military,* pp. 20–22, 32–36, and "The Idea of a Citizen Army," *Military Affairs,* XVII (1953), 30–33; Jacobs, *Beginning of the U.S. Army,* pp. 44–45, 245; Louis Morton, "The Origins of American Military Policy," *Military Affairs,* XXII (1958), 75–82; Louis Smith, *American Democracy and Military Power,* pp. 29–31, 309–10. For a history of American experience in mobilizing armies, see Marvin A. Kreidberg and Merton G. Henry, *History of Military Mobilization in the United States Army, 1775–1945.*

12. J. F. Callan, *The Military Laws of the United States,* pp. 87–93; Jacobs, *Beginning of the U.S. Army,* pp. 50–51, 68–71, 124–25.

13. Millis, *Arms and Men,* p. 50; Palmer, *Washington, Lincoln, Wilson,* pp. 15, 138–40. Thomas Jefferson took this view of the roles of regulars and militia; James D. Richardson, ed., *Compilation of the Messages and Papers of the Presidents,* I, 345.

14. *American State Papers, Military Affairs,* I, 6–13.   15. *Ibid.*

16. *Ibid.* At the time of Shays's Rebellion, Knox had already suggested a standing army for the support of the government against internal disorders. He early sought to persuade Washington to use armed force in dealing with the Whisky Rebellion. North Callahan, *Henry Knox: General Washington's General,* pp. 255, 306.

17. Bernardo and Bacon, *American Military Policy,* pp. 73–82; Palmer, *Washington, Lincoln, Wilson,* pp. 107–20; William H. Riker, *Soldiers of the States: The Role of the National Guard in American Democracy,* pp. 18–20.

18. Callan, *Military Laws,* pp. 95–100.

19. *American State Papers, Military Affairs,* I, 66, 69–71, 107.

20. *Ibid.,* p. 66.   21. Callan, *Military Laws,* pp. 126–27.

22. John C. Miller, *Alexander Hamilton: Portrait in Paradox,* p. 468.

23. Fitzpatrick, *Washington,* XXXVII, 47–48; Lodge, *Hamilton,* VII, 25.

24. Fitzpatrick, *Washington*, XXVI, 380.

25. *Ibid.*, XXXVII, 47–48; Lodge, *Hamilton*, VII, 25, 56–57.

26. Lodge, *Hamilton*, VII, 57.   27. *Ibid.*, pp. 55–56.

28. *Ibid.*, pp. 179–86.

29. *American State Papers, Military Affairs*, I, 133–44.   30. *Ibid.*

31. *Ibid.*, p. 142.

32. Stephen G. Kurtz, *The Presidency of John Adams: The Collapse of Federalism, 1795–1800*, pp. 316–17, 323, 354–56.

33. For Jefferson's attitude toward the army, see his annual messages to Congress in Richardson, *Messages of the Presidents*. The remark about obliterating the distinction between the civil and the military is in Julian P. Boyd, ed., *The Papers of Thomas Jefferson*, VII, 106. For the issue of the army in the election of 1800, Kurtz, *Presidency of John Adams*, pp. 336–45, 352–70.

34. Callan, *Military Laws*, pp. 141–49; Jacobs, *Beginning of the U.S. Army*, pp. 252–54; Palmer, *Washington, Lincoln, Wilson*, pp. 126–29; Richardson, *Messages of the Presidents*, I, 323.

35. R. Ernest Dupuy, *Where They Have Trod: The West Point Tradition in American Life*, pp. 21–46; Sidney Forman, *West Point: A History of the United States Military Academy*, pp. 20–35; Jacobs, *Beginning of the U.S. Army*, pp. 280–81. John McAuley Palmer points out that Washington and Jefferson conceived of a military academy as a means of disseminating military knowledge among the citizen soldiery, as well as of serving the regular army (*Washington, Lincoln, Wilson*, pp. 70–71, 124–25); but the principal point remains that the military academy would be a means of establishing and perpetuating professional military standards.

36. Jacobs, *Beginning of the U.S. Army*, pp. 268–69; Millis, *Arms and Men*, pp. 60–63.

37. Callan, *Military Laws*, pp. 211–17, 220–28, 230, 235–36, 238–40. Palmer, *Washington, Lincoln, Wilson*, pp. 126–33, points out the continued fondness, nevertheless, of both Jefferson and Madison for the militia. He emphasizes that like Washington they would have formed a ready reserve from the younger militia members; but it should be noted that they were much less specific and emphatic than Washington in demanding the most thorough training possible for the ready reserve.

III: *John C. Calhoun*

1. *The Works of John C. Calhoun*, V, 25–40.

2. *Ibid.*, pp. 80–93, especially p. 84 for the army with "nothing either to new model or to create."

3. *Ibid.*, pp. 81–82.

4. For sentiments of military amateurism in the Jacksonian era, see

John Hope Franklin, *The Militant South,* pp. 171–92; Millis, *Arms and Men,* p. 86.

5. Callan, *Military Laws,* pp. 306–9.

6. *Ibid.,* pp. 367–75, 378–87. On the Mexican War, Justin Smith, *The War with Mexico.*

7. Samuel P. Huntington, *The Soldier and the State: The Theory and Politics of Civil-Military Relations,* p. 216.

IV: *Dennis Hart Mahan*

1. On the Jacksonian enmity toward the militia system, see Ekirch, *Civilian and the Military,* pp. 67–68. On the development of the distinction between unorganized and organized militia and of the volunteer companies, Franklin, *Militant South,* pp. 171–75; Riker, *Soldiers of the States,* pp. 21–40.

2. Callan, *Military Laws,* pp. 408–9, 451–52; Ganoe, *History of the United States Army,* pp. 229–31, 249–53.

3. For the concept of the officer corps as a true profession as well as for the emergence of a genuinely professional officer corps in the United States, see Huntington, *Soldier and the State,* pp. 7–18.

4. Liddell Hart, *Ghost of Napoleon,* pp. 15–19; Ropp, *War,* pp. 24–42. 24–42.

5. Henry Barnard, *Military Schools and Courses of Instruction in the Science and Art of War;* Gordon A. Craig, *The Politics of the Prussian Army, 1640–1945,* pp. 45–46; Earle, *Modern Strategy,* pp. 172–74; Huntington, *Soldier and the State,* pp. 39–42, 45, 48–49.

6. Barnard, *Military Schools;* Huntington, *Soldier and the State,* pp. 42–43, 45–46, 49.

7. Dupuy, *Where They Have Trod,* pp. 62–182, 205–27; Forman, *West Point,* pp. 36–60.

8. *Dictionary of American Biography,* XII, 209–10, hereafter cited as *D.A.B.;* Dupuy, *Where They Have Trod,* pp. 192–202; W. D. Puleston, *The Life and Work of Captain Alfred Thayer Mahan,* pp. 1–17.

9. Dupuy, *Where They Have Trod,* pp. 228–40, and *Men of West Point: The First 150 Years of the United States Military Academy,* pp. 12–24. The French influence on Mahan continued to be great; in 1864, he testified that the French engineering school at Metz was a model for the whole world, *Army and Navy Journal,* II (1864–1865), 53.

10. D. H. Mahan, *An Elementary Treatise on Advanced-Guard, Out-Post, and Detachment Service of Troops . . . ,* p. 7. The 1864 edition of *Out-Post* is considerably enlarged over the early ones and is especially valuable for its new material on strategy and its review of the history of Napoleon's campaigns. Although the work of Henry W. Halleck to be discussed later was published earlier than the first edition of *Out-Post,*

Mahan's early preparation of his material for teaching purposes justifies calling his book "the first systematic American study of warfare."

11. *Ibid.*, pp. 217–18.   12. *Ibid.*, p. 33.   13. *Ibid.*, pp. 32–34.

14. Bruce Catton, *Mr. Lincoln's Army*, pp. 191–99; Millis, *Arms and Men*, pp. 127–30; Nickerson, *Armed Horde*, pp. 169–73; Ropp, *War*, pp. 143–46, 162–66.

15. Mahan, *Out-Post*, pp. 190, 198–99, 202.

16. *Ibid.*, pp. 185–96. For the remark that the spade is as important as the musket, see W. T. Sherman, *Personal Memoirs of W. T. Sherman*, II, 396.

17. Mahan, *Out-Post*, p. 77.   18. *Ibid.*, pp. 43–46.

19. *Ibid.*, p. 30.   20. *Ibid.*, pp. 30–31.

21. *Ibid.*, pp. 70, 77–78, 80–81.

22. *Ibid.*, pp. 83–86, 93–94, 105–6. Mahan recommended that a commander always carry out a personal reconnaissance of a prospective battlefield, *ibid.*, p. 273.

23. *Ibid.*, pp. 83–86.   24. *Ibid.*, p. 200.   25. *Ibid.*, pp. 36–37.

26. For Mahan's refraining from voting, *Army and Navy Journal*, II (1864–1865), 27. For his death, *D.A.B.*, XII, 210; Puleston, *Alfred Thayer Mahan*, pp. 50–51.

v: Henry W. Halleck and George B. McClellan

1. On the limitations of the Military Academy in the early nineteenth century, see especially Lloyd Lewis, *Sherman: Fighting Prophet*, p. 53.

2. On Jomini, see Earle, *Modern Strategy*, pp. 77–92, and the bibliography, pp. 524–25. R. Ernest and Trevor N. Dupuy, *Military Heritage of America*, pp. 173–82, considers Jomini in relation to his influence on American military thought. On this matter, an American military writer said in 1863, "Jomini's various works . . . have stood the test of time, and are at this moment more widely studied, probably, than those of any of his now numerous military contemporaries"; *Army and Navy Journal*, I (1863), 787–88. David L. Donald, *Lincoln Reconsidered: Essays on the Civil War Era*, pp. 88–102, considers Jomini's influence on the Civil War. Jomini's works exist in various editions: *Traité des grandes opérations militaires; Précis de l'art de la guerre*. Of the latter there is an English translation, *Summary of the Art of War*, trans. G. H. Mendell and W. P. Craighill. Jomini's nostalgia for eighteenth-century warfare is stated candidly in *Précis*, I, 96.

3. Henry W. Halleck, *Elements of Military Art and Science*, *passim*, especially pp. 59–60, 62–63, 140, 154. On Halleck, see *D.A.B.*, VIII, 150–52.

4. Halleck, *Elements*, pp. 144–45, 245–48, 323–26, 379–408, 445–46.

5. This conviction is implicit in Halleck's remarks on the value of studying the *Memoirs de Napoleon*, *ibid.*, pp. 59–60.

6. *Ibid.*, pp. 144–45, 382–83, 386–87.   7. *Ibid.*, pp. 379–86.
8. *Ibid.*, p. 378.   9. *Ibid.*, pp. 140–41.   10. *Ibid.*, pp. 147–48.
11. *Ibid.*, pp. 143–44.   12. *Ibid.*, pp. 150–51.
13. *Ibid.*, pp. 144–47.   14. *Ibid.*, p. 149.   15. *Ibid.*, pp. 324–25.
16. *Ibid.*, pp. 143, 324–26.   17. *Ibid.*, pp. 242–45.
18. *Ibid.*, pp. 397–404.   19. *Ibid.*, pp. 323–25.
20. *Ibid.*, p. 263.   21. *Ibid.*, p. 256.   22. *Ibid.*, pp. 153–54.
23. *Ibid.*, p. 324.   24. *Ibid.*, p. 406.   25. *Ibid.*, pp. 148–49.
26. *Ibid.*, pp. 39–40.   27. *Ibid.*, p. 43.   28. *Ibid.*, p. 63.
29. *Ibid.*, pp. 64–65.
30. Millis, *Arms and Men*, pp. 55, 57–58, 80–81, 101.
31. Halleck, *Elements*, pp. 155–209, 416–17.
32. *Ibid.*, p. 437.
33. On the other hand, Halleck anticipated Alfred Thayer Mahan in the field of naval strategy. He ruled out a strong home naval squadron as a substitute for coastal fortifications; the proper function of a navy, he said, is an offensive one. *Ibid.*, p. 209.
34. *Ibid.*, p. 91. At the same time, Halleck recognized the difficulties which would have attended an effort by Napoleon to supply his armies in Spain through regular depots, and the result was to leave his discussion of the Peninsular War ambiguous.
35. *D.A.B.*, XI, 581–85; George B. McClellan, *McClellan's Own Story.*
36. George B. McClellan, *The Armies of Europe*, pp. 5–6.
37. George B. McClellan, *Regulations and Instructions for the Field Service of the U.S. Cavalry in Time of War.*
38. McClellan, *Armies of Europe*, p. 386.   39. *Ibid.*, pp. 386–87.
40. *Ibid.*, pp. 389–93.   41. *Ibid.*, pp. 390–91.   42. *Ibid.*, p. 34.
43. *Ibid.*, pp. 34–35.   44. *Ibid.*, p. 35.   45. *Ibid.*, pp. 10–14.
46. *Ibid.*, p. 25.   47. *Ibid.*, p. 34.   48. *Ibid.*, pp. 34–35.
49. *Ibid.*
50. Richard Delafield, *Report on the Art of War in Europe in 1854, 1855, and 1856*, pp. 43–44; Alfred Mordecai, *Military Commission to Europe in 1855 and 1856: Report.*
51. *D.A.B.*, IV, 589–90.
52. George W. Cullum, review of Jomini's *Life of Napoleon* as translated with notes by Major General H. W. Halleck, *United States Service Magazine*, II (1864), 128–29.
53. *Ibid.*, pp. 136–37.   54. *Ibid.*, p. 125.   55. *Ibid.*, p. 126.

VI: *William T. Sherman and Ulysses S. Grant*

1. *Report of the Secretary of War*, 1871, p. 23; 1879, pp. 13–15; 1880, pp. 6–7; 1881, pp. 5, 36–39; 1883, pp. 44–45; 1887, p. 172; 1888, p. 6; hereafter cited as *R.S.W.*

2. *Ibid.*, 1879, p. 13.   3. *Ibid.*   4. *Ibid.*, 1881, pp. 36–37.

5. *Sherman, Memoirs,* II, 394–97. For European impressions of the Civil War, see Jay Luvaas, *The Military Legacy of the Civil War.*

6. Sherman, *Memoirs,* II, 394, 396–97.   7. *Ibid.*, p. 49.

8. *Ibid.*, pp. 396–97.   9. *Ibid.*, pp. 395–96.   10. *Ibid.*

11. *Ibid.*, p. 395.

12. Sherman to U. S. Grant, September 20, 1864, printed *ibid.*, p. 114.

13. *Ibid.*, pp. 220–21.

14. Sherman to H. W. Halleck, December 24, 1864, *ibid.*, p. 227.

15. *Ibid.*, p. 249.   16. *Ibid.*, p. 175.   17. *Ibid.*, pp. 111–12.

18. Sherman to James M. Calhoun *et al.*, September 12, 1864, *ibid.*, p. 126.

19. Sherman to H. W. Halleck, September 4, 1864, *ibid.*, p. 111.

20. Sherman to James M. Calhoun *et al.*, September 12, 1864, *ibid.*, p. 126.

21. *Ibid.;* Sherman as quoted in DeB. Keim, "Our Moral Weakness," *United States Service Magazine,* III (1865), 374.

22. Sherman as quoted in Keim, "Our Moral Weakness," *United States Service Magazine,* III (1865), 375.

23. Sherman to James M. Calhoun *et al.*, September 12, 1864, Sherman, *Memoirs,* II, 126.

24. M. C. Meigs, quoted in Russell F. Weigley, *Quartermaster General of the Union Army: A Biography of M. C. Meigs,* p. 285.

25. Keim, "Our Moral Weakness," *United States Service Magazine,* III (1865), 372.

26. *Ibid.*, p. 376. On Sherman's theories of war see also Lewis, *Sherman: Fighting Prophet* and B. H. Liddell Hart, *Sherman: Soldier, Realist, American.*

27. Grant to Sherman, September 12, 1864, printed in Sherman, *Memoirs,* II, 112–13, discusses a similar plan of marches from Mobile and Savannah. For an old, partisan, but good discussion of Grant's part in conceiving the march to the sea, see Adam Badeau, *Military History of U. S. Grant,* III, 39–67.

28. U. S. Grant, *Personal Memoirs of U. S. Grant,* I, 368–69.

29. *Ibid.*, *passim;* Bruce Catton, *Grant Moves South.* On the other hand, Dennis Mahan's teachings had anticipated Grant's mode of war by urging a campaign against the enemy's resources which would "make war feed war"; Mahan, *Out-Post,* p. 200.

30. Badeau, *Grant,* III, 109, 646.   31. *Ibid.*, p. 109.   32. *Ibid.*

33. *Ibid.*, p. 111.   34. *Ibid.*, pp. 642–44.

35. A. D. Wales, "Grant: His 'Mystery' and Genius," *Journal of the United States Military Service Institution,* XXXIX (1906), 5–6, hereafter cited as *J.M.S.I.*

36. *D.A.B.*, II, 258–59 for Bigelow's father and background.

37. John Bigelow, *The Principles of Strategy,* p. 81.

38. *Ibid.*, pp. 2–80, 105.   39. *Ibid.*, p. 20.

40. *Ibid.*, pp. 189–99, 211.   41. *Ibid.*, p. 263.

42. *Ibid.*, pp. 105, 224.

43. *Ibid.*, pp. 225–28. But Bigelow was inclined to place probably an excessive emphasis on the value of a long-established capital. He quoted with approval General John G. Barnard, that in the Civil War, "the preservation of the national cause" was identified with "the continuous tenure" of Washington. Surely the loss of Washington at any time would have been a tremendous blow to the Federal cause, but whether it would have meant the loss of the war is highly doubtful.

44. *Ibid.*, p. 229.   45. *Ibid.*, pp. 229–32.   46. *Ibid.*, p. 225.

47. *Ibid.*, p. 232.   48. *Ibid.*, pp. 232–33.   49. *Ibid.*, p. 264.

50. P. H. Sheridan, *Personal Memoirs of P. H. Sheridan,* II, 447–52; B. H. Liddell Hart, *The Revolution in Warfare,* p. 74.

vii: *Emory Upton*

1. *D.A.B.*, XIX, 128–30; Peter Smith Michie, *Life and Letters of General Emory Upton.*

2. A good account of Upton's attack at Spotsylvania is in Bruce Catton, *A Stillness at Appomattox*, pp. 111–18.

3. Michie, *Upton*, p. 108.   4. *Ibid.*, p. 109.

5. Emory Upton, *Infantry Tactics: Double and Single Rank.*

6. Michie, *Upton*, pp. 284–86, 289, 290, 298–303; W. T. Sherman Papers, Library of Congress, XXXVII, 4852, 4856, 4872; Emory Upton, *The Armies of Asia and Europe*, pp. v–ix.

7. Michie, *Upton*, p. 387; Upton, *Armies*, especially pp. 320–21.

8. Michie, *Upton*, pp. 386–87.   9. *Ibid.*, p. 418.

10. Upton, *Armies*, especially pp. ix, 317–18, 320–24, 367–70.

11. Emory Upton, *The Military Policy of the United States from 1775.*

12. Jacob D. Cox, "War Preparations in the North," in Robert Underwood Johnson and Clarence Clough Buel, eds., *Battles and Leaders of the Civil War* I, 94; Charles Winslow Elliott, *Winfield Scott: The Soldier and the Man*, pp. 718–20. For a caustic but not unfair discussion of the regular officer corps's general reluctance to accept the need to fight the Civil War with volunteers rather than regulars, see Palmer, *Washington, Lincoln, Wilson*, pp. 182–83, 187–97, 200–1, 211–12.

13. E.g., General George G. Meade's comments as late as October 5, 1862, in George Meade, *The Life and Letters of George Gordon Meade*, I, 317–18.

14. E.g., George W. Cullum's attitude as expressed in *United States Service Magazine*, II (1864), 135.

15. Richard B. Irwin, *ibid.*, pp. 225–28.

16. *Ibid.* It should be noted, however, that in 1866 this editorial

writer reverted to favoring a volunteer national guard. He continued to believe the Prussian military system the best in the world, but in the postwar period he concluded that the United States needed nothing so ambitious; *ibid.*, III (1866), 191–203.

17. Sherman, *Memoirs*, I, 381.

18. Richard C. Brown, "Emory Upton—The Army's Mahan," *Military Affairs*, XVII (1953), 125–31.

19. Upton, *Military Policy*, p. 248.   20. *Ibid.*, p. 4.

21. *Ibid.*, p. 67.   22. *Ibid.*, p. 297.   23. *Ibid.*, pp. 256–57.

24. *Ibid.*, p. 280.   25. *Ibid.*, p. 423.

26. *Ibid.*, *passim*, especially pp. 170, 198, 229, 374.

27. *Ibid.*, p. 67.   28. *Ibid.*, p. 145.   29. *Ibid.*, p. 194.

30. *Ibid.*, pp. 195, 222.   31. *Ibid.*, pp. 235–36, 428.

32. *Ibid.*, pp. 23–24.   33. *Ibid.*, pp. 61–62.   34. *Ibid.*, p. 229.

35. *Ibid.*, p. 62.   36. *Ibid.*, p. 71.   37. *Ibid.*, p. 9.

38. *Ibid.*, pp. 20, 67.   39. *Ibid.*, p. 120.   40. *Ibid.*, p. 116.

41. *Ibid.*, pp. 85, 91.   42. E.g., *ibid.*, pp. 67, 245.

43. *Ibid.*, p. 67.   44. *Ibid.*, pp. 234, 259–60, 420.

45. *Ibid.*, p. 257.   46. *Ibid.*, p. 85.   47. *Ibid.*, p. 417.

48. *Ibid.*, p. 336.   49. *Ibid.*, pp. 394–95.   50. *Ibid.*, p. 323.

51. *Ibid.*, p. 263.   52. *Ibid.*, p. 258.   53. *Ibid.*, p. 423.

54. *Ibid.*, p. 336.   55. *Ibid.*, pp. 144, 67.   56. *Ibid.*, p. 149.

57. *Ibid.*, p. 198.   58. *Ibid.*, p. 223.   59. *Ibid.*, pp. 416–17, 426–27.

60. *Ibid.*, pp. 67, 23.   61. *Ibid.*, p. 85.   62. *Ibid.*, p. 416.

63. *Ibid.*, pp. 208, 233–34, 312–13.

64. *D.A.B.*, XIX, 129–30; Michie, *Upton*.

65. Upton, *Military Policy*, p. 385.

66. Philip C. Jessup, *Elihu Root*, I, 242; Palmer, *America in Arms*, pp. 112–14, *Washington, Lincoln, Wilson*, pp. 264, 270–72.

VIII: *John A. Logan*

1. Grant, *Memoirs*, II, 365, 531.

2. *D.A.B.*, XI, 363–65. For Sherman's side of the controversy over the Army of the Tennessee, see Sherman, *Memoirs*, II, 85–86.

3. John A. Logan, *The Volunteer Soldier of America*, pp. 119–20.

4. *Ibid.*, pp. 487–89.   5. *Ibid.*, pp. 426–39.   6. *Ibid.*, p. 337.

7. *Ibid.*, pp. 439–50.   8. *Ibid.*, p. 441.   9. *Ibid.*, pp. 437–55.

10. *Ibid.*, pp. 394–425, 455–56.   11. *Ibid.*, pp. 457–58.

12. *Ibid.*, pp. 580–81.

13. *Ibid.*, *passim*, especially pp. 466–73, 558–60.

14. *Ibid.*, p. 600.   15. *Ibid.*, pp. 604–6.

16. *Ibid.*, pp. 606–7.   17. *Ibid.*, p. 464.

IX: *The Disciples of Emory Upton*

1. *R.S.W.*, especially 1869, pp. 23–30; 1871, pp. 22–23; 1877, pp. iii–vi; 1879, p. 4; 1880, pp. v–vi, 3–4; 1889, pp. 4–5; 1890, pp. 47–50; 1894, p. 68; 1895, pp. 74–75.

2. An Officer of the Army, "The Efficiency of the Army," *United Service*, VI (new series, 1891), 4–5; *R.S.W.*, 1893, pp. 47–48; 1884, pp. 49–50; 1889, p. 65; 1890, pp. 46–49; 1895, p. 68; Upton, *Military Policy*, pp. 77, 233–34.

3. Quartermaster General's Office, Letter Book 1876B, pp. 1222–23, National Archives.

4. Philip Sheridan to William T. Sherman, August, 1870, Sherman Papers, Library of Congress, XXVIII, 3796–97; Sheridan, *Memoirs*, II, 447–52.

5. An Officer of the Army, "The Efficiency of the Army," *United Service*, VI (new series, 1891), 10–13.

6. *R.S.W.*, 1890, p. 5.   7. *Ibid.*, 1869, pp. 31–32.

8. *Ibid.*, 1879, pp. xv–xvi; 1880, pp. xviii–xix.

9. *United States Statutes-at-Large*, XXIII, 434.

10. *R.S.W.*, 1886, pp. 32–33; 49th Congress, 1st Session, House Executive Documents, XXVIII (serial 2395, 2396), no. 49.

11. *R.S.W.*, 1887, pp. 118–21, 123–24; 1889, pp. 68–74; 1890, pp. 5–7; 1892, pp. 17, 46.

12. *Ibid.*, 1892, p. 17; 1893, pp. 15–16.

13. E.g., *ibid.*, 1893, p. 18.

14. Eugene Griffin, "Our Sea-Coast Defenses," *North American Review*, CXLVIII (1888), 71.

15. *Ibid.*, p. 65.

16. 49:1 House Executive Documents, XXVIII (serial 2395, 2396), no. 49.

17. Richard Wainwright, "Our Coast Defenses from a Naval Stand Point," *United Service*, II (new series, 1889), 48.

18. See *R.S.W.*, especially 1893, p. 14, which states: "The project of national defense, upon which this Department is now engaged, takes its origin in the act of March 3, 1885," that is, the act establishing the Endicott Board.

19. W. H. Carter, "One View of the Army Question," *United Service*, II (new series, 1889), 576.

20. E.g., *Army and Navy Journal*, XXXVI (1898–1899), 51, 356, 771, 877, 1072; XXXVII (1899–1900), 103, 960; *J.M.S.I.*, XXI (1897), 1–27, 225–56; XXII (1898), 449–70; XXIII (1898), 371–91; *United Service*, I (new series, 1889), 173; II (new series, 1889), 573–78; VI (new series, 1891), 1–15, 196; XIII (new series, 1895), 107–27. On

the professional journals see Max L. Marshall, "A Survey of Military Periodicals," M.A. thesis, University of Missouri, 1950. For official expressions of Uptonian expansible army views by secretaries of war and commanding generals, see *R.S.W.*, 1877, pp. iii–viii; 1879, p. 4; 1880, pp. v–vi, 31–34; 1881, p. 4; 1883, pp. 47–48; 1889, pp. 4–5; 1890, pp. 46–51; 1894, p. 68; 1895, pp. 74–75.

21. Arthur L. Wagner, "The Military Necessities of the United States, and the Best Provisions for Meeting Them," *J.M.S.I.*, V (1884), 237–71. Wagner as a faculty member did much to raise the standards of the School of Application at Fort Leavenworth; Ganoe, *History of the United States Army*, p. 363. It should be noted that the first honorable mention (second prize) essay was less Uptonian, for its author believed the militia might become highly useful with a minimum of federal training; Otho E. Michaelis, "The Military Necessities of the United States," *J.M.S.I.*, V (1884), 272–91. Sherman, who had encouraged Upton and who submitted Uptonian proposals to the Burnside Committee of Congress in 1878, but whose position on professionalism was not consistent, ranked Michaelis's essay first. The second honorable mention essay expressed views similar to Wagner's, *ibid.*, pp. 355–95.

22. *Ibid.*, pp. 237–71.

23. A. D. Schenck, "Organization of the Line of the Army," *United Service*, XIII (new series, 1895), 108. For the late nineteenth-century militia renaissance see Riker, *Soldiers of the States*, pp. 41–66. Some writers in the professional military journals of course argued that the existing militia system was substantially satisfactory: e.g., *J.M.S.I.*, XVIII (1896), 267–84; *United Service*, I (1878), 283–89; XII (new series, 1894), 365–75. But such articles were rare in comparison with those critical of the militia system.

24. E.g., *J.M.S.I.*, XVIII (1896), 477–506; *United Service*, I (new series, 1889), 519–32; VII (new series, 1892), 413–24; XIV (new series, 1895), 358–62, 395–405. On Social Darwinism and imperialism see Richard Hofstadter, *Social Darwinism in American Thought*.

25. J. G. Harbord, "The Necessity of a Well Organized and Trained Infantry at the Outbreak of War, and the Best Means to be Adopted by the United States for Obtaining such a Force," *J.M.S.I.*, XXI (1897), 2.

26. *Ibid.*, p. 4.

27. Ganoe, *History of the United States Army*, pp. 370–72; Walter Millis, *The Martial Spirit*, pp. 151–60; Spaulding, *Army in Peace and War*, pp. 378–79.

28. John A. Dapray, "Are We a Military People?", *J.M.S.I.*, XXIII (1898), 371–91. See also A. H. Russell, "What is the Use of a Regular Army in this Country," *ibid.*, XXIV (1899), 216–31, for a summary of views of leading military men on the unreadiness of the United States for war.

29. Frank Freidel, *The Splendid Little War;* Millis, *Martial Spirit,* pp. 196–292, 316–60.

30. Ganoe, *History of the United States Army,* pp. 399–408, 411–15; Frederic L. Huidekoper, *The Military Unpreparedness of the United States,* pp. 222–42, 260–68.

31. Bernardo and Bacon, *American Military Policy,* pp. 286–317; Ganoe, *History of the United States Army,* pp. 416–19; Jessup, *Root,* I, 240–68; Millis, *Arms and Men,* pp. 173–81; Elihu Root, *The Military and Colonial Policy of the United States: Addresses and Reports,* ed. Robert Bacon and James Brown Scott, pp. 121–29, 135–52, 349–478; Spaulding, *Army in Peace and War,* pp. 393–98.

32. Ganoe, *History of the United States Army,* p. 399.

33. Theodore Roosevelt to Henry Cabot Lodge, March 27, 1901, in Elting E. Morison, ed., *The Letters of Theodore Roosevelt,* III, 31–32.

34. Foster Rhea Dulles, *America's Rise to World Power, 1898–1954,* pp. 69–72.

35. Theodore Roosevelt to Sir Edward Grey, October 22, 1886, in Morison, *Theodore Roosevelt,* V, 463.

36. Alfred W. Bjornstad, "The Military Necessities of the United States and the Best Provisions for Meeting Them," *J.M.S.I.,* XLII (1908), 335–41. Expansible army views were also expressed in the second prize and honorable mention essays, *ibid.,* XLIII (1908), 1–24, 171–90.

37. E.g., *ibid.,* pp. 1–24.

38. Frederic L. Chapin, "Homer Lea and the Chinese Revolution" (Unpublished MS., Widener Library, Harvard University, 1950); *D.A.B.,* XI, 69–70; John P. Mallan, "The Warrior Critique of the Business Civilization," *American Quarterly,* VIII (1956), 216–30; Charles E. Van Loan, "General Homer Lea," *Harper's Weekly,* LVII (Jan. 4, 1913), 7.

39. Homer Lea, *The Valor of Ignorance,* and *The Day of the Saxon.* For *The Swarming of the Slav* see *Harper's Weekly,* LVII (1913), 7.

40. Lea, *Valor of Ignorance,* pp. 251–55.

41. *Ibid.,* especially pp. 260–61 on the ease of sending Japanese invasion armies to the United States.

42. *Ibid., passim,* especially pp. 8–57; Lea, *Day of the Saxon,* pp. 35–43.

43. E.g., *J.M.S.I.,* XXXVIII (1906), 36, 347–48; *United Service,* I (new series, 1889), 520–27; VI (new series, 1891), 510–12. On issues such as immigration see Richard G. Brown, "Social Attitudes of American Generals."

44. Cassius E. Gillette, "An American Uniform for the United States Army," *J.M.S.I.,* XXXVII (1905), 65.

45. See again Mallan, "The Warrior Critique of the Business Civilization," *American Quarterly,* VIII (1956), 216–30.

46. Lea, *Valor of Ignorance,* pp. 256–307.

47. Ignez Rodic, "The Prospects of an American-Japanese War,"

J.M.S.I., XLI (1907), 12–27. See also Theodore Roosevelt's observations on the European belief that the United States would lose a war with Japan, Morison, *Theodore Roosevelt*, V, 724–25.

48. Matthew A. Hanna, "Our Army a School," *J.M.S.I.*, XLI (1907), 143–51.

49. James S. Pettit, "How Far Does Democracy Affect the Organization and Discipline of Our Armies, and How Can Its Influence Be Most Effectually Utilized?", *ibid.*, XXXVIII (1906), 10.

50. *Ibid.*, pp. 31–35.   51. *Ibid.*, pp. 35–36.   52. *Ibid.*, pp. 3–8.
53. *Ibid.*, pp. 8–10.   54. *Ibid.*, pp. 29–30.   55. *Ibid.*, p. 9.
56. *Ibid.*, pp. 2, 38.

57. *Ibid.*, pp. 330–62. The two critics of Pettit's views were a major of the New York National Guard and Colonel Charles W. Larned, professor of drawing at West Point, who despite his position was a critic of conventional army thought and therefore a man whose views were dismissed elsewhere in the *Journal* as not those of a real soldier (*ibid.*, pp. 314–29). For views similar to Pettit's on the military advantages of monarchical government, see *United Service*, VII (new series, 1892), 347–56, and XVI (new series, 1896), 1–13.

58. *J.M.S.I.*, XXXVIII (1906), 358.   59. *Ibid.*, p. 368.

60. John Pope, address to the Army of the Tennessee, October 16, 1873, copy in W. T. Sherman Papers, Library of Congress, XXXVI, 4722–23.

x: *John M. Schofield*

1. *D.A.B.*, XVI, 452–54; John M. Schofield, *Forty-six Years in the Army.*

2. United States *v.* Eliason, 16 Peters 291, quoted in W. H. Carter, *Creation of the American General Staff*, 68:1 Senate Documents, II (serial 8254), no. 119, p. 15.

3. Bernardo and Bacon, *American Military Policy*, p. 252; Elliott, *Winfield Scott*, especially pp. 426–28, 648–58.

4. Elliott, *Winfield Scott*, pp. 426–28, 648–58.

5. Carter, *American General Staff*, pp. 2, 19–20, 33–35; Lewis, *Sherman: Fighting Prophet*, pp. 601–15; Schofield, *Forty-six Years*, pp. 406–10, 420–23, 468–76; W. T. Sherman Papers, Library of Congress, XXVII, 3570, 3789; XXVIII, 3798–3800.

6. *Revised Regulations for the Army of the United States, 1895*, p. 26.

7. *R.S.W.*, 1869, p. 28.

8. William Harding Carter, *The American Army*, pp. 185–97; John Gibbon, "Needed Reforms in the Army," *North American Review*, CLVI (1893), 212–18; Schofield, *Forty-six Years*, pp. 420–23, 469–72; John M. Schofield, "Needs of the Military Service, Especially in this Division [of

the Atlantic]," *R.S.W.*, 1887, pp. 116–18; W. T. Sherman Papers, Library of Congress, XXVII, 3616–17, 3646; XXXIII, 4437.

9. *R.S.W.*, 1887, p. 117.

10. Schofield, *Forty-six Years, passim,* especially pp. 404–11, 420–23, 468–76, 536–41.

11. This version of the famous statement is from the J. J. Graham translation of Clausewitz, *On War*, I, 3–4.

12. Schofield, *Forty-six Years,* pp. 336, 517–18.

13. *Ibid.*, pp. 364–66.   14. *Ibid.*, pp. 6, 539–41.

15. *Ibid.*, p. 457.   16. *Ibid.*   17. *Ibid.*, pp. 420–21.

18. *Ibid.*, p. 421.   19. *Ibid.*, pp. 422–23, 470.

20. *Ibid.*, pp. 421–22.   21. *Ibid.*, p. 410.

22. *Ibid.*, pp. 536–39.   23. *Ibid.*, p. 423; *R.S.W.*, 1892, I, 50.

24. 56:1 Senate Document 221, I (serial 3859), 115–16.

25. Jessup, *Root*, I, 251–53; Root, *Policy*, pp. 417–40.

26. Carter, *American General Staff*, pp. 31–32, 35–36; *Harper's Weekly*, XLVI (1902), 519; Jessup, *Root*, I, 260–61.

27. Jessup, *Root*, I, 259–62, 268; Millis, *Arms and Men*, 177–81; Williams, *Americans at War*, 104–5.

28. The early travail of the general staff system is surveyed in great detail in Otto L. Nelson, Jr., *National Security and the General Staff*, pp. 58–186. An excellent analysis of the Root reforms is in Paul Y. Hammond, *Organizing for Defense: The American Military Establishment in the Twentieth Century*, pp. 10–48. Williams, *Americans at War*, pp. 100–10, 123–24, includes penetrating observations on inconsistencies and imprecision in Root's own thinking. Hermann Hagedorn, *Leonard Wood: A Biography*, II, 95–125, describes Wood's role in rescuing the general staff from the verge of collapse.

XI: *R. M. Johnston*

1. Walter Goerlitz, *History of the German General Staff, 1657–1945,* p. 156.

2. R. M. Johnston, *Arms and the Race: The Foundations of Army Reform,* pp. 39–40.

3. Alexander Baltzly, "Robert Matteson Johnston and the Study of Military History," *Military Affairs*, XXI, 26–30; *D.A.B.*, X, 149–50.

4. Johnston, *Arms and the Race*, pp. 22–25.

5. *Ibid.*, pp. 46–48.   6. *Ibid.*, p. 49.   7. *Ibid.*, pp. 50–51.

8. *Ibid.*, pp. 67–71.   9. *Ibid*, pp. 71–72.   10. *Ibid.*, pp. 71–77.

11. *Ibid.*, pp. 77–81.

12. *Ibid.*, pp. 44–45, 34–37; R. M. Johnston, *Napoleon: A Short Biography*.

13. Johnston, *Arms and the Race*, pp. 34–37.

14. *Ibid.*, pp. 34–38, 52–57.

15. Liddell Hart, *Ghost of Napoleon*, pp. 101–4.

16. Johnston, *Arms and the Race*, pp. 37, 53–55.

17. *Ibid., passim*, especially pp. 34–57.

18. R. M. Johnston, *Bull Run: Its Strategy and Tactics, passim.*

19. *Ibid.*, pp. 100–3, 111–13.   20. *Ibid.*, pp. 161–62.

21. *Ibid.*, pp. 123–26, 136–48, 170–81.

22. *Ibid., passim*, especially pp. 52–81.   23. *Ibid.*, pp. 243–52.

24. Johnston, *Arms and the Race*, pp. 82–90, 95–100.

25. *Ibid.*, pp. 124–25.   26. *Ibid.*, pp. 120–44, 176–86.

27. *Ibid.*, pp. 192–215.   28. *Ibid.*, p. 212.

29. *Ibid.*, pp. 206, 212.   30. *Ibid.*, p. 214.

31. *Ibid.*, pp. 208–9; R. M. Johnston, *Leading American Soldiers*, pp. 224–25.

32. Johnston, *American Soldiers, passim*, especially pp. 157, 322–23.

33. *Ibid.*, pp. 176, 207–9.   34. *Ibid.*, pp. 175–76.

35. *Ibid.*, p. 176.   36. *Ibid.*, pp. 106, 121, 125, 131.

37. *Ibid.*, pp. 130–33; Johnston, *Bull Run, passim;* Kenneth P. Williams, *Lincoln Finds a General: A Military Study of the Civil War*, II, 793–96.

xii: *Leonard Wood*

1. E.g., *J.M.S.I.*, XXII (1898), 1–49; XXV (1899), 350–53.

2. T. Bentley Mott, "The Swiss Military Organization," *ibid.*, XXXVIII (1906), 246–63, 442–58, and XXXIX (1906), 18–9; A. C. Scharpe, trans., "Extracts from Regulations for Maneuvers for the Swiss Army," *ibid.*, XXXVIII (1906), 78–85.

3. Mott, "Swiss Military Organization," *ibid.*, XXXVIII (1906), 243, 453; XXXIX (1906), 23–27.

4. *Ibid.*, XXXIX (1906), 27–29.

5. *Ibid.*, XXXVIII (1906), 453–55.   6. *Ibid.*, XXXIX (1906), 23.

7. *Ibid.*, pp. 19–20.   8. *Ibid.*, pp. 20–23.   9. *Ibid.*, pp. 25–27.

10. *Ibid.*, p. 29.   11. E.g., *ibid.*, pp. 153–67, 210–16.

12. E.g., the *Nineteenth-Century Readers' Guide* for 1890–1899 contains approximately one-half column of entries under "United States Army"; the *Readers' Guide* for 1900–1909, three and one-half columns.

13. For the Plattsburg movement, see Hagedorn, *Wood*, II, 159–62, 193–96.

14. Leonard Wood Diary, Library of Congress, March 25, April 3, 13, 1912.

15. On the preparedness movement see Hermann Hagedorn, *The Bugle That Woke America*, and *Wood*, II, 146–203; Arthur S. Link, *Woodrow Wilson and the Progressive Era, 1910–1917* [1954], pp. 174–96; Henry F. Pringle, *Theodore Roosevelt*, pp. 585–87; William W.

Tinsley, "The American Preparedness Movement," Ph.D. thesis, Stanford University, 1939.

16. Huidekoper, *Military Unpreparedness*, pp. 1–272. Among Huidekoper's periodical articles on the preparedness question were "Is the United States Prepared for War?", *North American Review*, CLXXXII (1906), 161–78, 391–407; "The Truth Concerning the United States Army," *Infantry Journal*, VIII (1911), 848–63; "The United States Army and Organized Militia Today," *ibid.*, 43–60; and "Lessons of Our Past Wars," *World's Work*, XXIX (1915), 392–416.

17. Huidekoper, *Military Unpreparedness*, pp. 278, 284.

18. *Ibid.*, p. x.   19. *Ibid.*, *passim*, especially pp. 222–28.

20. *Ibid.*, pp. 545–46.   21. *Ibid.*, pp. 528–41.

22. *Ibid.*, pp. 532–35.   23. *Ibid.*, pp. 525–28, 541–52.

24. *Ibid.*, pp. 551–52.

25. *D.A.B.*, XX, 467–69; Hagedorn, *Wood*.

26. Hagedorn, *Wood*, II, 95–125; Millis, *Arms and Men*, pp. 200–1.

27. Hagedorn, *Wood*, II, 146–203. Walter Millis aptly calls Wood "a military evangelist," *Arms and Men*, p. 200.

28. Leonard Wood, *Our Military History: Its Facts and Fallacies*, pp. 34–36.

29. *Ibid.*, pp. 35–36.   30. *Ibid.*, p. 41.   31. *Ibid.*, p. 43.

32. On the much debated merits of Theodore Roosevelt's foreign policy a sympathetic account, perhaps excessively so, is William Henry Harbaugh, *Power and Responsibility: The Life and Times of Theodore Roosevelt;* critic ' of Roosevelt in its conclusions but not so much so in the body of the ,ork is Howard K. Beale, *Theodore Roosevelt and the Rise of America to World Power*.

33. Wood, *Military History*, pp. 31–49, 76.   34. *Ibid.*, pp. 39–40.

35. *Ibid.*, pp. 55–167, is a summary of Upton and Huidekoper on American military history. For Wood's views on the usual teaching of American history in schools and colleges, see *ibid.*, pp. 11–20.

36. Wood, *Military History*, pp. 76–86.

37. Wood, *The Military Obligation of Citizenship*, pp. 6–7.

38. Millis, *Arms and Men*, p. 201.   39. *Ibid.*, p. 217.

40. Wood, *Military History*, pp. 177–78.

41. Wood, *Military History*, pp. 197–207; *Military Obligation*, pp. 55–57.

42. Wood, *Military History*, pp. 207–13.

43. Leonard Wood, "What the War Means to America," in P. F. Collier and Son's *The Story of the Great War*, I, 12.

44. Quoted in Wood, *Military History*, p. 63.

45. *Ibid.*, pp. 214–27; Wood, *Military Obligation*, pp. 69–76.

46. Wood, *Military History*, pp. 185–87.

47. Wood, "What the War Means," *Story of the Great War*, I, 9. Among Wood's periodical articles for the preparedness campaign, see

"Training for War in Time of Peace," *Outlook*, XC (1909), 976–989; "Why We Have No Army," *McClure's*, XXXVIII (1912), 677–83; "The Army's New and Bigger Job," *World's Work*, XXVIII (1914), 75–84. There is a host of preparedness books reiterating Wood's arguments, many of them by Wood's friends and associates. E.g., William Freeman, *Awake! U.S.A.;* F. A. Kuenzli, *Right and Duty or Citizen and Soldier: Switzerland Prepared and at Peace, A Model for the United States;* Robert G. Schaefer, *Red, White and Blue;* Jennings C. Wise, *Empire and Armament: The Evolution of American Imperialism and the Problem of National Defence,* and *The Call of the Republic;* Eric Fisher Wood, *The Writing on the Wall: The Nation on Trial.* Carter, *American Army,* is an ambivalent book, whose author we have met as an Uptonian younger officer and as one of Root's assistants at the inauguration of the general staff. As a major general, Carter was a thoroughgoing regular; he had served in the army since he was a dispatch rider in the Civil War at the age of twelve and a half. He lauded Upton (pp. 13, 16, 30–31), and he devoted much of his book to rhapsodic praise of the regular army (e.g., pp. 79–89). But he now explicitly rejected the expansible army plan as injuring the effectiveness of the regulars (pp. 78, 111, 113), and he held that creating an adequate body of reserves from among discharged regulars, a favorite Uptonian scheme, was not feasible (pp. 103–10). He recommended that a reserve army be established by substituting federal volunteers for the state militia; curiously, he evaded the Uptonian question as to the effectiveness of such a citizen reserve.

48. Bernardo and Bacon, *American Military Policy*, pp. 340–44; Link, *Woodrow Wilson and the Progressive Era*, pp. 179–87; Millis, *Arms and Men*, pp. 217–18; Palmer, *Washington, Lincoln, Wilson*, pp. 315–17.

49. Millis, *Arms and Men*, pp. 222–25; Palmer, *Washington, Lincoln, Wilson*, pp. 317–18.

50. R.S.W., 1916, I, 155–208; *United States Statutes-at-Large*, XXXIX, pt. 2, 166–217; Bernardo and Bacon, *American Military Policy*, pp. 344–46.

51. Millis, *Arms and Men*, pp. 228–31.

52. John J. Pershing, *My Experiences in the World War*, I, 130–31.

xiii: *John McAuley Palmer and George C. Marshall*

1. Hagedorn, *Wood*, II, 290, 294–96; Huntington, *Soldier and the State*, pp. 280–82n.; Peyton C. March, *The Nation at War*, pp. 57–68.

2. William Frye, *Marshall: Citizen Soldier*, pp. 129–38; Pershing, *Experiences*, I, 150–56, 264–65.

3. On the Meuse-Argonne offensive, see especially Pershing, *Experiences*, II, 289–387. On Pershing's pride in his troops, *ibid.*, pp. 60, 63–64, 90–91, 273–74, 389–93.

4. Pershing called for a citizen army in testimony before a subcommittee of the Senate Military Affairs Committee in 1919, *Reorganization of the Army: Hearings before the Subcommittee of the Committee on Military Affairs, United States Senate, Sixty-fifth Congress, First Session, on . . . S.2715. . . .* II, 1572, 1579–80; hereafter cited as *Reorganization Hearings, S.2715.* Pershing's defense of the citizen army features of the National Defense Act of 1920 appeared in his article, "Our National Military Policy," *Scientific American*, CXXVII (1922), 83, 142. On his dispatch of Palmer to Washington, see Pershing's introduction to Palmer, *Washington, Lincoln, Wilson*, pp. xiii–xiv; Frye, *Marshall*, p. 175; Palmer, *America in Arms*, pp. 165–67.

5. *R.S.W.*, 1919, pp. 480–81.

6. James W. Wadsworth in his introduction to John McAuley Palmer, *Statesmanship or War*, p. xiv.

7. Frye, *Marshall*, p. 174; *Reorganization Hearings, S.2715* II, 1177; Wadsworth in Palmer, *Statesmanship or War*, pp. xi–xv.

8. Frye, *Marshall*, pp. 177–78; Palmer, *America in Arms*, pp. 168–70; *Reorganization Hearings, S.2715*, II, 1173–1232; Wadsworth in Palmer, *Statesmanship or War*, pp. xiv–xv.

9. *D.A.B.*, XIV, 187–88 (on Major General John McAuley Palmer of the Civil War); Palmer, *America in Arms*, pp. 101–3; Pershing in Palmer, *Washington, Lincoln, Wilson*, pp. xiii–xiv; *Reorganization Hearings, S.2715*, II, 1173–74; Wadsworth in Palmer, *Statesmanship or War*, pp. ix–x.

10. Palmer, *America in Arms*, p. 136.   11. *Ibid.*, pp. 136–37.

12. Dupuy, *Men of West Point*, pp. 45, 157; Palmer, *America in Arms*, pp. 137–47, *Washington, Lincoln, Wilson*, pp. 313–15; *R.S.W.*, 1912, pp. 71–153.

13. Palmer, *America in Arms*, pp. 147–48, 161–63, *An Army of the People, Washington, Lincoln, Wilson*, pp. 319–20; *Reorganization Hearings, S.2715*, II, 1173–74.

14. Dupuy, *Men of West Point*, pp. 156–59; Frye, *Marshall*, pp. 177–79; Palmer, *America in Arms*, pp. 170–87, *Washington, Lincoln, Wilson*, pp. 362–66; Wadsworth in Palmer, *Statesmanship or War*, pp. xv–xvii.

15. Palmer, *Statesmanship or War*, pp. 6–7, *America in Arms*, p. 141.

16. Palmer, *Statesmanship or War*, pp. 22–29.   17. *Ibid.*, p. 29.

18. *Ibid.*, pp. 2–8, *Washington, Lincoln, Wilson*, pp. 224–27, 232–39.

19. Palmer, *Statesmanship or War*, pp. 68–69. A Council of National Defense had been suggested earlier by Secretary Stimson in the annex to his annual report of 1912, which Palmer had helped to prepare, *R.S.W.*, 1912, pp. 127–28.

20. Palmer, *Statesmanship or War*, pp. 68–69.   21. *Ibid.*, p. 76.

22. *Ibid.*, pp. 16–22, *America in Arms*, pp. 93–95, *Washington, Lincoln, Wilson*, pp. 355–57.

23. Palmer, *Statesmanship or War*, pp. 30–34, 77–78, *Washington, Lincoln, Wilson*, pp. 325–26, 346–48.

24. Palmer, *America in Arms*, pp. 179–80.

25. Palmer, *Statesmanship or War*, pp. 38–39.

26. *Reorganization Hearings, S.2715*, II, 1174–75.

27. Palmer, *Statesmanship or War*, pp. 40–59, *Washington, Lincoln, Wilson*, pp. 304–5; *Reorganization Hearings, S.2715*, II, 1181–84, 1207–9.

28. Palmer, *America in Arms*, p. 173; *Reorganization Hearings, S.2715*, pp. 1208–9.

29. Palmer, *America in Arms*, p. 104.

30. Palmer, *Statesmanship or War*, pp. 59–64.

31. *Ibid.*, p. 63. Similar expressions appear in *Washington, Lincoln, Wilson*, pp. 173–76.

32. E.g., Palmer, *Statesmanship or War*, pp. 8–12, 80–102, *Washington, Lincoln, Wilson*, pp. 9–123, *passim.* Palmer rightly emphasized that Washington's disparagement of the militia referred to the untrained and badly organized militia of the Revolution but did not prevent him from advocating a trained militia as the foundation of American military policy in the 1780s and 1790s. He rightly pointed out (*America in Arms*, pp. 110–11, *Washington, Lincoln, Wilson*, pp. 263–81) that Upton distorted Washington through failing to discover Washington's 1783 recommendations to the Confederation Congress. But I think that Palmer in turn gave insufficient attention to Washington's support of Hamilton's proposals for strengthening the professional army in the 1790s, and I find in Washington's suggestions on military education more interest in building a professional officer corps and less enthusiasm for the possibilities of disseminating the knowledge required of military officers among the citizenry at large, than Palmer read into them. Washington consistently insisted on the highest professional military standards that the American situation would permit. Though he was not Emory Upton, he was nevertheless a founder of the conservative, professionalist military tradition in America, especially in view of the context of opinion in which he found himself.

33. Palmer, *Statesmanship or War*, pp. 86–89.

34. *Ibid.*, pp. 161–66.   35. *Ibid.*, p. 74.   36. *Ibid.*, p. 73.

37. 69:2 House of Representatives Committee on Military Affairs, *The National Defense: Historical Documents Relating to the Reorganization Plans of the War Department and to the Present National Defense Act;* Ganoe, *History of the United States Army*, pp. 479–82; Millis, *Arms and Men*, pp. 240–44; Palmer, *Statesmanship or War*, pp. 167–76 (including interpretations of the act by Pershing and Secretary of War John W. Weeks), *Washington, Lincoln, Wilson*, pp. 362–70; *United States Statutes-at-Large*, XLI, pt. 1, 759–812.

38. Pershing, "Our National Military Policy," *Scientific American,* CXXVII (1922), 83.

39. Palmer, *America in Arms,* pp. 187–90, *Statesmanship or War,* pp. 164–66, *Washington, Lincoln, Wilson,* pp. 367–70.

40. Palmer, *Washington, Lincoln, Wilson,* pp. 3–5, 146–48.

41. Palmer, *America in Arms,* pp. 196–200. During the 1930s Palmer published a biography of Baron von Steuben emphasizing Steuben's championship of a citizen militia as the basis for a permanent American military policy; John McAuley Palmer, *General von Steuben.*

42. Frye, *Marshall, passim,* especially pp. 159–60, 174.

43. Dupuy, *Men of West Point,* p. 158; Frye, *Marshall,* pp. 86, 91–92, 125, 174–79, 214.

44. Frye, *Marshall,* pp. 186–235, *passim.* On the Marshall-MacArthur feud, see Clark Lee and Richard Henschel, *Douglas MacArthur,* pp. 115–31. Despite the feud, MacArthur agreed with Marshall on the merits of the citizen soldier; see Frank C. Waldrop, ed., *MacArthur on War,* especially pp. 91–92 (from MacArthur's annual report as chief of staff, 1932), and Frederick Martin Stern, *The Citizen Army: Key to Defense in the Atomic Age,* pp. 151, 356–57.

45. Frye, *Marshall,* pp. 280–81.

46. Dupuy, *Men of West Point,* p. 410; Frye, *Marshall,* p. 367; Robert Payne, *The Marshall Story: A Biography of General George C. Marshall,* pp. 33–34.

47. Frye, *Marshall,* p. 367; Stern, *Citizen Army,* p. 150.

48. Cf. *Reorganization Hearings, S.2715,* II, 1176.

49. The President's Advisory Commission on Universal Training, *A Program for National Security,* pp. 397–99; Stern, *Citizen Army,* pp. 353–56.

50. President's Advisory Commission, *Program,* p. 393.

51. *Ibid.,* p. 395.   52. *Ibid.,* pp. 395–97.

53. Harry S. Truman, *Memoirs,* especially I, 510–12.

54. President's Advisory Commission, *Program,* p. 404.

55. *Ibid.,* pp. 401–3.

56. *Ibid., passim;* Truman, *Memoirs,* II, 53–55; *United States Statutes-at-Large,* LXV, 75–89.

57. The postwar political climate is perceptively discussed in Eric Goldman, *The Crucial Decade, 1945–1955.*

NOTES: *Epilogue*

1. Palmer, *Statesmanship or War,* especially pp. 16–22, 30–34, 76–78; R.S.W., 1919, p. 476.

2. The President's Advisory Commission on Universal Training argued in their *Report* that atomic weapons made universal military train-

ing more necessary, since universal military training could offer the means of preserving order and discipline in civil defense after an atomic attack. But the idea of giving all young men military training merely to enable them to participate better in civil defense at home never generated much political appeal. Stern, *Citizen Army*, also attempts to demonstrate that universal training is appropriate to the atomic age.

3. On the evolution of air force strategic doctrine, see Millis, *Arms and Men*, pp. 248–59, 268–71, 300. A brief survey of the evolution of American strategic doctrine in general which includes doctrine on air war is Dale O. Smith, *U.S. Military Doctrine: A Study and Appraisal.*

4. Fitzpatrick, *Washington*, XXXIII, 165–66.

Bibliography

DOCUMENTS

American State Papers, Military Affairs. 7 vols. Washington, Gales and Seaton, 1832–1861.
Callan, J. F. The Military Laws of the United States. Rev. ed. Philadelphia, G. W. Childs, 1863.
Journals of the Continental Congress. 13 vols. Philadelphia, Falwell, 1800–1801.
The President's Advisory Commission on Universal Training. A Program for National Security. Washington, Government Printing Office, 1947.
Quartermaster General's Office. Letter Book 1876B. National Archives.
Revised Regulations for the Army of the United States, 1895. Washington, Government Printing Office, 1895.
Richardson, James D., ed. Compilation of the Messages and Papers of the Presidents. 10 vols. and supplement. Washington, Government Printing Office, 1899–1903.
Secretary of War. Reports.
United States Congress.
    45:2 House Miscellaneous Documents, IV (serial 1818), no. 56.
    45:3 Senate Reports, I (serial 1837), no. 555.
    49:1 House Executive Documents, XXVIII (serial 2395, 2396), no. 49.
    56:1 Senate Document 221, I (serial 3859).
    65:1 Senate Committee on Military Affairs. Reorganization of the Army: Hearings before the Subcommittee of the Committee on Military Affairs, United States Senate, Sixty-fifth Congress, First Session, on . . . S.2715. . . .
    68:1 Senate Documents, II (serial 8254), no. 119.
    69:2 House Committee on Military Affairs. The National Defense: Historical Documents Relating to the Reorganization Plans of the War Department and to the Present National Defense Act.

OTHER SOURCES

Badeau, Adam. Military History of U. S. Grant. 3 vols. New York, Appleton, 1882.
Baltzly, Alexander. "Robert Matteson Johnston and the Study of Military History," Military Affairs, XXI (1957), 26–30.

Barnard, Henry. Military Schools and Courses of Instruction in the Science and Art of War. . . . Philadelphia, Lippincott, 1862.

Beale, Howard K. Theodore Roosevelt and the Rise of America to World Power. Baltimore, Johns Hopkins University Press, 1956.

Bernardo, C. Joseph, and Eugene H. Bacon. American Military Policy: Its Development since 1775. Harrisburg, Military Service Publishing Company [1955].

Bigelow, John. The Principles of Strategy. Rev. ed. Philadelphia, Lippincott, 1894.

Bjornstad, Alfred W. "The Military Necessities of the United States, and the Best Provisions for Meeting Them," *Journal of the United States Military Service Institution*, XLII (1908), 335–61.

Boorstin, Daniel J. The Americans: The Colonial Experience. New York, Random House, 1958.

Boyd, Julian P., ed. The Papers of Thomas Jefferson. 16 vols. to date. Princeton, Princeton University Press, 1950– .

Brown, Richard C. "Emory Upton, The Army's Mahan," *Military Affairs*, XVII (1953), 125–31.

—— "Social Attitudes of American Generals, 1898–1940." Ph.D. thesis, University of Wisconsin, 1951.

Calhoun, John C. The Works of John C. Calhoun. 6 vols. New York, Appleton, 1855.

Callahan, North. Henry Knox: General Washington's General. New York, Rinehart, 1958.

Carter, William H. The American Army. Indianapolis, Bobbs-Merrill [1915].

—— "One View of the Army Question," *United Service*, II (new series, 1889), 519–32.

Catton, Bruce. Grant Moves South. Boston, Little, Brown, 1959.

—— Mr. Lincoln's Army. Garden City, N.Y., Doubleday, 1949.

—— A Stillness at Appomattox. Garden City, N.Y., Doubleday, 1953.

Chapin, Frederic L. "Homer Lea and the Chinese Revolution," Unpublished MS., Widener Library, Harvard University, 1950.

Clausewitz, Karl von. On War. Translated by O. J. Matthjis Jollis. New York, Random House, 1943.

Craig, Gordon A. The Politics of the Prussian Army, 1640–1945. New York, Oxford University Press, 1956.

Cullum, George W. "Review of Jomini's Life of Napoleon," *United States Service Magazine*, II (1864), 125–37.

Dapray, John A. "Are We a Military People?", *Journal of the United States Military Service Institution*, XXIII (1898), 371–91.

Delafield, Richard. Report on the Art of War in Europe in 1854, 1855, and 1856. Washington, George W. Bowman, 1860.

Dictionary of American Biography. 21 vols. New York, Scribner's, 1928–1937.

Donald, David L. Lincoln Reconsidered: Essays on the Civil War Era. New York, Knopf, 1956.

Dorn, Walter L. Competition for Empire, 1740–1763. New York, Harper, 1940.

Dulles, Foster Rhea. America's Rise to World Power, 1898–1954. New York, Harper [1955].

Dupuy, R. Ernest. Men of West Point: The First 150 Years of the United States Military Academy. New York, Sloane [1951].

—— Where They Have Trod: The West Point Tradition in American Life. New York, Frederick G. Stokes, 1940.

Dupuy, R. Ernest, and Trevor N. Dupuy. Military Heritage of America. New York, McGraw-Hill, 1956.

Earle, Edward Meade, ed. Makers of Modern Strategy. Princeton, Princeton University Press, 1943.

Ekirch, Arthur A., Jr. The Civilian and the Military. New York, Oxford University Press, 1956.

—— "The Idea of a Citizen Army," *Military Affairs,* XVII (1953), 30–36.

Elliott, Charles Winslow. Winfield Scott: The Soldier and the Man. New York, Macmillan, 1937.

Fitzpatrick, John C., ed. The Writings of George Washington. 39 vols. Washington, Government Printing Office, 1932.

Forman, Sidney. West Point: A History of the United States Military Academy. New York, Columbia University Press, 1950.

Franklin, John Hope. The Militant South. Cambridge, Harvard University Press, 1956.

Freeman, William. Awake! U.S.A. New York, George H. Doran, 1916.

Freidel, Frank. The Splendid Little War. Boston, Little, Brown [1958].

Frye, William. Marshall: Citizen Soldier. Indianapolis and New York, Bobbs-Merrill [1947].

Fuller, J. F. C. The Conduct of War, 1789–1961. New Brunswick, Rutgers University Press, 1961.

Ganoe, William Addleman. The History of the United States Army. New York, Appleton-Century, 1942.

Gibbon, John. "Needed Reforms in the Army," *North American Review,* CLVI (1893), 212–18.

Gillette, Cassius E. "An American Uniform for the United States Army," *Journal of the United States Military Service Institution,* XXXVII (1905), 61–80.

Goerlitz, Walter. History of the German General Staff, 1657–1945. Translated by Brian Battershaw. New York, Praeger, 1953.

Goldman, Eric. The Crucial Decade, 1945–1955. New York, Knopf, 1956.

Grant, U. S. Personal Memoirs of U. S. Grant. 2 vols. New York,

Charles L. Webster, 1886. (One-vol. ed., E. B. Long, ed., New York, World Publishing Company, 1952).

Greene, Francis Vinton. The Revolutionary War and the Military Policy of the United States. New York, Schibner's, 1911.

Griffin, Eugene. "Our Sea-Coast Defenses," *North American Review,* CXLVIII (1888), 64–73.

Hagedorn, Hermann. The Bugle That Woke America. New York, John Day [1940].

—— Leonard Wood: A Biography. 2 vols. New York, Harper, 1931.

Halleck, Henry W. Elements of Military Art and Science; Or, Course in Instruction in Strategy, Fortifications, Tactics of Battle. . . . 3d ed. New York, Appleton, 1863.

Hammond, Paul Y. Organizing for Defense: The American Military Establishment in the Twentieth Century. Princeton, Princeton University Press, 1961.

Hanna, Matthew A. "Our Army a School," *Journal of the United States Military Service Institution,* XLI (1907), 143–51.

Harbaugh, William Henry. Power and Responsibility: The Life and Times of Theodore Roosevelt. New York, Farrar, Straus and Cudahy [1961].

Harbord, J. G. "The Necessity of a Well Organized and Trained Infantry at the Outbreak of War, and the Best Means to be Adopted by the United States for Obtaining Such a Force," *Journal of the United States Military Service Institution,* XXI (1897), 1–27.

Hatch, Louis C. The Administration of the American Revolutionary Army. Harvard Historical Studies, X. New York, Longmans, Green, 1904.

Hofstadter, Richard. Social Darwinism in American Thought. Philadelphia, University of Pennsylvania Press, 1944.

Huidekoper, Frederic L. The Military Unpreparedness of the United States. New York, Macmillan, 1915.

—— "Is the United States Prepared for War?", *North American Review,* CLXXXII (1902), 161–78, 391–407.

—— "Lessons of Our Past Wars," *World's Work,* XXIX (1915), 392–416.

—— "The Truth Concerning the United States Army," *Infantry Journal,* VIII (1911), 848–63.

—— "The United States Army and Organized Militia To-day," *Infantry Journal,* IX (1911), 43–60.

Huntington, Samuel P. The Soldier and the State: The Theory and Politics of Civil-Military Relations. Cambridge, Harvard University Press, 1957.

Jacobs, James Ripley. The Beginning of the U.S. Army, 1783–1812. Princeton, Princeton University Press, 1947.

Jensen, Merrill. The New Nation: A History of the United States during the Confederation. New York, Knopf, 1950.

Jessup, Philip C. Elihu Root. 2 vols. New York, Dodd, Mead, 1938.

Johnson, Robert Underwood, and Clarence Clough Buel, eds. Battles and Leaders of the Civil War. 4 vols. New York, The Century Company, 1884–1888.

Johnston, R. M. Arms and the Race: The Foundations of Army Reform. New York, The Century Company, 1915.

——Bull Run: Its Strategy and Tactics. Boston and New York, Houghton Mifflin, 1913.

—— Leading American Soldiers. New York, Henry Holt, 1907.

—— Napoleon: A Short Biography. New York, Henry Holt, 1909.

Jomini, Antoine Henri, Baron de. Précis de l'art de la guerre. 2 vols. Paris, Librairie militaire de L. Baudoin, 1894. (Translated by G. H. Mendell and W. P. Craighill as Summary of the Art of War, Philadelphia, Lippincott, 1864.)

—— Traité des grandes opérations militaires. 8 vols. Paris, 1804–1806.

Keim, DeB. "Our Moral Weakness," United States Service Magazine, III (1865), 369–76.

Kreidberg, Marvin A., and Merton G. Henry. History of Military Mobilization in the United States Army, 1775–1945. Washington, Government Printing Office, 1955.

Kuenzli, F. A. Right and Duty or Citizen and Soldier: Switzerland Prepared and at Peace, A Model for the United States. New York, National Defense Institute [1916].

Kurtz, Stephen G. The Presidency of John Adams: The Collapse of Federalism, 1795–1800. Philadelphia, University of Pennsylvania Press [1957].

Lea, Homer. The Day of the Saxon. New York, Harper [1912].

—— The Valor of Ignorance. New York, Harper, 1909.

Lee, Clark, and Richard Henschel. Douglas MacArthur. New York, Henry Holt, 1952.

Lewis, Lloyd. Sherman: Fighting Prophet. New York, Harcourt, Brace, 1932.

Liddell Hart, B. H. The Ghost of Napoleon. New Haven, Yale University Press [1933].

—— The Revolution in Warfare. New Haven, Yale University Press, 1947.

—— Sherman: Soldier, Realist, American. New York, Dodd, Mead, 1929.

—— Strategy. New York, Praeger, 1954.

Lodge, Henry Cabot, ed. The Works of Alexander Hamilton. 12 vols. New York, Putnam, 1904.

Logan, John A. The Volunteer Soldier of America. Chicago and New York, R. S. Peale, 1887.

Luvaas, Jay. The Military Legacy of the Civil War. Chicago, University of Chicago Press, 1959.

McClellan, George B. The Armies of Europe. Philadelphia, Lippincott, 1861.

—— McClellan's Own Story. New York, Charles D. Webster, 1887.

—— Regulations and Instructions for the Field Service of the U.S. Cavalry in Time of War. Philadelphia, Lippincott, 1861.

Mahan, D. H. An Elementary Treatise on Advanced Guard, Out-Post, and Detachment Service of Troops. . . . Rev. ed. New York, John Wiley, 1864.

Mallan, John C. "The Warrior Critique of the Business Civilization," American Quarterly, VIII (1956), 216–30.

March, Peyton C. The Nation at War. Garden City, N.Y., Doubleday, Doran, 1931.

Marshall, Max. "A Survey of Military Periodicals." M.A. thesis, University of Missouri, 1951.

Meade, George. The Life and Letters of George Gordon Meade, Major-General United States Army. 2 vols. New York, Scribner's, 1913.

Michaelis, Otho E. "The Military Necessities of the United States and the Best Provisions for Meeting Them," Journal of the United States Military Service Institution, V (1884), 272–91.

Michie, Peter Smith. Life and Letters of General Emory Upton. New York, Appleton, 1885.

Miller, John C. Alexander Hamilton: Portrait in Paradox. New York, Harper [1959].

Millis, Walter. Arms and Men: A Study in American Military History. New York, Putnam, 1956.

—— The Martial Spirit. New York, Literary Guild of America, 1931.

Mordecai, Alfred. Military Commission to Europe in 1855 and 1856: Report. Washington, George W. Bowman, 1861.

Morison, Elting E., ed. The Letters of Theodore Roosevelt. 7 vols. Cambridge, Harvard University Press, 1951–1954.

Morton, Louis. "The Origins of American Military Policy," Military Affairs, XXII (1958), 75–82.

Mott, T. Bentley. "The Swiss Military Organization," Journal of the United States Military Service Institution, XXXVIII (1906), 243–63, 442–58, and XXXIX (1906), 18–29.

Nef, John U. War and Human Progress. Cambridge, Harvard University Press, 1950.

Nelson, Otto L., Jr. National Security and the General Staff. Washington, Infantry Journal Press [1946].

Nickerson, Hoffman. The Armed Horde. New York, Putnam, 1940.

Palmer, John McAuley. America in Arms: The Experience of the United

States with Military Organization. New Haven, Yale University Press, 1941.

—— An Army of the People. New York, Putnam, 1916.

—— General von Steuben. New Haven, Yale University Press, 1937.

—— Statesmanship or War. Garden City, N.Y., Doubleday, Page, 1927.

—— Washington, Lincoln, Wilson: Three War Statesmen. Garden City, N.Y., Doubleday, Doran, 1930.

Payne, Robert. The Marshall Story: A Biography of General George C. Marshall. New York, Prentice-Hall [1951].

Pershing, John J. My Experiences in the World War. 2 vols. New York, Frederick A. Stokes, 1931.

—— "Our National Military Policy," Scientific American, CXXVII (1922), 83, 142.

Pettit, James S. "How Far Does Democracy Affect the Organization and Discipline of Our Armies, and How Can Its Influence Be Most Effectually Utilized?", Journal of the United States Military Service Institution, XXXVIII (1906), 1–38.

Pringle, Henry F. Theodore Roosevelt. New York, Harcourt, Brace [1931].

Puleston, W. D. The Life and Work of Captain Alfred Thayer Mahan. New Haven, Yale University Press, 1940.

Quimby, Robert S. The Background of Napoleonic Warfare: The Theory of Military Tactics in Eighteenth-Century France. New York, Columbia University Press, 1957.

Riker, William H. Soldiers of the States: The Role of the National Guard in American Democracy. Washington, Public Affairs Press [1957].

Rodic, Ignez. "The Prospects of an American-Japanese War," Journal of the United States Military Service Institution, XLI (1907), 12–27.

Root, Elihu. The Military and Colonial Policy of the United States: Addresses and Reports. Edited by Robert Bacon and James Brown Scott. Cambridge, Harvard University Press, 1916.

Ropp, Theodore. War in the Modern World. Durham, N.C., Duke University Press, 1959.

Russell, A. H. "What is the Use of a Regular Army in this Country," Journal of the United States Military Service Institution, XXIV (1889), 216–31.

Schaefer, Robert G. Red, White and Blue. New York, John C. Rankin, 1917.

Scharpe, A. C., translator. "Extracts from Regulations for Maneuvers for the Swiss Army," Journal of the United States Military Service Institution, XXXVIII (1906), 78–85.

Schofield, John McAllister. Forty-six Years in the Army. New York, The Century Company, 1897.

Sheridan, P. H. Personal Memoirs of P. H. Sheridan. 2 vols. New York, Charles L. Webster, 1888.

Sherman, W. T. Personal Memoirs of W. T. Sherman. 2 vols. New York, Charles L. Webster, 1892.

Smith, Dale O. U.S. Military Doctrine: A Study and Appraisal. New York, Duell, Sloan and Pearce [1951].

Smith, Justin. The War with Mexico. 2 vols. New York, Macmillan, 1919.

Smith, Louis. American Democracy and Military Power. Chicago, University of Chicago Press, 1951.

Spaulding, Oliver Lyman. The United States Army in Peace and War. New York, Putnam, 1937.

Stern, Frederick Martin. The Citizen Army: Key to Defense in the Atomic Age. New York, St. Martin's [1957].

Steuben, Friedrich Wilhelm Ludolf Gerhart Augustin, Baron von. A Letter on the Subject of an Established Militia, and Military Arrangements, Addressed to the Inhabitants of the United States. New York, J. M'Lean, 1784.

The Story of the Great War. 8 vols. New York, P. F. Collier, 1916–1920.

Tinsley, William W. "The American Preparedness Movement," Ph.D. thesis, Stanford University, 1939.

Truman, Harry S. Memoirs. 2 vols. Garden City, N.Y., Doubleday, 1956.

Turner, Gordon B., ed. A History of Military Affairs in Western Society since the Eighteenth Century. 3 vols. Princeton, Advisory Committee of the Princeton University Military History Project, 1952.

Upton, Emory. The Armies of Asia and Europe. New York, Appleton, 1878.

—— Infantry Tactics: Double and Single Rank. New York, Appleton, 1874.

—— The Military Policy of the United States from 1775. Washington, Government Printing Office, 1904.

Vagts, Alfred. A History of Militarism. New York, W. W. Norton, 1937. (Rev. ed., New York, Meridian [1959].)

Van Loan, Charles E. "General Homer Lea," Harper's Weekly. LVII (1913), 7.

Wagner, Arthur L. "The Military Necessities of the United States and the Best Provisions for Meeting Them," Journal of the United States Military Service Institution, V (1884), 237–71.

Wainwright, Richard. "Our Coast Defenses from a Naval Stand Point," United Service, II (new series, 1889), 46–50.

Waldrop, Frank C., ed. MacArthur on War. New York, Duell, Sloan and Pearce, 1942.

Wales, A. D. "Grant: His 'Mystery' and Genius," Journal of the United States Military Service Institution, XXXIX (1906), 1–10.

Ward, Christopher. The Delaware Continentals. Wilmington, Historical Society of Delaware, 1941.

—— The War of the Revolution. 2 vols. New York, Macmillan, 1952.

Weigley, Russell F. Quartermaster General of the Union Army: A Biography of M. C. Meigs. New York, Columbia University Press, 1959.

Williams, Kenneth P. Lincoln Finds a General: A Military Study of the Civil War. 5 vols. New York, Macmillan, 1949–1959.

Williams, T. Harry. Americans at War: The Development of the American Military System. Baton Rouge, Louisiana State University Press [1960].

Wise, Jennings C. The Call of the Republic. New York, Dutton, 1917.

—— Empire and Armament: The Evolution of American Imperialism and the Problem of National Defence. New York, Putnam, 1915.

Wood, Eric Fisher. The Writing on the Wall: The Nation on Trial. New York, The Century Company, 1916.

Wood, Leonard. The Military Obligation of Citizenship. Princeton, Princeton University Press, 1915.

—— Our Military History: Its Facts and Fallacies. Chicago, Reilly and Britton, 1916.

—— "The Army's New and Bigger Job," World's Work, XXVIII (1914), 75–84.

—— "Training for War in Time of Peace," Outlook, XC (1909), 976–89.

—— "Why We Have No Army," McClure's, XXXVIII (1912), 677–83.

Index

Adams, John, 17, 22
Adjutant general, powers of, 175
Air Force, United States, 252
Air power, 251-52
Alabama, 88, 103
Alaska, 191-92, 214, 238
Alexander the Great, 98
American Expeditionary Force, 223, 228
American Legion, 248
American Revolution, 1-11, 17-18, 25, 41, 65; Emory Upton's views on, 111, 114-16, 118, 189, 194-96
Annapolis, *see* Naval Academy
Appomattox Court House, Va., 193-94
Armaments industry, United States, 141-43
Army League, 204, 217
Army of Georgia, 100
Army of Northern Virginia, 86, 193
Army of Tennessee, 90, 100
Army of the Cumberland, 100, 228
Army of the Ohio, 100, 163
Army of the Potomac, 102, 112, 120, 193
Army of the Tennessee, 100, 107, 129
Army of Virginia, 120
Army Service Forces, 244
Army War College, 178, 193; founding of, 149, 175
Arthur, Chester A., 141
Artillery: problems of, 63, 138; development of, 66, 140-42; *see also* Weapons
Asia, armies, and Emory Upton, 104
Atlanta, Ga., 87, 163, 228; battle of, 129
Atlanta, U.S.S., 141
Auerstadt, battle of, 56
Australian army, 214
Austrian army, 74; in Napoleonic wars, 55, 185

Badeau, Adam, on Ulysses S. Grant's theory of war, 91-93, 98-99

Baltimore, Md., 65
Barnard, John G., 263n.
Bazaine, Achille, 99, 193
Beauregard, Pierre G. T., 187-90
Belgium, 190
Bennington, battle of, 7-8, 18
Berlin, 254
Berthier, Louis Alexandre, 56
Bigelow, John, Sr., 94
Bigelow, John: career, 93-94; theory of war, 93-99, 263n.
Bigelow, Poultney, 94
Bismarck, Otto von, 99, 182-83, 231
Bjornstad, Alfred W., military proposals, 151-52
Blackburn's Ford, Va., 189
Black Hawk War, 60-61
Blair, Francis P., Jr., 107
Blockade, Civil War, 96-97
Board of Ordnance and Fortification, 142
Boston, Mass., 142
Boston, U.S.S., 141
Bourcet, Pierre de, 40
Bowling Green, Ky., 90
Boyen, Hermann, 41
Braddock, Sir Edward, 237
Brandywine, battle of, 7, 189
British army: in American Revolution, 1, 4-5; in Napoleonic wars, 28-29; in Crimean War, 72, 75; in War of 1812, 97; age of officers, 139; in Boer War, 152; in World War I, 208, 224
Brown, Jacob, 29
Bryant, William Cullen, 94
Bull Run, first battle of, 101; R. M. Johnston on, 187-90
Bunker Hill, battle of, 18
Burgoyne, John, 7-8
Burke-Wadsworth bill, 241
Burnside, Ambrose E., 107
Butler, Benjamin F., 107

Calhoun, John C., military proposals,

Calhoun, John C. (*continued*) 30-35, 37, 40, 62; influence of, 109, 121-22, 244

California, 153, 191-92

Canada, 145

Caribbean Sea, 150

Carnot, Lazare, 3

Carolinas, the, campaign of (1865), 81, 86-88, 90, 96

Carter, William H.: influenced by Emory Upton, 144; and Root reforms, 174; career and military proposals, 272n.

Cavalry, problems of, 63, 69-71, 138

Cavalry Corps, Army of the Potomac, 193-94

Challemelle-Lacour, Paul Armand, 142-43

Charleston, S.C., 65, 89

Chase, Salmon P., 118

Chattanooga, Tenn., 163; battle of, 90

Chicago, U.S.S., 141

Chickamauga, battle of, 228

Chief of staff, evolution of office, 171-76; *see also* General staff

China: Emory Upton and, 104; Homer Lea and, 153; R. M. Johnston on, 191; Leonard Wood on, 211

Chippewa, battle of, 29

Cincinnati, Society of the, 6

Citizen army: idea of, 3-4, 7-9, 11-14, 18-19, 26, 199-202; John A. Logan on, 127, 129-36; Ulysses S. Grant on, 127-28; and modern conscription, 153, 203-4, 213-17, 220-22; John M. Palmer on, 233-40, 244-46; George C. Marshall on, 244-46; after World War II, 246-51

Citizen soldiers: value of, in American Revolution, 6-9; Thomas Jefferson on, 26-27; John A. Logan on, 127, 130-31, 134-36; Ulysses S. Grant on, 127-28; T. Bentley Mott on, 201-2; new interest in, 202-4; Frederic L. Huidekoper on, 206-8; Leonard Wood on, 212-17, 222, 224; in World War I, 224-25; John M. Palmer on, 229, 232-40; after World War II, 246-49, 253-54

Citizens' Military Training Camps, 240

Civilian control of the military: Emory Upton's criticisms of, 110-12, 118-21, 160, 177; James S. Pettit's criticisms of, 157-59; John Pope on, 160-61; John M. Schofield on, 162-

74, 176; R. M. Johnston on, 196-97; John M. Palmer on, 231-33, 238, 245-46; George C. Marshall on, 245-46

Civil War, 43-44, 75-77, 100-4, 127-29, 162-63, 165, 169-70, 197, 263n.; officer corps in, 77-78, 106-7, 131; and development of total war, 80-81, 195, 220-21; memoirs of participants, 83, 127-28; military lessons of, 83-101, 128, 138, 140, 187-90, 193-97, 213-14, 233; blockade, 96-97; influence on military thought, 107-8; Emory Upton's views on, 111-12, 114-15, 118-20, 123

Clarksville, Tenn., 90

Clausewitz, Karl von, 159; on nature of war, 3, 41, 56-57, 78, 80, 87, 168-70, 179, 181-82, 184, 186, 231, 255-56n.; influence in United States, 41, 56-57, 67

Cleveland, Grover, 141

Colorado, 193

Columbia, S.C., 100

Columbus, Ky., 90

Command problem, United States Army, 120-21, 149-50, 163-77; *see also* General staff

Compton, Karl T., 248

Concord, battle of, 8, 18

Confederacy, West Pointers in, 131

Congress (under the Confederation), and military organization, 10, 14-17

Congress (under the Constitution): military policy of, 18-22, 35, 65-66, 140-42, 164-65, 173-75, 177, 218-20, 226-28, 230, 232, 239-40, 248-49; Emory Upton on, 112-22; James S. Pettit on, 157-59

Connecticut, 42

Conscription: idea of, 3, 11-12, 153, 182; Emory Upton on, 123-24; John M. Palmer on, 234; *see also* Universal military training

Constitution, United States, 17-18, 164, 166, 170, 172; quoted, 1

Continental Army, 1-2, 4-7, 221

Continental Army plan (1916), 217-19

Continental Congress, military policy, 111

Cornwallis, Charles Cornwallis, First Marquis, 1, 4

Council of National Defense, suggested by John M. Palmer, 232; by Henry L. Stimson, 273*n.*

Craig, Malin C., 243

Crimean War, 68, 71-76

Cromwell, Oliver, 237

Cuba, 145-46, 148, 208, 210, 216; Cuban Insurrection (1868–1878), 137

Cullum, George W.: career, 75; military thought, 75-77

Cumberland River, 90

Dapray, John A., quoted, 147

Darwinism, 147, 170, 183

Davis, Jefferson, 165, 195

Defense Department, 244, 248-49; suggested by John M. Palmer, 232

Delafield, Richard, 55; military proposals, 74-75; on offensive war, 75

Delaware, troops, 1-2, 4, 221

Delaware River, 8

Democracy, relationship to a citizen army: 3, 7-9, 11-12, 26-27, 132-36, 220-22; Leonard Wood on, 213-17; John M. Palmer on, 227, 231-34, 238-39, 245; George C. Marshall on, 245

Democracy and armies: James S. Pettit on, 156-59; John Pope on, 160-61; John M. Palmer on, 227, 231-34, 238-39, 245; George C. Marshall on, 245

Democratic party, 131, 209, 218

Demosthenes, quoted, 199, 217, 238-39

Department of Missouri, 163

Department of National Defense, suggested by John M. Palmer, 232

Department of the Ohio, 163

Desaix de Veygoux, Louis Charles Antoine, 185

Dewey, George, 150

Dick Bill, 150, 175

Diedrichs, Otto von, 150

DuPont, Henry A., 125

École Polytechnique, 41

Eighteenth-century warfare (to the French Revolution), 1-4, 6-7, 179-80, 186, 255-56*n.*

Eighty-ninth Division (World War I), 223

Eisenhower, Dwight D., 248-49

El Caney, battle of, 148

Election of 1800, 27

Elkins, Stephen B., 172-73

Endicott Board, 141-44

Endicott, William C., 141

Engineers, Corps of, 27-28, 42, 66, 142

Europe, military methods and thought of: 2-7, 20, 26, 28, 40-42, 55-57, 68-77, 80-81, 169, 172-73, 175-87, 193-95, 198, 207-8, 255-56*n.*; Emory Upton on, 104-6, 112, 119-21, 123-24, 153; Ulysses S. Grant on, 128

Eutaw Springs, battle of, 7

Expansible army idea, 22-23, 31-34, 62-63, 73, 105-6, 108-9, 121-25, 136, 145, 152-53, 157, 178, 192, 201, 226, 238, 240-41, 267*n.*

Fallen Timbers, battle of, 18

Falmouth, Me., burning of, 65

Federalist party, 22, 27

Fifteenth Army Corps (Civil War), 129

Filipino Insurrection, 148-49

Financial problems, military, 61; Emory Upton on, 112-13

First Army, United States (World War I), 242-43

First Division (World War I), 224, 242

First Military District, 209

Florida, 60

Foch, Ferdinand, 110

Foreign policy, United States: in 1890s, 146-47; after Spanish War, 210-11, 250; after World War I, 226, 250; World War II and after, 242, 246, 250-51

Forrest, Nathan Bedford, 107, 236-37

Fort Assiniboine, Mont., 94

Fort Donelson, Tenn., 90

Fort Henry, Tenn., 90

Fort Leavenworth, Kansas, cavalry and infantry school, 82, 266*n.*; Staff College, 229, 242

Fort Monroe, Va., artillery school, 82

Fort Riley, Kansas, 137

Fort Sumter, S.C., 140

Fortifications, 65-67, 74-75; coastal, 65-67, 71-74, 140-44, 194

Fourteenth Army Corps (Civil War), 228

France: threat of war with, 21-22; in Napoleonic wars, 28; in World War I, 190-91, 223-25, 228; in World War II, 241

Franco-Prussian War, 99, 110, 138, 182-84, 188
Franklin, battle of, 163
Franklin, William B., 118, 145
Frederick II, the Great, 2-3, 179, 194
Fredericksburg campaign, 101-2, 194
Frémont, John C., 107
French army: in French Revolution, 3-5, 20, 26, 180-82; in Napoleonic wars, 28, 55-57, 67, 185-86; professionalism in, 41, 76-77; influence on United States, 41-43, 55, 76-77, 105, 220, 259n.; in Crimean War, 72, 75-76; Emory Upton's views of, 105; at beginning of twentieth century, 152; in Franco-Prussian War, 183-84; in World War I, 224
French Revolution, wars of, military methods, 3, 5, 20, 26, 80, 179-82, 220

Garrison, Lindley M., 217-19, 229
General in chief, Emory Upton on, 120; role of, 164-68, 171-74
General staff, Emory Upton on, 120-21, 149-50; R. M. Johnston on, 186-87
General staff, United States: founding of, 149-50, 173-75; evolution of, 175-76, 240; organizational proposals of, 217-18, 226-27, 230, 240-41; *see also* Command problem
Georgia, campaign of (1864), 81, 84, 86-87, 90, 96-97, 163, 196, 228
German army: in Franco-Prussian War, 99, 182-83, 186-88; Emory Upton's views on, 104-6, 109-10, 121-24; influence on United States Army, 105-6, 109-10, 121-24, 153, 175-77, 207-8, 220, 226-27, 230-31; at beginning of twentieth century, 152, 177; in World War I, 207-8, 220, 225; in World War II, 244-45; *see also* Prussian army
Germantown, battle of, 7
Germany: possibility of war with, 146, 150-53; Homer Lea on, 153-54; in World War I, 190-91, 233-34; Bismarckian system, 230-31; in World War II, 241
Gettysburg, battle of, 95
Gibbes, Wade Hampton, 101
Giles, James Branch, 21
Goldsboro, N.C., 100

Gondrecourt, France, 224
Gordon, John B., 107
Governor's Island, N.Y., 209
Gneisenau, August Neidhardt, Count, 41
Grant, Ulysses S.: career, 79-80, 89-90, 165, 171, 193-94, 236; theory of war, 80-81, 89-93, 100-1; on Sherman's march to the sea, 97; on citizen army, 127-28; as commanding general, 165, 168, 172
Great Britain: in Napoleonic wars, 28; possibility of war with, 65, 145-46; Homer Lea on, 153-54; in World War I, 233
Greene, Nathanael, 1, 7, 197; quoted, 5-6; John A. Logan on, 130-31
Gribeauval, Jean Baptiste Vaquette, 180, 186
Grolman, Karl Wilhelm Georg von, 41
Guibert, Charles Benoît, Comte de, 40
Guilford Court House, battle of, 1-2, 7
Gulick, John W., 230
Gun Foundry Board, 141
Gurney-Wadsworth bill, 246

Haig, Sir Douglas, 110
Halleck, Henry W., 55; military proposals, 54, 57-67, 261n.; career, 57-58, 236-37, 259-60n.; on offensive war, 64; theory of war, 67, 91; translation of Jomini, 75; influence of, 122
Hamilton, Alexander: on professional versus citizen soldiers, 10; chairman of congressional military committee, 10; military proposals, 14-16, 20-26, 35, 221, 274n.; on a military academy, 16; inspector general, 22; influence of, 109, 122
Hanna, Matthew A., quoted, 156
Hannibal, 98
Harbord, James G., 147
Harmar, Josiah, 18
Harper's Weekly, 174
Harrison, William Henry, 130
Harvard Medical School, 209
Harvard University, 178
Hawaii, 146, 151, 191-92, 238
Hay, James, 218-19
Herkimer, Nicholas, 130
Hickman, Ky., 90
History, military, value of, 45-46, 58-59, 77
Hitler, Adolf, 241

Hoar, George F., quoted, 142-43
Hobkirk's Hill, battle of, 7
Hood, John B., 129, 163
Hooker, Joseph, 107
Horseshoe Bend, battle of, 116
House Military Affairs Committee, 218, 230, 239
Hudson River, 7, 53
Huidekoper, Frederic L.: in preparedness movement, 203, 208, 210; military proposals, 203-8, 213, 217-18; reflects Emory Upton's influence, 204-5, 207-8; on militia, 205-6; on state military powers, 205-6; on regular army, 206; on possibilities of citizen soldiers, 206-8; on reserves, 206-8; influence of Leonard Wood on, 213
Huntsville, Ala., 88

Illinois, 128, 228
Immigration: officers' views, 155; Leonard Wood on, 212
India, 191
Indian wars, 8, 18-19, 60-61, 113, 116
Infantry regiment, organization, Emory Upton on, 124, 138, 149
Italian campaign (1800), 185

Jackson, Andrew, 29, 130, 236-37
Jackson, Thomas Jonathan (Stonewall), 194-95, 236
Jacksonian democracy, 38-39
Japan: possibility of war with, 146, 150-52, 203; in Russo-Japanese War, 150-52; war scare of 1907, 151; Homer Lea on, 153-56; R. M. Johnston on, 191
Japanese army: in Russo-Japanese War, 151-52, 158; in World War II, 244-45
Jefferson, Thomas, military ideas, 26-28, 215-16, 218, 220, 244, 257-58n.
Jena, battle of, 40, 56, 110
Johnson, Andrew, 163
Johnston, Joseph E., 187, 189-90
Johnston, R. M.: on nature of war, 177-87, 190, 196-98; career, 178-79; on rise of mass armies, 179-87, 197-98; on limitations of mass armies, 184-90; on Civil War, 187-90; military proposals, 190-98; on improving regular army, 192-93; on value of mobility, 193-94; on value of the offensive, 193-95; on value of small,

mobile army, 193-95, 197-98; on civilian supremacy, 196-97
Jomini, Antoine Henri, Baron de: career, 55-56; military thought, 56-57, 77-78; influence in United States, 57, 67, 75-77, 260n.

Kansas, 223
Keim, DeB., quoted, 89
Kellermann, François Étienne, 185
Kentucky, 163
King's Mountain, battle of, 8, 18
Kitchin, Claude, 218
Knox, Henry, military proposals, 19-20, 135, 215, 221, 257n.; on Militia Act of 1792, 21
Knoxville, Tenn., 90
Korean War, 248-49, 252
Kriegsakademie (Prussia), 23-24, 41, 45

Lacour, *see* Challemelle-Lacour
Lake Champlain, 7
Lamont, Daniel S., 172-73
Larned, Charles W., 268n.
Las Guásimas, Cuba, 148
Latin America, 146-47, 192; independence movement, 30-31
Lea, Homer, career and ideas, 153-56
Lee, Richard Henry, quoted, 205, 216
Lee, Robert Edward, 43, 86, 95, 193-95, 236
Legion of the United States, 18
Liddell Hart, B.H., on Napoleon, 186
Limited war theory, after World War II, 252-53
Lincoln, Abraham, 89, 168; Emory Upton on, 111-12, 115; R. M. Johnston on, 197
Lloyd, Henry, 40
Lodge, Henry Cabot, 209
Logan, John A.: and command of the Army of the Tennessee, 107, 129; on citizen army, 127-36, 236-37; career, 128-29, 136, 228, 236; on Military Academy, 131-33; on regular army, 133-34; death, 136; influence, 228, 236-37, 244
Long Island, battle of, 18, 189
Luce, Stephen B., 144
Lundy's Lane, battle of, 29

MacArthur, Douglas, 243, 275n.
McCarthy, Joseph R., 248
McClellan, George B., 55; military pro-

McClellan, George B. (*continued*)
posals, 54, 68-75; career, 67-69, 107, 193-94; on offensive war, 72-73; Emory Upton on, 112; as commanding general, 168
Macdonough, Thomas, 130
McDowell, Irvin, 118; in First Bull Run campaign, 187-90
McHenry, James, 24
Machiavelli, Niccolò, 52
Madison, James, 28, 258n.
Mahan, Alfred Thayer, 110, 144, 146-47, 261n.
Mahan, Dennis Hart: military proposals, 38, 44-52, 54, 259-60n., 262n.; career, 42-44, 52-53; on offensive war, 46-49, 54, 194-95; influence, 44-45, 54-55, 77, 140, 149, 194, 221; death, 53
Malakoff Redoubt, 74-75
Manila Bay, 150
March, Peyton C., 223, 226-27, 239, 243, 250
Marcy, William B., 122, 165
Marengo, battle of, 185
Marlborough, John Churchill, First Duke of, 179
Marshall, George C.: military ideas, 223, 243-47; on universal military training, 223, 244-47; career, 242-44, 248-49; and John M. Palmer, 242-46; and Harry S. Truman, 247
Maryland, troops, 1-2, 4, 221
Massachusetts Institute of Technology, 248
Mass armies: rise of, 3, 20-21, 85-86, 100-1, 125, 152-53, 177-85, 197-99, 208, 218, 220-22, 229, 234-35, 242, 246, 251; limitations of, 171, 179, 184-95, 249, 251-54
Medical Corps, 209
Meigs, M. C., quoted, 89, 138
Melas, Michael, Baron, 185
Memphis, Tenn., 90
Merritt, Wesley, 174-75
Metz, France: engineering school, 43, 259n.; seige of (1870), 99, 193
Meuse-Argonne offensive, 225, 228, 242
Mexican War, 36, 52, 60, 68, 74; Emory Upton on, 112-13
Mexico: possibility of war with, 145; in 1916-1917, 219
Michie, Peter Smith, 101, 125
Miles, Nelson A., 174-75

Military Academy, United States, 163; first proposals for, 16, 23-24; founding, 27-28; suggestions for improvement, 32, 135, 193; development, 36-37, 40, 42-45, 54-55, 75, 77-78, 221; Emory Upton on, 105; preference shown to graduates, 107; John A. Logan on, 130-35
Military Division of the Atlantic, 163
Military Division of the Pacific, 163
Military Service Institution, United States, 145, 151, 156
Military Training Camps Association, 241
Militia, United States: evolution of, 5-9, 20-21, 38-39, 116-18, 146-47, 150; suggestions for improving, 12-16, 19-20, 74, 108, 135-36, 145, 192, 200-2, 205-7; ineffectiveness, 28-29, 116-19, 146, 205-6; Jacksonian hostility toward, 38-39; Emory Upton on, 116-19; *see also* National Guard
Militia Act of 1792, 20-21, 117, 197
Mindanao, 208
Missiles, ballistic, 249, 251-52, 254
Mississippi River, 216
Missouri, 163
Mobile, Ala., 90
Moltke, Helmut von, 99, 159, 184
Monarchy and military power, James S. Pettit on, 158-59
Monmouth, battle of, 7
Monroe Doctrine, 151
Monroe, James, 30, 35, 42
Montfaucon, France, 225
Mordecai, Alfred, 55, 74
Morocco crisis (1905), 211
Moslem world, 191
Mott, T. Bentley, military proposals, 200-2
Murat, Joachim, 55-56

Napoleon, 28, 40-42, 55-56, 67, 76-77, 98, 179, 261n.; Dennis Hart Mahan's admiration for, 47-49; R. M. Johnston on, 185-86, 188-89, 194
Napoleonic wars, 28, 185-86
Nashville, Tenn., 90
National Army (World War I), 220, 224, 230
National Defense Act of 1916, 175, 219-20
National Defense Act of 1920, 230, 239-41
National Guard: evolution of, 146,

148, 218-20, 224, 239-41; Dick Bill, 150, 175; suggestions for improvement, 229; *see also* Militia

Naval Academy, United States, John A. Logan on, 130, 132

Naval Gun Factory, 141

Naval war: Civil War blockade, 96-97; Henry W. Halleck on, 261*n.*; *see also* Fortifications, coastal

Navy, United States: George Washington on, 11; naval militia, 19; evolution of, 63, 141, 147, 151; Civil War blockade, 96-97; John A. Logan on, 133; first steel ships, 141

Navy Department, 232

New Deal, 248

New Jersey, 4; campaign of (1776), 18, 114

New Orleans, battle of, 29

New York City, 142; campaign of (1776), 7

New York *Evening Post,* 94

Ney, Michel, 55

North Carolina, 218

Northwest Territory, 18

Nuclear weapons, 246, 249, 251-52, 254, 275-76*n.*

Offensive warfare, value of, 46-48, 64-67, 72-73, 75, 85, 95, 140, 194-95, 224

Officer corps, European, 6

Officer corps, United States: problems of developing, 5-6, 16, 23-24, 31-32, 36-37, 40, 53, 58-59, 62-64, 71, 75-76, 106-7, 130-36, 193, 215, 236-37; evolution of, 6, 36-37, 39-46, 75-78, 139, 221-22; isolation from American life, 77-78, 220-21, 250; military ideas of, 107-8, 127-29, 138-39, 144-49, 156, 220-24, 228, 240-41, 248-50, 266*n.*; as an aristocracy, 132-34; pessimism of, 137, 147-51, 156, 159-62, 177-78, 194, 224; age of, 139; on immigration, 155; on civilian supremacy, 167-68; gradually changing attitude toward citizen soldiers, 199-200, 202-3; *see also* Military Academy

Open Door policy, 150-51

Opequon, battle of the, 103

Organized Reserves, 240-41

Pacific Ocean, 154-56, 191

Palmer, John M., Sr., 228-29

Palmer, John McAuley: military proposals, 223, 225-59; career, 225-30, 239-49; genesis of his ideas, 228-29; on citizen soldiers, 229, 233-42, 244-46; rejection of Emory Upton, 229-32, 237-38, 251; and National Defense Act of 1920, 230, 239-40; on civilian supremacy, 231-34; on democracy, 231-34, 238-39, 245; on Swiss army, 233-36, 244; on universal military training, 234-35, 239, 241-42; on regular army, 235, 238, 240-41; on George Washington, 236-37, 241, 274*n.*; attempt to reconcile conflicting military traditions, 239, 244; and George C. Marshall, 242-46; and post-World War II military planning, 244-46

Panama Canal Zone, 192, 238

Patterson, Robert, 187

Peninsular Campaign (1862), 101, 111, 193

Pennsylvania, 204

Perry, Oliver Hazard, 130

Pershing, John J., 236; in World War I, 223-25, 228, 242; military ideas, 223-27, 240, 242; and George C. Marshall, 242-43

Pétain, Henri Philippe, 110, 225

Petersburg, Va., 193-94

Pettit, James S.: military proposals, 137, 156-59, 178; contemporary appraisals, 159-60

Philadelphia, 114; campaign for (1777), 194

Philippine Islands, 148-52, 192, 208, 210, 238; Homer Lea on, 154

Plattsburg movement, 203, 215, 240-41

Poland, 241

Polk, James K., 36, 197

Pope, John, 107; on the regular army in a democracy, 160-61

Preparedness, necessity for American, 34, 60, 82, 127, 139-40, 145-49, 151-52, 190-92, 210-12, 216-17, 250-54

Preparedness movement, World War I, 203-4, 208-9, 217-22

Presidency, military powers of the: Emory Upton on, 111-12, 120, 122, 164-76; James S. Pettit on, 158; John McAuley Palmer on, 232; *see also* Command problem

President's Advisory Commission on Military Training, 248, 275-76n.

Princeton, battle of, 194-95

Proctor, Redfield, 172-73; quoted, 139

Professional armies, idea of, 1-14; development of, 2-3, 6

Professionalism, military, growth of, 6, 39-42, 44-46, 53-60, 76-78, 149, 220-22, 253-54, 255n.

Progressive movement, 218

Prussian army, 159; under Frederick the Great, 2; in era of reformers, 40-41, 182; influence on United States, 108; see also German army

Public opinion, on American army, 8-9, 15-18, 20, 34-35, 38-39, 77-78, 127, 147, 162, 203-4, 248-49; James S. Pettit on, 158-59

Puerto Rico, campaign of (1898), 148, 216

Quartermaster's Department, 138

Racism, among officers, 155; see also Social Darwinism

Radicals (Civil War era), 89

Rappahannock Station, Va., 102

Regular army, United States: evolution of, 1-2, 4-9, 15, 17-19, 22, 27-29, 35-37, 39, 63, 82-83, 113-15, 122, 137-40, 148-51, 174-76, 219-20, 224-25, 239-41, 252-54; value of (as seen by George Washington), 1-2, 4-11, 16, 21-24 (by Alexander Hamilton), 22-26 (by John C. Calhoun), 30-35 (by Henry W. Halleck), 58-64 (by George B. McClellan), 71 (by officer corps), 77-78 (by Emory Upton), 113-15 (by Arthur T. Wagner), 145-46 (by R. M. Johnston), 192-95; suggestions for improvement, 22-25, 30-35, 108-9, 119-24, 145-46, 152-53, 192-93, 206, 214, 217-20, 226-27, 229; in Civil War, 106-7, 114-15; in civil disturbances, 115-16; John A. Logan on, 133-35

Regulations, on command of the army, 166

Republican party, 128, 204, 209

Reserve forces: George Washington's plan, 12-14; Alexander Hamilton's plan, 14-15, 23; Henry Knox's plan, 19-20; Frederic L. Huidekoper's plan, 206-8; Leonard Wood's plan,

214-15; Continental Army plan, 218; John McAuley Palmer's plan, 229, 234-36; Organized Reserves, 240-41; see also Expansible army, Militia, National Guard

Reserve Officers' Training Corps, 219, 240

Rhodes, James Ford, 197

Richmond, Va., 196

Riedesel, Friedrich Adolf, Freiherr von, 8

Rochambeau, Jean Baptiste Donatien de Vimeur, Comte de, 4

Rodic, Ignez, 155-56

Roosevelt, Franklin D.: and George C. Marshall, 243; on universal military training, 246-47

Roosevelt, Theodore, 155; on threat of war with Germany, 150; on regular army, 151; on Root reforms, 174; stimulates military interests, 203, 209; friend of Leonard Wood, 209, 211; foreign policy, 211; on moral forces, 217

Root, Elihu: Emory Upton's influence on, 125-26, 149, 175-76; reforms, 149-50, 173-77

Rough Riders, 148, 208

Russia: Homer Lea on, 154; R. M. Johnston on, 190-91; after World War II, 247, 249, 251, 254

Russian army: in Crimean War, 56, 69, 73-75; in Russo-Japanese War, 152; in Napoleonic wars, 186

Russian campaign (1812), 186

Russo-Japanese War, 150-52, 211

St. Clair, Arthur, 18

St. Cyr (France), 41

St. Louis, Mo., 163, 165

St. Mihiel offensive, 242

Samoa, 146, 150

San Francisco, Calif., 142, 155

San Juan Hill, battle of, 148, 208

Santiago de Cuba, 148, 208

Saratoga, campaign of, 7-8, 18

Savannah, Ga., 87, 100

Saxe, Maurice, Comte de, 40, 193

Scharnhorst, Gerhard David von, 41

Schenck, A. D., on militia, 137, 145

Schofield, John M., 125; study of ordnance and fortification, 142; career, 162-68; on civilian supremacy and the command problem, 162-77

Schofield Board, 142

School of Application for Engineers and Artillery (France), 43, 259n.
Schools, military, 23-24, 41, 43, 45, 105-6, 149, 193, 259n.; United States, founding of schools of application, 82, 145; see also Army War College, Military Academy
Schuyler, Philip, 130
Science and war: John M. Schofield on, 171; Leonard Wood on, 216-17
Scott, Winfield, 29, 37; views on fighting Civil War, 106-7; on expansible army, 122; as general in chief, 164-65, 167-68, 171-72, 175; in First Bull Run campaign, 187
Secretary of war: Emory Upton on, 120; James S. Pettit on, 158; role of, 164-69, 171-76; John M. Schofield on, 167-69, 171-76
Sedan, France, 225
Selective Training and Service Act of 1940, 241
Selma, battle of, 103
Seminole War, 60-61; Emory Upton on, 113
Senate Military Affairs Committee, 174, 226-28, 230, 234, 239, 242-44
Senate War Investigating Committee, 247
Service journals, 108, 144-45
Sevastopol, siege of, 71-75
Seven Weeks War, 110
Seward, William H., 104
Shays's Rebellion, 115-16, 257n.
Shenandoah Valley, 187, 189; campaign of (1864), 81, 90-91, 103; campaign of (1862), 195
Sheridan, Philip H.: in Shenandoah Valley, 81, 90, 92, 103; in Franco-Prussian War, 99, 138; as commanding general, 165-66, 168, 171-72, 175, 209; as cavalry commander, 193-94
Sherman, William Tecumseh: theory of war, 79-81, 85-89, 95-97, 100-1, 220-21, 252; career, 79-81, 236; Georgia campaign, 81, 84, 86-88, 90, 96-97, 100, 196; Carolina campaign, 81, 86-88, 90, 96; as commanding general, 81-82, 94, 165-66, 168, 171-72, 175, 209; and military education, 81-83; on lessons of Civil War, 83-89, 108; and Emory Upton, 104, 125; and John A. Logan, 129; on coastal fortifications, 140-41; on

prize essay committee, 145, 266n.
Shiloh, battle of, 90, 128
Sickles, Daniel E., 130
Sierra Nevada, 154-55
Sixth Army Corps (Civil War), 99, 102
Social Darwinism, 147, 154-55, 170, 183, 190, 210
South, the, 218
South Carolina, campaign of (1865), 87
Soviet Union, see Union of Soviet Socialist Republics
Spain: Napoleon's campaign in, 67, 261n.; possibility of war with, 145
Spanish-American War, 146-50, 173, 203, 250; war investigating committee, 173
Spencer, John C., quoted, 61
Spotsylvania, battle of, 102-3
Staff College (United States), 229, 242
Staff departments, 62, 166-67, 173-75, 209
Stanton, Edwin M., 163
Starke, John, 130
States, military powers of, 20; Emory Upton on, 117-20; T. Bentley Mott on, 200-1; Frederic L. Huidekoper on, 205-6
Steele, Matthew F., quoted, 159
Steuben, Friedrich Wilhelm, Baron von, military ideas of, 13-15
Stevenson, Adlai, 253
Stimson, Henry L., 229, 246, 273n.
Stone's River, battle of, 228
Subsistence Department, 138
Sun Yat-sen, 153
Supreme Court, United States, cited, 164
Swiss army, 12, 190, 199-202, 207-8, 214, 222, 233-36, 244
Switzerland, 190

Tactics: in American Revolution, 6-7; Dennis Hart Mahan's, 47, 49-51; in Civil War, 84-85; Emory Upton's, 104
Taft, William Howard, 175, 246
Taylor, Zachary, 130
Teil, Jean Pierre, Baron du, 180
Tennessee, John Bell Hood's invasion, 163
Tennessee River, 90
Terry, Alfred H., 130
Thayer, Sylvanus, 42-43, 149
Thirty Years War, 81

Thomas, George H., 228
Thomas, Lorenzo, 118
Total war, rise of, 85, 101, 169-71, 195-96, 220-21, 249, 251-52
Tower, Zealous B., 145
Training, military, problems of, 12-13, 15, 19-20, 23, 25, 59-60, 69-71, 85, 122-23, 135-36, 201-2, 224-25, 235-36
Trenton, battle of, 8, 194-95
Truman, Harry S., and universal military training, 247-49
Twenty-ninth Division (World War I), 228

Ulm, battle of, 55
Uniforms, military, 155
Union of Soviet Socialist Republics, 247, 249, 251, 254
Universal military training: Leonard Wood on, 213-17; Peyton C. March on, 226; general staff plan (1916), 230; John McAuley Palmer on, 234-35, 239, 241-42, 244-46; George C. Marshall on, 244-46; after World War II, 246-49, 251-54, 275-76n.
Upton, Emory: military proposals, 100, 103-4, 109-26; on expansible army, 100, 121-25, 136, 178; career, 101-6, 124-26; on Civil War generalship, 103; tactics, 104; marriage, 104; tour of Asia and Europe, 104-5; admiration for European armies, especially German, 104-5, 109-10, 119-22, 149-50, 177; pessimism, 109-10, 125, 137, 148-49, 156-62; on civilian control of the military, 110-12, 119-21, 160, 163, 165-71, 177; on regular army, 113-15, 119-24, 254; on George Washington, 114-15, 274n.; on militia and citizen soldiers, 116-19, 178, 205-6, 228; on military powers of the states, 117-20, 148-49; on general in chief, 120; on general staff, 120-21, 175-76; on conscription, 123-24; on infantry organization, 124, 138; death, 124-25; influence, 125-26, 137, 144-45, 148, 151-52, 156-62, 175-76, 178, 194, 204-5, 207-8, 211-12, 220-22, 224, 226, 228-29, 240-41, 250-51; publication of *The Military Policy of the United States*, 125-26, 149; ideas rejected by John McAuley Palmer, 229-32, 237-39, 244, 251

Upton, Maria, 101

Valley Forge, 5
Venezuela, 146
Vermont, 8
Veterans of Foreign Wars, 248
Virginia, 218
Virginia Military Institute, 243
Volunteer army: in Civil War, 107; Emory Upton on, 118; R. M. Johnston on, 192; National Defense Act of 1916, 219

Wadsworth, James W., Jr., 226-27, 230, 241, 246
Wagner, Arthur L.: Uptonian views, 145-46; career, 145, 266n.
War, nature of, 2-5, 7-9, 56-57, 67, 80-81, 85-101, 143-44, 168-71, 177-87, 190, 196-98, 246, 249, 251-54
War Department, 164, 173, 226-27, 229-30, 232, 246
War Department Circular 347, 244-46, 248
War Department Special Staff, 244
War Hawks (1812), 28
War of 1812, 28-30, 65, 97; Emory Upton on, 113-14, 116-17, 123
War Plans Division, general staff, 226
Washington, D.C., 165, 187, 189, 204, 263n.; burning of, 65
Washington, George: on professional army, 1-2, 4-11, 16, 21-24, 121, 222; military proposals, 1-2, 4-16, 21-24, 121, 200, 205, 215, 221-22, 244, 254; conservatism of, 3; generalship, 4-5, 189, 194-95; on militia and citizen soldiers, 5, 8, 12-14, 205, 215, 222; on officers, 5-6; on navy, 11; on Swiss army, 12, 200; on a military academy, 16, 258n.; recalled to military service, 22, 26; on reconnaissance, 50; Emory Upton on, 114-15, 274n.; as a citizen soldier, 130, 236-37; John McAuley Palmer on, 236-37, 241, 246, 274n.
Washington University, St. Louis, 163
Watervliet Arsenal, 141
Wayne, Anthony, 18
Weapons, development of, 66, 84-85, 140-43, 246, 249, 251-52, 254, 275-76n.
West Point, *see* Military Academy, United States
Whisky Rebellion, 257n.

Willett's Point, N.Y., engineering school, 82
Williams, Kenneth P., 197
Wilson, Sir Henry Hughes, 110
Wilson, James, 103
Wilson, Woodrow, and preparedness, 204, 209, 217-20
Wood, Leonard: career, 175, 204, 208-11, 223; as chief of staff, 175, 209, 229; on citizen army, 199, 213-17, 222, 225; and Army League, 204; influence, 204, 208-10, 217-18, 226, 230, 241, 244; and preparedness movement, 204, 208-11; military proposals, 210-17; and Theodore Roosevelt's foreign policy, 211; on American military history, 211-12; reflects Emory Upton's influence, 211-12; on value of citizen soldiers, 212-17, 222, 224; on conscription and universal military training, 213-17, 219-20, 222, 224; on regular army, 214; on reserve forces, 214-15; in World War I, 223
World War I, 175, 182, 190-91, 198, 203, 205, 210, 233-35; United States Army in, 222-25, 228, 242
World War II, 239, 241-42, 246, 251
Wright, Horatio G., 102

XYZ Affair, 21

Yorktown, siege of, 4, 7